The Melody of Theology

The Melody of Theology

A Philosophical Dictionary

Jaroslav Pelikan

Harvard University Press
Cambridge, Massachusetts
London, England

Library of Congress Cataloging-in-Publication Data

Pelikan, Jaroslav Jan, 1923—
  The melody of theology.

  Includes index.
  I. Theology—Dictionaries. I. Title.
BR95.P36 1988   230   88-690
ISBN 0-674-56472-3 (alk. paper) (cloth)
ISBN 0-674-56473-1 (paper)

Without ceasing and without silence, they praise the goodness of God, in that venerable and thrice-illumined melody of theology.

—Nicephorus of Constantinople

The virtuosity (or special calling) of a person . . . is the melody of that person's life.

—Friedrich Schleiermacher

▪ Contents

▪ Preface

Several years ago, Aida Donald of Harvard University Press invited me to prepare a "middle-size book" that "could amount to a kind of autobiography in small bites—for it has the beguiling simplicity of being organized by the alphabet." Such books by senior scholars, she explained, "are a kind of *summa* of their work and life." She suggested that in my case "it would be a *summa* of theology." Unfortunately, that title had already been preempted seven centuries ago, and the "small bites" are in this case "small bytes," but the invitation was, in Calvin's language, a *vocatio irresistibilis.* Three of the greatest autobiographies of all time, bearing the titles *Confessiones, Dichtung und Wahrheit,* and *Apologia pro vita sua,* by, respectively, AUGUSTINE OF HIPPO, JOHANN WOLFGANG VON GOETHE, and JOHN HENRY NEWMAN, have been my constant companions for most of my life. As the hymn says, "We follow in their train."

Any intellectual autobiography is, by definition, an exercise in self-indulgence, based as it on the assumption that a sufficient number of readers will have sufficient curiosity about how the author's mind has evolved. An intellectual autobiography in the form of a "philosophical dictionary" permits the additional self-indulgence of employing the seeming objectivity of some eighty-two dictionary entries, arranged in the impersonal sequence of alphabetical order, to express a completely personal set of prejudices. My research trips and lecture tours of the past several years have permitted me the still further self-indulgence of being able to compose several of the entries in special places—DOSTOEVSKY in his city of Saint Petersburg/Leningrad, BYZANTIUM in Constantinople/Istanbul, HARNACK in Estonia, SLAVS in Prague, SÖDERBLOM in Uppsala, and of course ROME in Rome and LUTHER in Saxony. As is my wont, I have interspersed highly personal judgment, rather technical scholarly analysis, and audacious historical-theological generalization. Preparing this dictionary has also given me the opportunity to recycle for my own use material I had originally written for other people's less philosophical dictionaries, but it has also obliged me, after years of working to sustain a narrative "story line" through an entire volume or even through several, to compress each topic into a self-contained unit, while avoiding any but the most necessary overlap and duplication; cross-references in "small caps" are an effort to handle this problem.

Biblical quotations are, almost without exception, from *The New English Bible;* I have followed its style of setting verse, but have felt free to add italics. Other quotations from works originally written in other languages are adopted—but also adapted—from various translations, including my own. Within the limits of convention, I have striven for consistency in handling the vexing question of the capitalization of nouns referring to theological topics: thus "gospel" and "revelation" are capitalized when books of the New Testament are meant, but not when they are used as synonyms for "the Christian message." Almost all proper names are identified by date, on the assumption that no one reader will need all the identifications but that different readers may need different ones; I have followed the convention of identifying popes by their official names and by the years of their pontificate.

The book bears no dedication, but a pair of epigraphs instead, partly in order to explain its title; the passages from which they are taken are given in full in the entry on MELODY. If there were a dedication, it would have been inscribed to George V. Florovsky (1893–1979), who, more than any other person except my late father, taught me to sing "the melody of theology" this way.

The Melody of Theology

· Angel

Everybody knows what angels look like—those enormous little cherub *putti* at Saint Peter's, the figure of Gabriel in a Botticelli Annunciation, the powerful Michael of countless Greek and Slavic icons. Oliver Gant's angel, as Thomas Wolfe described it in *Look Homeward, Angel,* "held a stone lily delicately in one hand. The other hand was lifted in benediction, it was poised clumsily upon the ball of one phthisic foot, and its stupid face wore a smile of soft stone idiocy."

Yes, everybody knows what angels look like—everybody except another Thomas, the one from Aquino. For although THOMAS AQUINAS and the other scholastics have a reputation for claiming to be better acquainted with the habits of angels than they had any right to be, the Thomistic doctrine of angels is actually a carefully circumscribed effort to make systematic sense of this puzzling phenomenon as it had been presented by the Bible and the Christian tradition. What connected human life with the life of the (other) animals was a physical nature; what connected humanity with the Creator was the IMAGE OF GOD. But here were beings that biblical monotheism forbade calling gods, but that were not animals or human beings either—and yet they definitely were creatures. Denouncing what it called "angel-worship" (Col. 2:18), the New Testament had clearly insisted that angels and spirits, too, belonged on this side of the boundary line between Creator and creature. The apostle Paul was "convinced that there is nothing in death or life, in the realm of spirits (Greek *angeloi*) or superhuman powers, in the world as it is or the world as it shall be, in the forces of the universe, in heights or depths [perhaps a reference to the astrological zenith and nadir]—nothing *in all creation* that can separate us from the love of God in Christ Jesus our Lord" (Rom. 8:38–39). And so angels needed to be fitted into the order of creatures: they were rational, as God and human beings were rational; they were created, as human beings and animals were created; yet they were not physical, as human beings and animals were physical.

They were, moreover, divided into good and evil angels. Although the narrative of the Fall in the Book of Genesis spoke only of a "serpent" that was "more crafty than any wild creature that the Lord had made" (Gen. 3:1) and did not mention the Devil by name, Christian exegetes had early concluded that the agent of the temptation could not have been a mere reptile, regardless of how crafty, but must have been a fallen angel. All the powers appertaining to angels had here been put into the service of evil. The Latin epigram *corruptio optimi pessima* ("There is nothing worse than the corruption of the best"), for which contemporary life often seems determined to provide such ample documentation, was apparently invented by the scholastics to cover the case of the fallen angels. As *Paradise Lost* demonstrates, it is extremely difficult to do justice to this complex of qualities in the evil angels without making them either semidivine or else so *simpático* as to dull the moral and religious edge of the entire biblical drama.

Within the Gospel accounts, angels appear at many of the most crucial junctures: an angel announces to Mary that Jesus is to be born (Luke 1:26–38); an angel strengthens Jesus during the agony in the Garden of Gethsemane (Luke 22:43); an angel announces to the bewildered followers that Jesus has been raised from the dead (Matt. 28:1–7), and again that he has ascended into heaven (Acts 1:10–11). They serve chiefly as messengers from God, but in the Hebrew Bible these messengers could pack a lot of power, as when "the angel of the Lord went out and struck down a hundred and eighty-five thousand in the

Assyrian camp" from the army of Sennacherib (2 Kings 19:35). None of Thomas Wolfe's "soft stone idiocy" here!

A decisive and influential chapter in the history of the doctrine of angels was contributed by the treatise *On the Celestial Hierarchy,* composed by the mysterious Christian Neoplatonist who wrote under the pseudonym "Dionysius the Areopagite." That had been the name of one of the relatively few Athenians whom the apostle Paul managed to convert during his brief visit (Acts 17:34). Quite naturally, he is listed quite early as having become the first bishop of Athens. But early in the sixth century a corpus of writings surfaced, bearing his name and presenting a blend of Christian and Neoplatonic ideas. As the putative disciple of Paul, the author carried an all but apostolic authority; moreover, the ideas he presented corresponded to the deepest intuitions of many Christian thinkers. In the doctrine of angels he found the biblical key to the Neoplatonic theory of the "great chain of being," which extended between the spiritual-physical being of a created humanity and the spiritual being of a Creator God a hierarchy of spiritual creatures, rank upon rank, up the ladder of heaven. (In the eyes of the bishops and other church authorities it did not harm his cause a bit that the Pseudo-Dionysius wrote a companion treatise, *On the Ecclesiastical Hierarchy,* in which the parallels between the church in heaven and the church on earth, therefore between angels and bishops, could be traced.)

Putting all of this together, the scholastics came up with an account that located angels along the chain of creatures, as non-physical rational beings that God had made. By embedding them firmly within the natural order, scholastic philosophical theology sometimes spoke in ways that have reminded present-day physicists (at any rate, those who have read Thomas Aquinas) of the qualities now ascribed to quarks and other equally mysterious creaturely forces. As the scholastics pondered the comings and goings of angels in the biblical accounts, moreover, they sought to make sense of their remarkable means of locomotion between the heavens (wherever and whatever those might be) and earth as we know it. As a consequence, medieval angelology must be reckoned as the most ambitious sustained effort in Western intellectual history to imagine what extraterrestrial rational beings might be like—even though they did not possess bodies. In this sense it belongs to the history of scientific speculation as well as to the history of theological and philosophical speculation and to the history of art—even if no one knows for certain just what angels do look like.

▪ Apocatastasis

Although its history goes back to the cosmology of Aristotle, this Greek term for "restoration" acquired great importance only with the Christian thought of the first three centuries. It appears in one single passage of the New Testament, when Peter speaks of "the time of universal restoration" (Acts 3:21).

On that slender foundation the greatest speculative genius of those early centuries, who was arguably the greatest speculative genius in all of Christian history, ORIGEN OF ALEXANDRIA, constructed a breathtaking vision of the cosmic design of God. To deal with the dilemma that has been faced for twenty centuries by every effort at a systematic understanding of the Christian message—how to assert the eternal providence of an omnipotent God and harmonize it with human free will and responsibility—Origen projected a pedagogical view of history in which "the end is as the beginning." God would allow free will its fullest possible expression, but would—not by force but by patience—lure it back to its intended goal, until eventually, with their free will preserved intact but now fulfilled, all creatures would come to a universal restoration, an apocatastasis. And by "all creatures" Origen meant just that: the Devil and the other fallen angels, too, would finally find a place in the renewed cosmos of divine love.

Origen combined the term apocatastasis from the Book of Acts with the most universalistic of the language employed by the apostle Paul to describe his own vision of the end: Christ "is destined to reign until God has put all enemies under his feet . . . And when all things are thus subject to him, then the Son himself will also be made subordinate to God who made all things subject to him, and *thus God will be all in all*" (1 Cor. 15:26–28). Could God ever be truly "all in all," Origen dared to wonder, if anywhere in the universe there remained any pockets of resistance to divine love? If not, then apocatastasis ought to imply universal salvation, achieved not by the tyranny of divine omnipotence but by the providence of divine love.

Of course he could not propound this as a dogma, but he did feel entitled to ask the question. Yet even for that he has been condemned. The message of the gospel is inseparable from the missionary imperative, which would appear to be rendered utterly nugatory if God planned to save everyone anyway, regardless of faith or unfaith. Yet the Origenist vision of apocatastasis has refused to be dismissed so easily. Confronted as they believed they were by a choice between the universalism of an Origen and the predestinarianism of an Augustine or a Luther, many Christians have nourished such a vision. The justice of God demanded that there be a hell, but the mercy of God permitted (or perhaps even required) that we pray for it to be empty. Dante in the *Paradiso* agonized over the problem of the damnation of noble pagans and repeatedly raised the painful question of whether it had to be true, without explicitly modifying the official position. But readers of Dante—or of Augustine or Luther—have turned again and again to Origen's vision. The issue of apocatastasis as doctrine was perhaps put best by the nineteenth-century Pietist churchman and theologian, Christian Gottlieb Barth (1799–1862): "Anyone who does not believe in the universal restoration is an ox, but anyone who teaches it is an ass."

▪ Apophatic

Apophasis is the Greek word for "negation," and an apophatic theology is a negative theology. But because speaking about a negative theology sounds—how should one put it?—too negative, the Greek adjective *apophatikos* has been Anglicized and pressed into use. The counterpart of *apophasis* is *kataphasis,* "affirmation"; hence the terms "apophatic" and "cataphatic." (As with APOCATASTASIS in place of the Greek *apokatastasis*—and as, for that matter, with the Latin *pelicanus* in place of *pelekanos*—the Greek "kappa" becomes a "c" in Latin and then in English.)

Much of the history of Christian apophatic theology is Eastern and Greek. To explain the mystical meaning of the doctrine of angels, the title of the third chapter of *The Mystical Theology* by Pseudo-Dionysius the Areopagite puts the question: "Which are the cataphatic theologies, and which are the apophatic?" The text replies that the central doctrines of the Catholic faith, such as the Trinity and the incarnation, are genuine affirmations. "But," the Pseudo-Dionysius continues, "my argument now rises from what is below up to the transcendent," from the data of REVELATION to trying to speak about the Revealed. "And the more it climbs, the more language falters, and when it has passed up and beyond the ascent, it will turn silent completely, since it will finally be at one with him who is indescribable." For in fact, as he says in another of the treatises of the *Corpus Areopagiticum,* "the Deity is far beyond every manifestation of being and life." That was why the Bible resorted to such negative terms as "invisible," as in the oxymoron of the *locus classicus* for NATURAL THEOLOGY (Rom. 1:20): "His invisible attributes, that is to say his everlasting power and deity, have been visible"—in their very "invisibility," that is. For "God is in no way like the things that have being, and we have no knowledge at all of his incomprehensible and ineffable transcendence and invisibility."

Pseudonymously or not, the unknown author was summarizing here a major theological presupposition that had come down through Christian theology from Origen and the Cappadocians: that because all languages were human (even and especially Greek), the MYSTERY of the divine being transcended the categories of speech. By its clarity (even and especially in Greek), cataphatic language gave the illusion of saying something affirmative concerning transcendent reality, but that was "always unfitting to the hiddenness of the inexpressible." Therefore the apophatic way of speaking "appears to be more suitable to the realm of the divine." Despite its etymology in both Greek and Latin as an "unveiling," revelation did not grant to the initiate an opportunity to peek into the secrets of ultimate Being. Rather, biblical revelation deliberately chose for these transcendent realities such as angels metaphors that were obviously dissimilar, "so completely at variance with what they really are," that their transcendence and otherness might become palpable. That is why the entries under "alpha" in a DICTIONARY like G. W. H. Lampe's *A Patristic Greek Lexicon* bulk so large; for what grammarians call the "alpha-privative" in Greek, like the prefix *in-* in Latin or *non-* in English, makes its affirmations by negating. Language must be apophatic in order to be cataphatic in the only way in which it is possible to be cataphatic about transcendence.

Throughout the history of patristic theology, Eastern but also Western, this accent on the apophatic had functioned as a check, and one that was often necessary, on the pretensions of theologians. Augustine warned, in the midst of his masterful exposition of the dogma of the Trinity, that the purpose of its technical terminology was "not that [the mystery] might be spoken, but that it not be left unspoken"; he spoke only in order not to remain completely silent. Similarly, the Cappadocians had to deal with a heresy that claimed to be as well informed about the true nature of God as God was. Unfortunately, orthodoxy has sometimes encouraged such pretensions and claims in its adherents as well. On the other hand, the serenity with which a theologian like Thomas Aquinas proceeded in his *Summa* has sometimes been allowed to obscure the genuinely apophatic nature of his cataphatic statements. "Immaterial substances," Thomas said, "cannot be known by us in such a way that we apprehend 'what they really are'" (their *quidditas*). The reason, as he had just explained, was that "there is no proper and adequate proportion between material things and immaterial things"; and as his authority for this he cited Dionysius. Therefore it was only by "the method of negation" (*via remotionis*) that theology could proceed properly.

In recent times, apophatic theology has occasionally shown dangerous signs of becoming trendy, sometimes as a cloak for an agnostic outlook that denies the reality of revelation and incarnation altogether. Therefore the study of apophaticism as a theological and philosophical outlook needs to stress its place in the history of Christian doctrine, including its dialectical relation to creed and dogma.

· Atheist/Agnostic

Popular parlance, which often ignores the nice distinctions developed by theologians, philosophers, and historians, tends to use these two terms (along with "skeptic," "infidel," and others, perhaps even "deist") quite indiscriminately. And there probably are still atheists who prefer to call themselves agnostics, because atheism appears to imply an absolute and doctrinaire position, which, even when it espouses the nonexistence of God, is anathema to them. Nevertheless, it is useful to distinguish between atheist and agnostic doctrine.

An agnostic position is one that leaves open the question whether there exists a god or gods, professing to find such a question unanswered or even unanswerable. For the atheist, the question has been answered, and in the negative: "There is no God." The words that introduce that quotation in Psalm 14:1, "The impious fool says in his heart, 'There is no God,'" have often been repeated as the first and last word of the Christian tradition on the issue. Christianity has usually confronted other kinds of theism, not atheism. But especially since the EN-

LIGHTENMENT, which vigorously debated the question of which was worse, atheism or superstition, theology has been obliged to look at it more deeply, and the encounter with Marxism has made it a matter of existential concern in the twentieth century. Meanwhile, the intellectual and moral relativism of the secular zeitgeist, in the West at least as much as in the East, has compelled new attention to the agnostic alternative as well.

To include all that is designated as atheism, it is necessary to distinguish, as theologians in dialogue with Marxism have, between theoretical and practical atheism. Theoretical atheism is the denial, in principle, that there is a god or gods. Most often, the term has been used polemically to label the position of an opponent who denies one's conception of the Divine. The Jews and early Christians were accused of atheism by the Romans, despite the obvious theism of Jewish and Christian beliefs, because they refused to acknowledge the Roman gods, including the emperor, as truly divine. The response of Christian apologists such as Augustine was to turn the accusation back on the Romans themselves. Orthodox Christians employed the term "atheist" in their polemics against various kinds of heresy, notably against those which, while affirming the existence of God, denied the doctrine of the Trinity in the form in which it was confessed by the church as dogma. A philosophical thinker like Baruch Spinoza (1632–1677), together with a theologian such as Schleiermacher whose doctrine of God he affected, earned the label because both of them, according to their critics, did not distinguish accurately enough between God and the world and thus appeared to deny the transcendence of the Divine.

From these examples it is evident that theoretical atheists in the absolute sense are not so numerous as the frequent use of the term might suggest. At the same time, it is not accurate to maintain, as some have, that there are no atheists. A thoroughgoing materialism or mechanism has sometimes led to the flat declaration that there is no Being deserving the title or the attributes of deity. To maintain that the universe is fully self-explanatory, or that human life neither has nor needs the help of any Holy to which to turn in penitence, prayer, and adoration, is an atheistic philosophy. The effort of certain modern philosophers and philosophical theologians to posit a "finite God," and the pantheism of others, tend to limit the applicability of the label "theoretical atheism" in modern thought.

Practical atheism, on the contrary, is not limited to the intelligentsia, but represents the working philosophy of large numbers of those to whom the Christian message is addressed. Practical atheism is the denial, in practice, that there is a god, or an attitude according to which the question of the existence of God is irrelevant to the meaning of life and the decisions of human existence. The discovery of scientific explanations for phenomena formerly attributed to supernatural causes has diminished the realm of MYSTERY and produced a "dis-enchanted world." Similarly, the elimination of the influence of organized religion from spheres of activity such as medicine, education, and the arts has led to a worldview in which ideas of God and of a life after death play no significant role. The term "secularism" was coined in the middle of the nineteenth century to identify such a philosophy of life. When pressed in a debate, its adherents may assert their belief in God, that is, their acceptance of the idea that there is a god, but apart from such debate they appear to have no need for this hypothesis. Most theologians would call such an outlook atheistic; for if the term "god" has any meaning, they would argue, that meaning must include an obligation to enter into significant relations with the Divine, whatever form those relations may assume.

"Agnostic" both as a term and as the identification of a philosophical position seems to have been coined in 1869 by the British biologist and scientific philosopher Thomas Huxley (1825–1895) to designate someone who repudiated Judeo-Christian theism and yet disclaimed doctrinaire atheism, transcending both in order to leave such questions as the existence of God in abeyance. In his *Science and the Christian Tradition* Huxley himself defined agnosticism as the principle "that it is wrong for a man to say that he is certain of the objective truth of any proposition unless he can produce evidence which logically justifies that certainty." This ruled out not only dogmatic belief in the propositions of the Christian tradition, but "the profession of disbelief in such inadequately supported propositions" as well.

From this definition and from the use of the word in ordinary speech it is evident that "agnostic" can cover two related but nevertheless distinct viewpoints. It may mean no more than the suspension of judgment on ultimate questions because not all the evidence has come in—or because all the evidence can never come in. In this sense even the New Testament's description of faith in Hebrews 11:1 as that which "gives substance to our hopes, and makes us certain of realities we do not see" might, by Huxley's definition, be called agnostic in its tenor, for it asserts that the final grounds of belief lie beyond the realm of evidence and experience. As doubt has been a path to conversion in the thought and development of Christian thinkers like Luther and Dostoevsky, so being agnostic in this sense belongs to the biblical interpretation of the relation to God. Agnosticism in this sense of the word is a position with which Christian APOPHATIC theology, whether ancient or modern, manifests affinities that some theologians find promising and others disturbing.

The context of Huxley's definition, however, makes it clear that this species of Christian faith and apophaticism was the intended polemical target of his charge of agnosticism, for the suspension of judgment on ultimate questions was thought to invalidate Christian beliefs about "realities we do not see." Huxley's essay on "Agnosticism and Christianity" was actually a discussion by a biologist of such nonbiological questions as the Mosaic authorship of the Pentateuch and the superiority of the ethic of the Sermon on the Mount. Hence the inventor of the word "agnostic" was himself responsible for its nontechnical use as a designation for only one of the combatants in the struggle that Andrew Dickson White (1832–1918) described in his *History of the Warfare of Science with Theology in Christendom*. Huxley's role in the warfare between evolution and creationism helped to establish this connotation as the primary one in the definition of the label "agnostic" and, contrary to his stated intention, to make the distinction between atheist and agnostic more difficult than ever to maintain.

• Atonement

The most surprising historical instance of the distinction between what became DOGMA and what did not is the contrast between the doctrine of the incarnation and the doctrine of the atonement or redemption through the work of Christ.

During the formative centuries of the doctrine of the incarnation, there had been many ways of describing the atonement, most of them having some precedent in biblical speech. One of the most prominent was the biblical metaphor of ransom: Satan held the human race captive in its sin and corruptibility, and the death of Christ was the ransom paid to the Devil as the price to set it free. A related metaphor for atonement was that of the victory of Christ: Christ entered into mortal combat with Satan for the human race, and the winner was to be lord; although the crucifixion appeared to be Christ's capitulation to the enemy, his resurrection broke the power of the Devil and gave the victory to Christ, granting to humanity the gift of immortality. From the Old Testament and the Epistle to the Hebrews came the image of Christ as both the priest and the sacrificial victim who was offered up to God to still the divine anger. From the sacrament of penance came the idea that the death of Christ was a vicarious satisfaction rendered to God for the human race. Following the New Testament (1 Peter 2:21), the church fathers could admonish their hearers to learn from the example of the death of Christ how to suffer patiently. They could also point to the suffering and death of Christ as the supreme illustration of how much God loves a sinful creature. As in the New Testament, therefore, so in the tradition of the church there were many figures of speech—not at all seen as mutually exclusive, but as complementary—to represent the atonement effected by the life, death, and resurrection of Christ.

These figures of speech strove to meet two needs simultaneously: to emphasize that the atonement was an act of God and to safeguard human participation in that act. Some theories were so objective in their emphasis upon the divine initiative that the human race seemed to be a pawn in the transaction between God-in-Christ and the Devil. Other theories so subjectively concentrated their attention on the human involvement and the human response that the divine aspect of the atonement could vanish from sight. Anselm of Canterbury (ca. 1033–1109), who decisively affected the development of natural theology, was also the theologian who most effectively brought together elements from many theories into one doctrine of the atonement, summarized in his book *Cur Deus homo?* (*Why God Became Man*). According to this doctrine, sin was a violation of the honor of God. God offered life to the descendants of Adam and Eve if they rendered satisfaction for that violation; but the longer human history went on, the deeper the debt became. Only a life that was truly human and yet had infinite worth could give satisfaction to the violated honor of God on behalf of the entire human race. Such a life was that of Jesus Christ, whom the mercy of God sent as a means of satisfying the justice of God. Because he was truly human, his life and death could be valid for humanity; but because he was truly divine, his life and death could be valid for *all* humanity. Accepting the fruits of his life and death conferred the benefits of his satisfaction.

With some relatively minor alterations—such as including the "active obedience" of the life of Christ along with the "passive obedience" of his death as the price of satisfaction—Anselm's doctrine of the atonement passed over into the theology of the Western church, forming the basis of both Roman Catholic and orthodox Protestant ideas of the work of Christ and helping to guarantee loyalty to the orthodox doctrine of incarnation, on which it had been based. It owed its acceptance to many factors, not the least of them being the way it squared with the liturgy and art of the West, Protestant as well as Catholic: not only the *Pietà* of Michelangelo Buonarroti (1475–1564) but the *Saint Matthew Passion* of Johann Sebastian Bach

(1685–1750) could be taken as expressions of this doctrine of the atonement. By this means, the doctrine said to have been implicit in the *lex orandi* of WORSHIP could be seen as having found its explicit formulation in the theological *lex credendi*. Unlike the incarnation, however, it did not achieve the status of a dogma of the universal church, whose only ecumenical statement of faith, the Nicene Creed, contented itself with saying that the life, death, and resurrection had been "for" humanity, without specifying how and why.

▪ Augustine of Hippo (354–430)

Convert, theologian, and (to paraphrase Alexander Souter) perhaps not the greatest of Latin writers, but almost certainly the greatest man who ever wrote Latin.

It seems likely that we are better informed about the intellectual and spiritual development of Augustine than that of any other theologian in Christian history, thanks to his composition of the *Confessions* in 397–401. To appreciate the special quality of this book, it is necessary to read it alongside the only writing from classical antiquity with which it deserves in any way to be compared, the *Meditations* of Emperor Marcus Aurelius (121–180 C.E.); but saying that merely reinforces its uniqueness. Although the genre of autobiography comprises many styles (including this autobiographical "philosophical dictionary"), the term does not do justice to Augustine's enterprise in the *Confessions*. It is a confession of sins to the God who forgives sins, and it is at the same time a confession of praise for the mystery of providence and GRACE.

Apart from its biographical and literary importance, the book belongs to the history of Christian theology for at least two reasons. The odyssey it charts for its readers is psychological, moral, and spiritual, but it is theological as well. It takes Augustine through the Neoplatonic philosophical theologians—chiefly, it seems, Plotinus (205–270 C.E.)—and through the dualistic theology of Manicheism to the doctrines of the Catholic Church; and therefore Augustine's description and defense of his personal religious development deals at length with the comparison between these theological systems, becoming a standard document for such comparisons and a source for later treatments of them. Yet the *Confessions* belongs to the history of theology for another and somewhat less obvious reason: through this book, more perhaps than through any other, the interpretation of the theologian's personal experience established itself as a legitimate component, in some sense even a source, of the theological task, and the person of the theologian became part of the theology.

The break with Manicheism was the first of a series of theological controversies in which Augustine was to be involved for all of his adult life; each was to elicit from him doctrinal formulations that would affect the subsequent history of Christian thought. To counteract Manichean dualism, he had to clarify his doctrine of the intrinsic goodness of creation in relation to the presence of evil in the world, and the reality of free will despite human sin. As that dispute was ending, he became embroiled in a defense of the Catholic Church of North Africa against the charge of the Donatists that, by harboring in its episcopate men who had betrayed the faith under the pressure of persecution, it had invalidated its ministry; his response, which was to become fundamental in the medieval understanding of the holiness of the church, was to insist that this holiness did not depend on the subjective moral state of clergy or faithful, but on the objective gift of grace conferred through the sacraments, which in turn depended for their validity on the institution of Christ and on the preservation of the unity of the Catholic Church as their locus. During the final decades of his life Augustine carried on the debate for which he was to be known best in later centuries, that against the Pelagians. His prayer in the *Confessions* asking God to "give what thou commandest, and command what thou wilt" seemed to his contemporary, the Irish monk Pelagius, to be treating individual moral responsibility with inadequate seriousness: every person faced the moral choices faced by Adam and Eve and was to be held accountable for the outcome of those choices. What Augustine interpreted as the Pelagian argument forced him to formulate his doctrine of original sin as the unavoidable consequence of the fall of Adam and Eve passed on to all their natural descendants, together with his doctrine of sovereign grace as the unearned gift of God to those who were the objects of divine election.

An older controversy, only vestigially remaining by Augustine's time, was the fourth-century conflict that issued in the orthodox doctrine of the TRINITY. "This is my faith, since it is also the Catholic faith": with these words Augustine inaugurated *On the Trinity*, which would become, for the Latin West at any rate, the classic summation of the central teaching of Christianity. In it he carefully rehearsed the biblical evidence for the trinitarian dogma, piecing it together from the many passages in both Old and New Testament that had to be considered. Engaged as he was during the same years with preparing his *Tractates on the Gospel of John*, he gave special attention to the passages from the Fourth Gospel that had figured so prominently in the development of that dogma. Its opening words, "When all things began, the Word (*Logos*) already was," identified the Logos with God in a manner that, in Augustine's eyes, made the doctrine of the Trinity necessary. On the other hand, those passages in the Fourth Gospel that seemed to contradict the orthodox teaching, notably the saying of Jesus, "The Father is greater than I" (John 14:28), had to be explained away. On that exegetical foundation Augustine proceeded to build the second and more speculative part of the treatise, in which he formulated his highly original and influential theory of the IMAGE OF GOD as an image of the entire Trinity, reflected in the structure of the human mind and in the nature of human thought and experience. A strong case can be made that *On the Trinity* must be accounted his most brilliant intellectual and theological achievement.

As is the case with the *Contra Celsum* of Origen within the apologetics of the Greek church fathers, so Augustine's *City of God (De civitate Dei)* stands in the Latin tradition as the most important monument of the defense of Christianity against outside attack. In this case it was principally the attack of those who blamed the church and the gospel for the fall of the Roman Empire. By the time he had completed his response, however, Augustine had not only rejected such arguments as a failure by the Romans to understand the endemic evils in the empire that had brought on its demise (thus anticipating EDWARD GIBBON), but had also formulated what was to become the classic Christian theory of the philosophy of history: that the providence of God was at work, through the events of human history, in leading the elect to the heavenly City of God, of which they were already citizens, and that the history of earthly and political cities such as Rome, whatever proximate good it might accomplish, was subordinated to that providence. In the process he had also begun to articulate a theological interpretation of politics, whose implications were to become a matter of debate especially in the aftermath of the Reformation.

During the Reformation, Protestants were as assiduous as Roman Catholics in laying claim to the heritage of Augustinian theology. His emphasis against the Donatists on the unity of the Catholic Church as the *conditio sine qua non* of Christianity seemed to support the Roman Catholic side, but his defense of sovereign grace against the Pelagians seemed to favor the Reformers against the scholastics, many of whom the Reformers therefore charged with being "Semi-Pelagian." Renewing that charge within the circle of Roman Catholic theology, Jansenism in the seventeenth century presented itself as the only authentic Augustinianism, but was condemned in the name of the synthesis of Augustine and THOMAS AQUINAS that had come out of the Council of Trent (1545–1563) after the Reformation.

Loyalty to the teachings of Augustine has not been confined to these disputing churches and theological parties. Étienne Gilson has suggested that the philosophical method of René Descartes (1596–1650) was an adaptation of the Augustinian procedure of moving through subjective doubt to objective affirmation of the self, the world, and God. In the twentieth century Augustine remains the only figure from early

Christianity—arguably, the only figure from all of late antiquity—whom we can still read with understanding and empathy.

· Authority

Lurking behind every theological issue is the problem of authority. As it is possible to stop any argument in its tracks by raising the epistemological question, "How do you know that, and how is that related to the way you know other things?" so the appeal to authority carries the specious appearance of promising to resolve all other matters of theological inquiry by making them its corollaries. Then the correlative of authority, which is obedience to Bible or CHURCH, assumes the position of the principal virtue from which all others can be derived.

As a result, authority has repeatedly become the *a priori* consideration in Christian doctrinal controversy. One of the first controversies in Christian history, already evident in some of the later books of the New Testament, was the confrontation with various systems of cosmic redemption that are now usually grouped under the title of Gnosticism. The confrontation involved many of the most fundamental teachings in Christian dogmatics and ethics: the place of evil in a good world allegedly created by a God of love; the reality of the incarnation in a truly human body of a Logos who was nevertheless coequal in the Trinity; the promise and hope of eschatology as the outcome of the divine plan. Every one of those doctrines would have been redefined if the Gnostics had succeeded in achieving respectability for their theologies, and in its response to them the ORTHODOXY of the church was obliged to consider its position on each. Yet it was above all by clarifying its schema of authority that orthodoxy triumphed. As formulated by Irenaeus of Lyons (ca. 130–ca. 200), the orthodox conception of authority rested on a tripartite foundation: the apostolic canon of the New Testament, together with the reaffirmed canon of the Old Testament; the apostolic CREED, as the normative "rule of faith" in accordance with which the Scriptures were to be interpreted; and the apostolic episcopate, as the guardian and repository by which apostolic Scripture and apostolic rule of faith could be recognized.

Once it had been defined through the controversy with Gnosticism as the doctrine on the basis of which all other doctrines could be dealt with, the appeal to authority remained a decisive factor in debates between theologians or between churches. To judge by its prominence in the polemical literature, the major dogmatic question dividing East and West in the controversy between Byzantium and Rome was the legitimacy of the doctrine of Filioque. That in turn frequently came down to differing conceptions of TRADITION (and implicitly of development of doctrine) and consequently of authority. The East charged the West with having arrogated to itself an authority over the text of the Nicene Creed that properly belonged to a general council, whereas the West, once it had been challenged in this manner, asserted that a council was ecumenical and therefore authoritative only if it was approved by the Holy See. This interpretation of the East-West conflict as ultimately a dispute over the authority of the papacy in the church seemed to find confirmation when, with the achievement of unanimity on authority, compromise formulas about the Trinity found acceptance on both sides, if only temporarily, as in the Union of Florence in 1439.

Within Western Christendom itself, the East-West schism was in many ways overshadowed by the divisions of the Reformation. In Luther's own religious and theological development, the central issue was the content of the gospel, which he equated with the Pauline doctrine of justification by faith. That led in turn to the fundamental divergences between the Reformation and Roman Catholicism over the relation of nature and grace. Nevertheless, both sides repeatedly interpreted the *status controversiae* on all these issues as a function of the prior division over the relative authority of Bible and tradition. At the center of Reformation debates over authority was a formula coined by Augustine in his controversy with Manicheism, a controversy that was in many ways a continuation of the battle of the earlier centuries against Gnosticism: "I would not believe the Gospel itself," Augustine had declared, "unless I were compelled to do so by the authority of the Catholic Church." Roman Catholics maintained that Augustine's position vis-à-vis Manicheism was paralleled in their stance against the Reformation's effort to dissociate the authority of the Gospel and of Scripture from that of the Catholic Church; Protestants denied that Augustine elevated the church over the Scriptures, and tried to limit this authority to the church's recognition of the canon of the New Testament as authentic, because Augustine himself had elsewhere refused to allow his own books and those of other theologians to be placed on the same level as the Bible. Both Protestants and Roman Catholics frequently gave the impression that if the nature and locus of authority could be identified, reconciliation on everything else would naturally follow.

The multiplication of theological differences and divisions within Protestantism, which supposedly agrees on the supreme (or even sole) authority of Scripture, has done little to confirm that simplistic view; nor does it, on the other hand, tend to substantiate the no less simplistic claim of Roman Catholic anti-Reformation polemics that the recovery of a proper definition of authority and the reestablishment of obedience to it would put all other doctrines in their proper place. Like the epistemological question, to which it may be seen as the theological corollary, the place of authority in a theological system is often understood better *a posteriori* than *a priori*. Those theologians, such as the Cappadocians and Luther (however great their differences), who have introduced authority only after their exposition of other doctrines may initially have confused their hearers about the grounds for their teachings, but they have avoided giving the impression that their theology was a system analogous to Euclidean geometry, in which all other doctrines emerged as deductions from the prolegomena on authority. That may or may not be theologically or philosophically satisfying, but it is at any rate how doctrines—including and especially the doctrine of authority itself—have developed.

• Baptism

As the initiatory rite of the Christian Church, baptism has been observed well-nigh universally by all who call themselves Christian. The meaning and effect of baptism, however, have been the subject of considerable controversy, especially since the Reformation.

Although some critical scholars have been inclined to dispute the claim that Christian baptism was instituted by Jesus himself, such was the unanimous teaching of the early church. There is no actual account of the institution of baptism, but the Gospel of Matthew closes with the "Great Commission" issued by the risen Christ to his followers: "Go therefore and make all nations my disciples; baptize men everywhere in the name of the Father and the Son and the Holy Spirit, and teach them to observe all that I have commanded you" (Matt. 28:19). Other passages in the New Testament, such as John 3:5, substantiate the impression that Jesus had instituted baptism earlier. Around this basic rite a wealth of imagery and meaning was centered, as the Epistles of the New Testament, especially those of Paul, indicate. Baptism was likened to the deluge in the time of Noah (1 Peter 3:20–22)—a prefigurement that achieved wide circulation among early Christian writers. In Romans 6:3–4 Paul said that baptism granted a share in the death and resurrection of Christ, and that it communicated the forgiveness of sins. It was associated with the gift of the HOLY SPIRIT, as a passage such as Acts 9:17–19 suggests. On the basis of these and similar declarations by the writers of the New Testament it must be concluded that in the Christian community of the first century baptism was regarded as essential to the new birth and membership in the kingdom of God.

The Gospel of John claims the authority of Jesus Christ himself for this interpretation of baptism: "No one can enter the kingdom of God without being born from water and spirit" (John 3:5). Neither the New Testament nor other early Christian literature makes explicit reference to the custom of baptizing infants, although they do make it clear that the gift of salvation belonged to children as well as to adults (Acts 2:39) and draw a parallel between Christian baptism and Jewish circumcision (Col. 2:11–13). On the basis of such evidence it has been argued that infant baptism was a custom that had come down from the apostles themselves, as Origen seems to have been the first to maintain. On the other hand, Tertullian (ca. 160–ca. 225) seems to have been the first to object to infant baptism; this suggests that by the end of the second century it was already a practice of the church, and one over which there was no serious controversy.

What did produce controversy in the early church was the question of whether baptism by heretics was valid and whether, consequently, those who came over to orthodox Christianity from the heretical groups were to be baptized a second time. During the third century the North African church was enforcing such a requirement, which provoked a controversy with the bishop of Rome, who argued for the objective validity of baptism even when it was administered by a heretical priest. The same question, though in a different form, came up two centuries later. The Catholic answer, as formulated by AUGUSTINE, was that not the "who" but the "what" in baptism determined its validity. If, therefore, a heretic or even a pagan baptized according to the prescribed form and intended the act to be the baptism of the church, this would be a valid baptism. Such is the position Roman Catholic, Orthodox, Anglican, and Lutheran theologians have all taken.

In the East the doctrinal development did not contradict

such Western emphases, but it did manifest emphases of its own. One of the favorite motifs of the Greek fathers was the idea that baptism prepared the Christian for resurrection. Connected with this idea was the "seal of the Holy Spirit," which was said to impart to the candidate an "indelible character." Another favorite metaphor was the notion of "illumination" (Greek *phōtisma*) through baptism. In the structure of SACRAMENTS in Eastern churches baptism is accompanied by confirmation; thereafter the candidate receives the Eucharist even as an infant. The baptismal formula of some Eastern churches was (and still is): "This servant of Christ is baptized in the name of the Father and of the Son and of the Holy Spirit," instead of the "I baptize you . . ." employed in the West. Despite some theological conflict over the propriety of the Eastern formula, the Western Church finally declared it acceptable, while retaining its own; it also took over into its piety and its theology many of the emphases characteristic of the baptismal thought of the Greek Christians. The Nicene Creed spoke for all of Christendom when it declared: "We acknowledge one baptism for the remission of sins."

Drawing upon both biblical and traditional themes of baptismal theology, the scholastics gave this doctrine a precision it had not always had in the earlier writers of the church, incorporating it into a comprehensive sacramental system, in which the doctrine of baptism both shaped and was shaped by the church's definition of the sacraments in general. According to scholastic teaching baptism was a means of grace in which, through the use of water and the divinely instituted formula, the neophyte was admitted to membership in the visible church; SIN, both original and actual, was forgiven, an indelible character was implanted, and the gift of the Holy Spirit was conferred.

This traditional doctrine of baptism was not, as such, a primary target of criticism in the Reformation. Most of the Anglican reformers, here as elsewhere, took a position that manifested continuity with the medieval teaching. Baptism was regarded as a means of GRACE, and it worked both regeneration and forgiveness, even in infants. Luther taught that baptism granted forgiveness of sins, life, and salvation. John Calvin (1509–1564) also acknowledged that baptism effected regeneration, but only in the predestined; in general, there was less room in Calvin's system than in Luther's for a doctrine of the means of grace. Ulrich Zwingli (1484–1531) took a more extreme position than either Calvin or Luther in his stand against Roman Catholic sacramentalism. The logical outcome of Zwingli's position would have been to question not only the sacramental definition of baptism, but its very necessity.

This conclusion was drawn not by the "magisterial Reformation," but by the Anabaptists. Their hostility to the union of church and state caused them to look for a believers' church, into which one would come not automatically by birth and infant baptism, but consciously by the decision of faith. This view of the church and of the individual represented a fundamental break with the baptismal tradition. Instead of infant baptism the Anabaptists insisted upon believers' baptism, which would follow faith rather than create it. Although the lines of descent from Anabaptism to more recent Protestant denominations are not easy to draw, this insistence did set the pattern for several denominations to formulate doctrines of baptism that differed from the medieval doctrine much more sharply than the teachings of the Reformers had. Because they hold that the church, as holy, is composed of true believers who have made personal confession of their faith, these denominations argue that the decision of faith may be neither anticipated nor taken away from the child by its parents and the church. Therefore baptism must be postponed until such a time as the child becomes capable of making this decision personally. This shift in baptism was of a piece with the more general revision of traditional sacramentalism by Protestant theology, and it regained the attention of theologians when it was given a vigorous statement in 1947 by Karl Barth (1886–1968).

▪ Bible

Much of the material that is in this philosophical dictionary—and much more that is not—could, in one way or another, be part of a book-length article on the Bible and its place in the history of theology. It makes more sense, therefore, to make this what editors of encyclopedias usually call an "article on articles," an expanded cross-reference.

The entry AUTHORITY considers the role of the Bible in the life and teaching of the CHURCH; the entries TRADITION and DEVELOPMENT OF DOCTRINE examine some of the ways the use of the Bible has worked itself out in history. For the Christian definition of the Old Testament, also in comparison with the way it is defined within Judaism, the entry CANON OF HEBREW SCRIPTURE (THE OLD TESTAMENT) serves as a guide. It is paralleled by CANON OF THE NEW TESTAMENT, for the books added to the Hebrew Bible by the church to form the Christian Scriptures. The theological and scholarly issues in the determination of variant readings in the manuscripts of the New Testament are the subject of the entry TEXT OF THE NEW TESTAMENT. An overview of the methods by which biblical interpreters have derived religious and theological meaning from the canon and text of the Bible, once agreed upon as authoritative, appears under the entry HERMENEUTICS. It is supplemented by individual articles on some of the major figures in the history of biblical interpretation, such as ORIGEN OF ALEXANDRIA, AUGUSTINE OF HIPPO, and MARTIN LUTHER.

▪ Byzantium

Like "medieval," the historical category "Byzantine" is burdened with pejorative connotations. Although the entry on "Byzantine" in *Webster's Third New International Dictionary* deals exclusively with the significance of the term for art history and ecclesiastical history, its meaning in today's usage would seem to be: unnecessarily complicated or involuted, perhaps also devious and hypocritical. Often linked with the adverb "downright," the term seems frequently to be invoked in exasperation, especially as a result of confrontations with bureaucratic regulations or with intellectual abstractions. For example, an earlier volume in this series of "philosophical dictionaries" describes a sequence of events in which "what had been simplicity in the first years now quickly became Byzantine in complexity and also in opulence."

There was, it must be admitted, much in the life and history of the Byzantine Empire to justify such usage. For example, in the practice of divorce Byzantine style it was said to have been possible for an emperor to put away his wife by asking her to stand as godmother to his illegitimate child; the spiritual kinship between the parent and the godparent of a child, as defined by Byzantine theology and canon law, made marriage between them a form of incest, and so the marriage could be annulled.

Earlier connotations of "Byzantium" and "Byzantine" were no less pejorative. One of the most widely circulated descriptions is that of GIBBON, in Chapter 53 of *Decline and Fall of the Roman Empire*: "They held in their lifeless hands the riches of their fathers, without inheriting the spirit which had created and improved that sacred patrimony; they read, they praised, they compiled, but their languid souls seemed alike incapable of thought and action. In the revolution of ten centuries, not a single discovery was made to exalt the dignity or promote the happiness of mankind." Yet even Gibbon had been obliged, a few paragraphs earlier, to acknowledge, albeit grudgingly, that "the Byzantine Greeks . . . by the assiduous study of the ancients, have deserved *in some measure* the remembrance and gratitude of the moderns" (emphasis added). For young scholars who overdosed on Gibbon in their early teens, these caricatures were their first introduction to Byzantium. Those fortunate enough to be using the edition of Gibbon prepared by J. B. Bury (1861–1927) learned from his introduction that this issue was probably the one on which Gibbon was weakest (except, Bury added, "perhaps on the Slavonic side of the history of the Empire"). Bury himself went on to help turn Byzantine studies around in the West, above all by his own *History of the Later Roman Empire,* published in 1923 and still indispensable.

Whether because they find that "Slavonic side of the history of the Empire" personally intriguing or because they are interested in the continuities of Byzantine orthodoxy with the early Greek Christianity of the CAPPADOCIANS, scholars in historical theology have increasingly turned to Byzantium. For many of them in twentieth-century America, their mentor and *patēr pneumatikos* was George V. Florovsky (1893–1979), through whom they learned that this continued preoccupation with the Byzantine heritage could in turn help them to understand the West.

▪ Canon of Hebrew Scripture (The Old Testament)

The Christian movement was born with a Bible in its hand: the Hebrew Scripture that constituted the Bible of Judaism. This appears to have been transmitted within the Jewish community in at least two divergent collections: the broader collection reflected in the Septuagint, the translation of the Hebrew Bible into Greek carried out by Alexandrian Jews in the second century B.C.E., and a narrower canon accepted in Palestine and then adopted by the assembly of rabbis at Jamnia about 90 or 100 C.E. under the leadership of Rabbi Akiba (ca. 50–132 C.E.). Eventually Christians came to call the Hebrew Bible the "Old Testament," to correspond with the "New Testament" of specifically Christian Scripture. Not only did the church give the Hebrew Bible a special name, and through its schematism of prophecy and fulfillment develop a distinctive system of HERMENEUTICS for interpreting it; it also made the determination of its normative canon a task for Christian theologians and eventually for a council of the Roman Catholic Church.

The Holy Scripture for Jesus and the early Christians was the Hebrew Bible of the Jewish community, but no list of books it included exists. To ascertain its scope it is necessary, therefore, to scrutinize the Old Testament quotations and references that appear in the New Testament. Such scrutiny has occupied generations of biblical scholars, who have identified references and allusions to most of the books of the Old Testament, though not to all of them. Among the books to which the New Testament refers are several of the so-called Apocrypha belonging only to the list of books in the Septuagint, as well as some books, such as Enoch (see Jude 9), that do not belong to any canon. Some scholars have even attempted to identify two canons of the Old Testament lying behind the New; they contend that the Old Testament used by the Epistle to the Hebrews was the Septuagint, whereas that used by other portions of the New Testament was the narrower Palestinian canon. Such attempts, however, have not proved convincing to the majority of biblical historians. The study of Old Testament quotations in the New Testament has led to an ambiguous conclusion regarding the state of the Old Testament canon in the first century C.E.

That ambiguity makes it understandable that the early fathers of the Christian Church were unclear about the canon of the Old Testament. Melito of Sardis (d. ca. 190) is said by Eusebius of Caesarea (ca. 260–ca. 340) to have inquired among Eastern rabbis about the scope of their canon. The catalogue they gave him, as reproduced by Eusebius, corresponds neither to the Hebrew nor to the Greek list of books: it contains the Wisdom of Solomon, but it does not contain the Book of Esther. A list given by Origen includes Esther but puts it at the very end; the catalogue of Athanasius of Alexandria (ca. 296–373) omits Esther altogether. For most of the early Christian fathers the Old Testament meant the Septuagint, because few of them other than Origen knew both biblical LANGUAGES. Although they were aware of the divergence between the canon as accepted by the Jews and the list of books contained in the Septuagint, the examples of Melito, Origen, and Athanasius suggest that the status of the disputed books remained in doubt during the first four centuries of the Christian era.

Jerome (ca. 347–ca. 420) was one of the few Christians in those centuries to learn Hebrew. What he learned from Jewish rabbis caused him to distinguish sharply between the canon as approved by the Jews and the catalogue represented in the Septuagint. As he came to prefer the Hebrew text to the Septuagint, so he also assigned primary authority to the Jewish canon and put the deuterocanonical books, or Apocrypha, into at best a secondary position. Jerome's contemporary AUGUSTINE, on the other hand, provides a catalogue of Old Testament writings that includes these books. Thoughout the medieval period the status of the deuterocanonical books remained doubtful. Some theologians followed Jerome and excluded them altogether from the Bible; others followed Augustine and accepted them with little hesitation; still others had reservations but used them as Holy Scripture. Contact between Jewish and Christian scholars, which was commoner during the Middle Ages than is often supposed, served to point out to many Christian theologians the discrepancies between their Old Testament and the Bible of the Jews. But it was not until the period of Renaissance and Reformation that the issue once more became a matter of concern and controversy to Christian thinkers.

As part of their insistence that the church return to the authority of the Bible rather than that of tradition, the Protestant Reformers called for the elimination of the deuterocanonical books from the Bible. Luther's translation of the Bible included them in a separate section as Apocrypha, to be read but not to be put on the same level as canonical Scripture. The other Reformers were even more vigorous in their opposition. Believing that the Old Testament canon in use among the Jews of their own time was also the Bible of Jesus and of the early Christians, they refused to accept quotations from the Apocrypha as support for Christian teaching. The use of certain passages in the Apocrypha to support prayers for the dead (2 Macc. 12:43–45) and other Roman Catholic practices and doctrines only strengthened them in this refusal. During the nineteenth century Protestants in England went so far as to prohibit the printing of Bibles that included the Apocrypha, even with an explanatory note like the one in Luther's translation. Not until the twentieth century did it become possible once more to issue the Apocrypha within the covers of Protestant Bibles, and that only in some few editions.

In antithesis to the position of the Reformers, the Roman Catholic Council of Trent (1545–1563) made the larger canon, including the deuterocanonical books, the official list of biblical books for the church. More than a century later, in 1672, the Synod of Jerusalem established the Old Testament canon for the Eastern Orthodox churches, accepting four of the books in the Septuagint (Tobit, Judith, Wisdom, and Ecclesiasticus) but rejecting Baruch and the Books of the Maccabees.

Ever since the sixteenth and seventeenth centuries, therefore, the churches of Christendom have had a clearly defined canon of the Old Testament—or, rather, three canons, one each for Roman Catholicism, Protestantism, and Eastern Orthodoxy. The canons of Protestantism and Judaism are identical, although the order of the books is different. One consequence of ecumenical cooperation is that Christian theologians on all sides have come to approach the question of the Old Testament canon less polemically and more historically. The new understanding between Jews and Christians of every tradition has given the Jewish canon a certain presumptive force also among Roman Catholics, while the new understanding of postbiblical tradition has caused Protestants to look at the Apocrypha with greater sympathy.

▪ Canon of the New Testament

In addition to, and alongside, the CANON OF HEBREW SCRIPTURE (THE OLD TESTAMENT), which it received from Judaism, the early church had an oral TRADITION about Jesus Christ, which lies behind the New Testament and is presupposed by it. Only gradually, however, did the codification of that tradition in the books of the New Testament evolve into a parallel biblical canon.

Several factors seem to have been responsible for the rise of the New Testament canon; church historians vary in the amount of weight they assign to each. One factor certainly was the sheer passage of time, as the church needed to discover whatever resources it could to bind it to its past and to guarantee its continuity in the tradition of the faith; the "memoirs of the apostles" were one such resource. Also responsible for the establishment of the canon was the circulation of writings that bore the names of apostles but did not contain apostolic teaching (as that teaching was being interpreted by the church). The only way to eliminate these forgeries was to define the limits of the apostolic writings. Such a definition became a crucial necessity when the heretic Marcion of Pontus (d. ca. 160) compiled a canon of the New Testament containing his edition of the epistles of PAUL and of the Gospel of Luke, which he regarded as the only genuine GOSPEL. Although it now appears that Marcion alone did not cause the church to establish its canon, he did accelerate the process. Another heretical movement that helped to accelerate it was Montanism, whose claim of speaking in the name of the Holy Spirit could be countered only by reference to the genuine authority of the Spirit in the apostolic witness of the New Testament writings. The task of sifting through the writings of the early church and of identifying this apostolic witness occupied Christians well into the fourth century. Eusebius of Caesarea (ca. 260–ca. 340) suggested the division of the New Testament writings into *homologoumena,* those that were acknowledged almost universally as part of the New Testament, and *antilegomena,* those that were disputed but finally accepted.

The earliest pieces of Christian literature to be collected seem to have been the Epistles of Paul, but it would appear, despite 2 Peter 3:16, that they did not qualify as Scripture. From the liturgical usage of the church at Rome it seems that the Gospels were the first Christian books to be added to the canon of Hebrew Scripture as supplementary Scripture, and that this had happened by the middle of the second century. Also from Rome, and also apparently from the second century, comes the oldest extant list of New Testament writings, the Muratorian fragment, so named because it was published by the scholar and theologian Lodovico Antonio Muratori (1672–1750). It was written in Latin, perhaps in translation from a Greek original, and contains the names of the books being read at Rome about 200. By about that time, as the writings of Irenaeus (ca. 130–ca. 200) and Tertullian (ca. 160–ca. 225) suggest, both Lyons and Carthage were using the Gospels, the Epistles of Paul, and some other Epistles as Scripture. A few years later the works of Origen make it clear that he was working with a similar though not identical collection.

From these four places—Rome, Lyons, Carthage, and Alexandria—may be compiled a list of books on which they all agreed. That list would include the following, given in the order now employed in the New Testament: Matthew, Mark, Luke, John, Acts, Romans, 1 Corinthians, 2 Corinthians, Galatians, Ephesians, Philippians, Colossians, 1 Thessalonians, 2 Thessalonians, 1 Timothy, 2 Timothy, Titus, Philemon, and 1 John.

From these same sources and from several church fathers quoted by Eusebius may be assembled also a list of the books that were disputed on one or another ground, but that eventually were included in the canon of the New Testament. The Epistle to the Hebrews belongs to this category. It seems to have been accepted in the Eastern section of the church but disputed in the West, for it does not appear in the Muratorian canon and is also questioned by other writers. The Epistle of James was in doubt among even more writers. Although 1 Peter is almost universally acknowledged, it is absent from the Muratorian catalogue. 2 Peter, on the other hand, was questioned by many fathers who accepted 1 Peter. The Epistle of Jude appears in the Muratorian canon but was rejected elsewhere. Sometimes 2 John and 3 John were included with 1 John as one book, but they did not receive the universal support that it did. Presumably because of its apocalyptic ESCHATOLOGY, the Book of Revelation was the object of more antagonism than any other of the books eventually canonized. The Montanist movement made apocalyptic literature suspect in the orthodox church, and some writers did not believe that the same man had written the Gospel of John and Revelation.

The writings of Eusebius and Athanasius make it evident that agreement on the disputed books was approaching by the middle of the fourth century, and that the canon of the New Testament that now appears in the Bible was gaining general, if not quite universal, acceptance. That canon appears for the first time in the thirty-ninth Festal Letter of Athanasius, written in 367.

After the Festal Letter other traditions held their own for a time. The school of Antioch accepted only three of the so-called catholic Epistles—James, 1 Peter, and 1 John—although one of its most illustrious representatives, Theodore of Mopsuestia (ca. 350–428), rejected the whole of this section of the canon. The West followed the lead of Athanasius. In 382 a synod was held at Rome under Pope Damasus (366–384) at which the influence of Jerome (ca. 347–ca. 420) secured the adoption of a list of books answering to that of Athanasius. This was ratified by Pope Gelasius (492–496). The same list was confirmed independently for the province of Africa in a series of synods at Hippo Regius in 393 and at Carthage in 397 and 419 under the leadership of Augustine. The Second Trullan Council of 692, the Quinisextum, may be taken to have formally closed the process of the formation of the canon for East and West. Yet Eusebius's distinction between *homologoumena* and *antilegomena* did not disappear completely from the church. It was revived by Luther in his objections to the Epistle of James, and it formed part of the basis for the modern reconsideration of the canon.

▪ Cappadocians

During the fourth century of the Christian era, the Roman procuratorial province of Cappadocia in Asia Minor—like Florence in the fifteenth century or colonial Virginia in the eighteenth—became the scene for a remarkable outpouring of literary and philosophical genius, lending its name to three outstanding leaders of Christian thought whose theological accomplishments were, and still are, classics of courageous speculation even as they represent the golden age of Greek Christian ORTHODOXY.

All three of them were born in Cappadocia within a few years after the Council of Nicea of 325, at which the orthodox doctrine of the Trinity had been promulgated. Although that doctrine owed its official standing in both church and state to the decrees of the council, it owes its intellectual standing above all to the defense and exposition of the Nicene decrees first by Athanasius of Alexandria (ca. 296–373) and then by the three Cappadocians. As the heirs simultaneously of Greek learning and of Christian faith, they brought to their exposition and defense the theological and exegetical insights they had inherited from the Greek PATRISTIC tradition, as well as the analytic and rhetorical skills that had come to them from the Greek philosophical tradition. In a time like our own, which is inclined to ignore rhetorical skill, dismissing it as "mere rhetoric"—and which is therefore highly vulnerable to its suasions—it may be necessary to explain that the study of rhetoric, like the study of the law with which it had many connections, was a preparation for many areas of public service in state and church. The philosophical analyses of the Cappadocians make use of the categories of Neoplatonism for the statement of Christian doctrine. Far from representing merely a HELLENIZATION of the gospel, this combination of traditions made Cappadocian thought the intellectual fulfillment of the saying of Jesus: "Be wary as serpents, innocent as doves" (Matt. 10:16).

Basil the Great (ca. 330–379), bishop of Caesarea, is most widely remembered as the founder of Greek cenobitic monasticism, whose monastic Rule set down the principles and practices of the ascetic life in a form that has continued to stand in Eastern communities and that significantly influenced the development of monasticism in the West as well. The theological significance of Basil's Rule, set against heretical forms of asceticism, lies chiefly in its successful combination of the imperative to deny the self and the world with a vigorous affirmation of the goodness of the creation. That affirmation was part of Basil's recognition, stated in his influential educational treatise, *Exhortation to Youths as to How They Shall Best Profit by the Writings of Pagan Authors,* that the natural world and natural reason were God's good gift and were to be received with thanks. Principally, however, Basil earned his place in the history of theology by his masterpiece *On the Holy Spirit (De Spiritu Sancto).* Because of the peculiar difficulties of the doctrine of the Holy Spirit, the methods employed for arriving at dogma in the doctrine of the Trinity did not quite fit the doctrine of the Holy Spirit, and it was necessary to revise the techniques and the terminology in articulating the faith of the church regarding the Third Person of the Trinity. Basil took the formula of baptism as stated in Matthew 28:19–20 as the basis for an argument that the logic of the church's confession stated there and of the church's CREED as stated at the Council of Nicea made it obligatory to coordinate the Holy Spirit with the Father and the Son in dogma as well as in the *lex orandi* of the doxologies and baptismal rites in its worship.

His younger brother Gregory (ca. 330–ca. 395), who was bishop of Nyssa for a quarter century and thus is known to history as Gregory of Nyssa, also was trained in rhetoric and considered the possibility of a career in it. But thanks to the guidance of their elder sister, Macrina, the church and theology drew not only Basil but Gregory, who went on to become the most creative of the reinterpreters of the thought of ORIGEN, bringing it into line with the theological conclusions to which orthodoxy had come since Origen's pioneering explorations. As an Origenist he is noteworthy especially for his effort—concerning whose success there is continuing controversy—to formulate an orthodox version of the doctrine of APOCATASTASIS. The subtlety of his philosophical thought enabled him to meet challenges both pagan and heretical on their own ground, above all in his treatise *Against Eunomius,* in which he sometimes seems to come close to making the unity of the Trinity in God a special and supreme instance of the Platonic doctrine of universals. Because it was also the heresy of Eunomius (d. 394) to claim (according to his orthodox opponents) that he knew the nature of God as well as God did, Gregory's affirmation of the abiding mystery of the divine nature even after revelation and incarnation stands as a major document in the history of orthodox APOPHATIC theology. In his exegetical works, Gregory continued and refined the hermeneutics of Origen, and in such commentaries as his exposition of the Song of Songs he pressed mystical theology to the limits of the church's teachings, but not beyond them.

It was, however, another Gregory (329–389), bishop of Nazianzus and then (briefly) of Constantinople, who acquired the epithet "the Theologian" or "the Divine." This title, which recognized him as the expounder of the meaning of the doctrine of God as Trinity, was applied preeminently to the evangelist John, who was taken to be the author of the Gospel bearing his name (which provided the most elaborate proof for the Trinity) as well as of the three Epistles of John and of the Book of Revelation (which is therefore still known as "the Revelation of Saint John the Divine"). Gregory's right to the title comes chiefly from his five *Theological Orations.* Like Basil's *On the Holy Spirit,* they were called forth by the debate over the propriety of calling the Holy Spirit by the name "God" in the same way as the Father and the Son; but he was much less hesitant than Basil about the use of that name. The *Theological Orations* rooted the doctrine of the Holy Spirit in a comprehensive interpretation of the relation of the One and the Three, and the ecclesiastical-speculative Eastern doctrine of the Trinity, in its distinction from the trinitarian speculations of Augustine, owes much to this exposition. As one scholar has put it, "it is Gregory's great merit to have given for the first time a clear definition of the distinctive character of the divine persons."

It is the great merit of all three Cappadocians together to have given a comprehensive systematization of the Greek understanding of the gospel, not only as a statement of the doctrine of the Trinity, but as an entire spiritual and intellectual system. In its treatment of such doctrines as sin and the atonement, the corpus of spiritual and theological works produced by the Cappadocians also manifested a treatment of the question of nature and grace that did not have to rely on the categories of Augustine. Whenever someone asks whether there exists a succinct but profound statement of that spiritual and intellectual outlook, with at least some of the subjective and yet objective flavor of the *Confessions* of Augustine, the most appropriate answer is probably the *Life of Macrina* by Gregory of Nyssa. In it she appears as the decisive force in the shaping of the faith of her two eminent brothers, but also as a substantial theologian in her own right. Her dying prayer reported there, as Harnack recognized, "expresses the hopes and the consolation of Greek Christianity in an unsurpassed way, without permitting one to miss the peculiar animation of feeling that belongs to the essence of this Christianity." The blending of these elements in their thought helps to explain the hold that the Cappadocians have had on the interpreters and followers of Eastern Orthodoxy from their time to our own.

· Church

Even in the Gospels as edited by the church, there are only two passages (Matt. 16:18; Matt. 18:17) in which the word "church" (Greek *ekklēsia*) appears in the sayings attributed to Jesus, by contrast with the many in which Jesus speaks about the kingdom of God. Yet by the time the canon of the New Testament was established, the church had acquired the inchoate institutional structures that are presupposed in the Epistles to Timothy and to Titus, and it was being spoken of in the grandiloquent language of the Epistles to the Ephesians and Colossians as Christ's "body [which] as such holds within it the fullness of him who himself receives the entire fullness of God" (Eph. 1:23). A confession of "the holy church" belonged to the earliest recensions of the CREED or rule of faith; and although the doctrine of the church has not had the same sort of continuous history that has marked the doctrine of the incarnation, but has moved to the center of theological interest only from time to time, its prominence in the New Testament and in the creeds has assured it a place in most expositions of Christian belief. The most influential formulation of ecclesiology has been that of the Niceno-Constantinopolitan Creed: "And [we believe] in one holy catholic and apostolic church." Countless manuals of DOGMA—in Greek and Latin, German and Russian—have made these four *notae ecclesiae* (marks of the church) the outline for their presentation of the doctrine.

The creedal statement that the church is "one" has been variously employed: as the description of an empirical reality; as a doctrinal affirmation to be held in spite of empirical reality; or as an imperative to change empirical reality to conform with the doctrinal affirmation. Everyone's New Testament has contained the "high-priestly prayer" of Jesus on the night before his death, "May they all be one" (John 17:21). Nothing more indelibly confirms the persistence of the sense that the church was intended by its founder to be one than the sometimes desperate efforts of those who live in an empirically divided Christendom to prove that the church has nevertheless preserved its oneness. One way to achieve this is to identify the church with one's own church; another is to define the church (and hence its unity) as essentially invisible, regardless of the state of the visible church or churches. On the grounds for the unity there has also been continuing disagreement. Some have found oneness in the sharing of Christian service to the world; some have sought the unity in the institutional affiliation of all parts of the church with one another through a hierarchical structure; others have insisted on a unity of faith and doctrine as prerequisite to unity of any kind. The ECUMENICAL movement, by its attention to "Faith and Order" as well as to "Life and Work," has gone beyond these differences of definition to work for unity—and reunion—simultaneously on all these grounds.

Of the four marks of the church, the designation "holy" is the earliest to appear in a creed; but as the term has carried a variety of meanings when applied to persons, so also the "holiness" of the church has led to fundamental disagreements. The dispute between Augustine and his Donatist opponents dealt with the relation between the first and the second of the attributes of the church: they argued that fundamentally compromising the moral holiness of the church by tolerating the continued ministry of clergy who had committed mortal sin (as, in their judgment, the Catholic Church had done) vitiated the authentic unity of the church and the integrity of its sacraments; he maintained that the unity was prerequisite to the holiness and therefore had to be preserved as the *summum bonum,* because only a church that was one could help its members and clergy grow toward the ideal of holiness. Also in the name of the holiness of the church various systems of church discipline have evolved; their beginnings are evident in the New Testament, both in the instruction of Jesus about how to proceed if your "brother commits a sin" (Matt. 18:15–17) and in the actual dealings with such cases in early Christian congregations, notably with the incest that had appeared among the Corinthians (1 Cor. 5:1–5). In protest against what they took to be the excessive laxity of the church in the medieval period, several REFORMATION groups made the restoration of strict church discipline and the enforcement of the imperative of holiness an essential component of their doctrine of the church.

The attribute "catholic" has seemed to be the easiest of the four to confirm empirically. For if it meant, in Augustine's phrase, that the church is "dispersed throughout the world," the achievements of the Christian missionary enterprise— Roman Catholic, Orthodox, and Protestant—made the catholicity of the church visible. Whatever may have been true of the British Empire, it is certainly the case that the sun never sets on the Christian Church. Nevertheless, theologians have repeatedly suggested that such an understanding of the catholicity of the church can be quite superficial. The church was already truly "catholic" when it was confined to the congregations described in the New Testament, in the sense that it existed as the universal church beyond any such individual local body. Upon hearing the term "Catholic Church," most people would think of the Roman Catholic Church. Yet its own leaders, by their recognition of the validity of the Eastern Orthodox tradition and churches as well as by their acknowledgement that through baptism the sacramental boundaries of the church are greater than its institutional boundaries, have extended the title "Catholic" beyond that simple identification. Particularly since the work of Newman and the Oxford Movement, "Catholic" has often been employed as a title for those churches, and those movements within various churches, that have emphasized CONTINUITY with the doctrine, polity, and liturgy of the patristic and medieval periods.

When the New Testament speaks of the church as "built upon the foundation laid by the apostles and prophets" (Eph. 2:20), it specifies that the true church must be able to call itself "apostolic." Since an apostle was "one sent"—the old parsonage joke was that this was as much as some people were willing to give—calling the church apostolic, whatever else it may have meant, implied that the church was in mission to the world, as the apostles themselves were. But since the second century formulations of orthodoxy as summarized by Irenaeus of Lyons (ca. 130–ca. 200), apostolicity has taken on the special meaning of accepting and obeying the AUTHORITY of the apostles, as this had been expressed through the apostolic Scriptures, through the apostolic tradition and creed, and through the apostolic office of the bishops. When the leaders of the Protestant Reformation broke with this understanding, it was in the name of a more authentic apostolicity, expressed above all in the conformity of the church's teaching and preaching with the message of the Bible. In the debates of the ecumenical movement, the designation of the church as apostolic has become controversial particularly through the insistence of some upon the restoration of the "historic episcopate," understood as the doctrine of the apostolic succession of ordaining bishops.

During the nineteenth century, when the DEVELOPMENT OF DOCTRINE was changing the perspective of theologians, it became fashionable for them to speak of their own time as "the age of the church," by which they meant that after other doctrines had had their own special eras—Trinity in the patristic centuries, sacraments in the medieval period, justification in the age of the Reformation—it was now the turn of the doctrine of the church to develop. Across a wide spectrum of denominational and geographical distribution, many theologians of that period did turn their attention to it in fresh and powerful ways; and in many ways the rise of an ecumenical theology has been the fruit of those labors.

· Continuity

Practically every day for nineteen and one-half centuries, Christians somewhere in the world have gathered around consecrated bread and wine in commemoration of their Lord and in celebration of his presence. Although there is no conceivable way to provide documentary proof for so apodictic a generalization, most students of Christianity would probably acknowledge it to be true. If it is true, this repetition of the sacrament of the Eucharist for nearly three-fourths of a million days in a row stands as a massive instance of the continuity of the church across changes of culture and language, liturgy and theology.

Yet a reader will have to go far to find any reference to this continuity—or to most of the other continuities—in present-day manuals of ecclesiastical history. The first such manual, that of Eusebius of Caesarea (ca. 260–ca. 340), does open with the words: "The continuities with the holy apostles" (Greek *tas tōn hierōn apostolōn diadochas*), together with the times that have elapsed from our Savior's day down to our own." But a modern historian of ideas is much more representative of the conventional wisdom when he declares that "the term 'Christianity' . . . is not the name for any single unit of the type for which the historian of specific ideas looks." Although he grants, not without a touch of condescension, that "ecclesiastical historians should write books on the history of Christianity," he dismisses that history as "a series of facts which, taken as a whole, have almost nothing in common except the name," as well as, he feels obliged to add, "the reverence for a certain person, whose nature and teaching, however, have been most variously conceived, so that the unity here too is largely a unity of name." All of this makes it possible for him to describe the continuity of Christian history as a "superficial appearance of singleness and identity."

Singleness and identity are the claims that were made for the history of Christian faith in the most widely disseminated principle by which to measure continuity of doctrine, the so-called Vincentian canon: *quod ubique, quod semper, quod ab omnibus creditum est* (what has been believed everywhere, always, and by all). In his *Commonitory for the Antiquity and Universality of the Catholic Faith against the Profane Novelties of All Heresies,* Vincent of Lérins (d. ca. 450) was confronting the awkward reality of doctrinal pluralism: although the canon of Scripture was "complete, and sufficient of itself for everything, and more than sufficient," it was obvious that "all do not accept it in one and the same sense, but one understands its words in one way, another in another, so that it seems to be capable of as many interpretations as there are interpreters." Vincent's answer to this predicament was to invoke, as the authority for Christian doctrine, not only the Bible but Christian tradition, therefore "universality, antiquity, and consent." Each of these three criteria (or subcriteria) had a share in the determination of what could legitimately identify itself as the catholic doctrine of the universal CHURCH.

"We shall follow universality," according to Vincent, "if we confess that one faith to be true which the whole church throughout the world confesses." This was a definition of continuity as an ecumenical confession across the whole of contemporary Christendom. Its most celebration formulation had come from Augustine: "The universal church is in its judgments secure of truth" (*Securus judicat orbis terrarum*). When these words were brought to his attention, Newman said, they "struck me with a power which I never had felt from any words before." He paraphrased them to mean "that the deliberate judgment in which the whole church at length rests and acquiesces is an infallible prescription and a final sentence against

such portions of it as protest and secede." For Newman personally, the definition of continuity as universality "absolutely pul-
verized" his efforts, as an Anglican, to lay claim to authentic
"catholicity" while remaining separate from the See of Rome,
and he made his submission in 1845.

It also acted as a countervailing force to a definition of continuity as antiquity, which he now found to be simplistic. The
Anglican Oxford Movement, of which he had been a leading
member, had altered the order of the criteria in the Vicentian
canon, putting antiquity first: *quod semper, quod ubique, quod ab
omnibus* was the form in which the canon was and still usually is
quoted. Augustine's words about authority were, Newman asserted, "antiquity deciding against itself." In its original intent
as well as in its use, however, the Vincentian canon did make
antiquity, or more precisely continuity since antiquity, a necessary component. "If we in no wise depart from those interpretations which it is manifest were conspicuously held by our holy
ancestors and fathers," according to Vincent, that would assure
catholicity in doctrine. Despite the *semper,* of course, there were
periods of doctrinal history that had special force in providing
such assurance; and as the Vincentian canon came to be used in
medieval theology, and then especially in the controversies of
the Reformation, that privileged position was accorded to PA-
TRISTIC doctrine.

In the debates over the relative priority of universality and
antiquity as measures of continuity, the third of Vincent's standards, consent (*ab omnibus*), has received less attention than it
deserves. He himself presented it as a principle of control on the
authority of antiquity; for "in antiquity itself," he explained,
"we should adhere to the consentient definitions and determi-
nations of all, or at least of almost all, priests and [theological]
doctors." The escape clause, "or at least of almost all," was
meant to prevent the principle from sanctioning a determination of continuity by an ongoing plebiscite; and the specifica-
tion of priests and theologians is reminiscent of Aristotle's mis-
givings about democracy as a system in which the least qualified
make the decisions. In many periods of church history, for ex-

ample during the Enlightenment, the orthodoxy of the common people may well have exceeded that of "priests and doctors."

To Newman the stipulation of "almost all" also suggested that "the rule of Vincent is not of a mathematical or demonstrative character, but moral, and requires practical judgment and good sense to apply it." As the critical historiography of doctrine, during the century since Newman, has meticulously examined the texts of patristic, medieval, and Reformation theology, not only consent, but universality as well as antiquity must appear to be illusory. It was in response to the corrosive effects of such a relativism that Harnack moved from his historical researches to an effort at defining "the essence of Christianity," and even those who are uncomfortable with the outcome must acknowledge the validity of the concern. There are at least two refinements, less corrections than clarifications, that need to be appended to the Vincentian canon if it is to make historical sense (and probably if it is to make theological sense as well). Continuity must be measured not only by the writings of the "priests and doctors" on scholars' shelves, but also by the dialectic between *lex orandi* and *lex credendi* in WORSHIP. Both the writings and the *lex orandi,* moreover, must be set into the context of a dynamic rather than static definition of tradition, seen in the light of its "inner dimension," DEVELOPMENT OF DOCTRINE. In the words that John Henry Newman quoted from Vincent of Lérins, "Let the soul's religion imitate the law of the body, which, as years go on, develops indeed and opens out its due proportions, and yet remains identically what it was."

▪ Creeds of Christendom

Under this title, Philip Schaff (1819–1893), "father of church history in America," published in 1877 a collection of the principal creedal statements, both universal and particular, that had been produced since the ancient church. The work went into a second edition less than a year later, and ever since it has stood as a convenient and reliable compilation to which scholars of every denomination (or of none) have been able to turn for historical and textual information about creeds. The first volume is subtitled *History of Creeds,* the second *Greek and Latin Creeds* (which includes creed-like passages in the New Testament and in early Christian writers), and the third *Evangelical Creeds.* Although efforts were made after Schaff's death to keep the collection up-to-date, the time has probably come to redo completely the introductions and texts of all three volumes, adding such recent creedal affirmations as the Barmen Declaration of the German Protestant churches against the Nazi ideology in 1934, the promulgation of the dogma of the assumption of the Virgin Mary in 1950, various ecumenical statements of faith during the twentieth century, and the doctrinal constitutions of the Second Vatican Council of 1962–1965. Nevertheless, Schaff's table of contents, given here in the current version of his formulations and titles, is still the most balanced list available of the historic Christian creeds:

Ecumenical Creeds.
> The Apostles' Creed.
> The Nicene Creed, A.D. 325 and 381.
> The Creed of Chalcedon, A.D. 451.
> The Athanasian Creed.
> The Creed of the Sixth Ecumenical Council against the Monothelites, A.D. 680.

Roman Creeds.
> The Canons and Dogmatic Decrees of the Council of Trent, A.D. 1563.
> The Profession of the Tridentine Faith, A.D. 1564.
> The Decree of Pope Pius IX on the Immaculate Conception of the Blessed Virgin Mary, A.D. 1854.
> Papal Syllabus of the Principal Errors of Our Time, A.D. 1864.
> The Dogmatic Decrees of the [First] Vatican Council, Concerning the Catholic Faith and the Church of Christ (the Infallibility of the Pope), A.D. 1870.

Greek and Russian Creeds.
> The Orthodox Confession of the Eastern Church, A.D. 1643.
> The Confession of Dositheus, or the Eighteen Decrees of the Synod of Jerusalem, A.D. 1672.

The Longer Catechism of the Russian Church, Prepared by Philaret, Revised and Approved by the Most Holy Synod, A.D. 1839.
Old Catholic Union Creeds.
The Fourteen Theses of the Old Catholic Union Conference with Greeks and Anglicans, A.D. 1874.
The Old Catholic Agreement on the Filioque Controversy, A.D. 1875.
The Creeds of the Evangelical Lutheran Church.
The Augsburg Confession, A.D. 1530.
Luther's Catechism, A.D. 1529.
The Formula of Concord, A.D. 1576.
The Saxon Visitation Articles, A.D. 1592.
The Creeds of the Evangelical Reformed Churches.
The Sixty-Seven Articles of Ulrich Zwingli, A.D. 1523.
The Ten Theses of Berne, A.D. 1528.
The First Helvetic (or Second Basle) Confession, A.D. 1536.
The Second Helvetic Confession, A.D. 1566.
The Heidelberg or Palatinate Catechism, A.D. 1563.
The Gallican Confession, A.D. 1559.
The Belgic Confession, A.D. 1561.
The First Scotch Confession, A.D. 1560.
The Second Scotch Confession, A.D. 1581.
The Thirty-Nine Articles of the Church of England, A.D. 1563 and 1571. With the American Revision, 1801.
The Anglican Catechism, A.D. 1549, 1662.
The Lambeth Articles, A.D. 1595.
The Irish Articles, A.D. 1615.
The Arminian Articles, A.D. 1610.
The Canons of the Synod of Dort, A.D. 1619.
The Westminster Confession of Faith, A.D. 1647. With the American Alterations.
The Westminster Shorter Catechism, A.D. 1647.
Modern Protestant Creeds.
Congregational Confessions.
The Savoy Declaration, A.D. 1658.
The Declaration of the Congregational Union of England and Wales, A.D. 1833.
The Declaration of the Boston National Council, A.D. 1865.
The Declaration of the Oberlin National Council, A.D. 1871.
Baptist Confessions.
The Confession of 1688 (the Philadelphia Confession).
The New Hampshire Confession, A.D. 1833.
The Free-Will Baptist Confession, A.D. 1868.

Presbyterian Confessions.
   The Confession of the Waldenses, A.D. 1655.
   The Confession of the Cumberland Presbyterian Church (American),
      A.D. 1829.
   The Auburn Declaration (American), A.D. 1837.
   The Confession of the Free Evangelical Church of Geneva, A.D. 1848.
   The Confession of the Free Italian Church, A.D. 1870.
  The Confession of the Society of Friends, Commonly Called Quakers,
      A.D. 1675.
  The Easter Litany of the Moravian Church, A.D. 1749.
  The Methodist Articles of Religion, A.D. 1784.
  The Reformed Episcopal Articles of Religion (American), A.D. 1875.
  The Nine Articles of the Evangelical Alliance, A.D. 1846.
  The Second Helvetic Confession in English.
Recent Confessional Declarations and Terms of Corporate Church Union.
  Confessions and Creeds since 1880.
   The American Congregational Creeds, 1883, 1913.
   The Articles of Faith: The Presbyterian Church of England, 1890.
   The Revision of the Westminster Confession: The Presbyterian
      Church, U.S.A., 1903.
   The Brief Declaratory Statement of the Reformed Faith, 1902.
   The Confessional Statement of the United Presbyterian Church, 1925.
   Recent Protestant and Roman Catholic Catechisms.
  The Union of Church Bodies: Bases and Terms.
   Reunion of the Cumberland Presbyterian with the Presbyterian
      Church, U.S.A., 1906.
   Unions within the Lutheran Family, 1918, 1930.
   The United Church of Canada: Basis of Union, 1925.
   The Union of the Scottish Churches, 1929.
   The Wesleyan Churches in England, 1932.
  Proposals Looking toward Church Unions.
   The Lambeth Quadrilateral, 1886, 1888.
   The Lambeth Quadrilateral and the Free Churches of England,
      1921–25.
   The Lambeth Conference and the Union of Churches in South India,
      1930.
   The Anglican and Protestant Episcopal Churches and the Orthodox
      Eastern and Old Catholic Churches.
   The Church of England and the Roman Catholic Church, 1896, 1921–25.
   Proposals of the Protestant Episcopal Church.
   Congregational Proposals of Union.
   Presbyterian Proposals of Union.
  Church Alliances and Federations of Churches.

· Dante Alighieri (1265–1321)

Florentine poet, philosopher, lay theologian, and author of *The Divine Comedy.*

Although Dante's place in a dictionary dealing with world literature would be unquestionable, his right to be included here may require justification. The justification is not, *pace* the Dominican Thomist scholar Pierre Mandonnet (1858–1936), author of the highly influential *Dante le théologien,* that the poet was a disciple of Thomas Aquinas, in the light of whose *Summa Theologiae* Dante's *Divine Comedy* was to be read, with Beatrice (whether or not she ever existed) standing for theology. Rather, the justification is to be found in the specific theological content of various of Dante's works. Dante was not a disciple of Thomas; it would come closer to historical truth to see him as a disciple of Augustine—which is, of course, what Thomas Aquinas believed himself to be.

The doctrine with which Dante dealt the most directly, and the most "theologically," was the doctrine of the CHURCH. His treatise on church and state, *De Monarchia,* had to take up the theology of the church in order to criticize certain theories of the papacy and its relation to the civil order. Those who have read *De Monarchia* as essentially an anti-ecclesiastic tractate have misunderstood the subtlety of its argument. Dante was not an enemy of the church as Christ had intended it to be, but he was a critic of the church as men had perverted it. As he had the apostle Peter say in the *Divine Comedy,* "It was not our meaning that the keys which were committed to me should become the device on a standard for warfare on the baptized." In *De Monarchia,* therefore, Dante took the words of Christ to Pontius Pilate, "My kingdom does not belong to this world" (John 18:36), to mean that the assumption of political authority by the church was deleterious not only to secular politics but also to the authentic sacramental life of the church. The authority of the state came from God, but it did not come through the church, which had its own identity and should have its own integrity.

Although it is not accurate to describe Dante as a Thomist, it does seem appropriate to invoke the Thomistic interpretation (which is also an Augustinian interpretation) of the relation between GRACE and nature as a key to the central structure of the *Comedy.* As he appeared in Dante's *Inferno,* Vergil (70–19 B.C.E.) was not the historical figure of the Roman poet, but the pagan who, in his Fourth Eclogue, had in some measure anticipated the coming of Christ; therefore he could guide Dante up to, but not into, the gate of Paradise. And whoever the historical Beatrice may have been, she took over from Vergil as Dante's guide to represent, and in some sense to vindicate, the truth claims of revelation. What nature and reason, for which Vergil was the spokesman, had been able to perceive was valid, but it was not sufficient for salvation. The mystery of the word and will of God went beyond human insight and achievement. Yet that did not mean abolishing nature and reason, but perfecting them by the authority of divine revelation and the doctrines disclosed through it.

In Dante's great poem, every major doctrine of Christian theology—and almost every major Christian theologian—comes in for notice. The vision of God that inspired Dante's *Divine Comedy* is explicitly and eloquently the vision of the Trinity. "The Love that moves the sun and the other stars" celebrated in its closing line is the love that, according to Augustine's *On the Trinity,* binds Father, Son, and Holy Spirit together eternally:

> Three circles
> appeared to me; they had three different colors,
> but all of them were of the same dimension;
> one circle seemed reflected by the second,
> as rainbow is by rainbow, and the third
> seemed fire breathed equally by these two circles.

So even the Western doctrine of FILIOQUE could receive poetic affirmation. Repeatedly Dante takes up even technical dogmatic details of the orthodox doctrine of the person of Christ and of the incarnation formulated by the various councils, and demonstrates his grasp of terminology as well as content. In Canto 24 of the *Paradiso* he has himself subjected to a rigorous theological examination, patterned after a disputation in a university, on central issues of medieval theology: the definition of faith, the identification of authority in matters of doctrine, the proper method of argumentation, and the nature of theological proof. "It is appropriate for us," he says here, "to propound our syllogisms by starting with believing," sounding the scholastic theme of "faith in search of understanding."

Yet if one were pressed to identify one doctrine whose treatment in the *Divine Comedy* makes it a leitmotiv of Dante's poetry and theology, it would have to be the doctrine of Mary, "the name of that fair flower which I always invoke, at morning and at evening." In Paradise she is "the Queen to whom this realm is subject and devoted," the Queen of heaven before whom the angels dance and play. Dante's language about Mary becomes APOPHATIC as he confesses:

> Even if my speech were rich as my
> imagination is, I should not try
> to tell the very least of her delights.

So transcendent is her glory as Dante describes it that, in the opinion of some literary commentators and of some theological critics, she eclipses Christ himself by the end of the poem. Dante's interpretation of the relation between the Christian devotion to Christ and the Christian devotion to Mary is put, fittingly enough, into the mouth of Bernard of Clairvaux (1090–1153), whose celebration of Mary had been a high point of Marian theology and piety:

> Look now upon the face that is most like
> the face of Christ, for only through its brightness
> can you prepare your vision to see him.

Whatever one may think of the Mandonnet thesis, Dante's evocation of the MELODY of doctrine in his poetic version of medieval Mariology shows itself to be "theological" at least in the sense that, like most other theologians, he raises more problems than he solves, leaving it to later scholars to puzzle out what he meant. It is almost a cliché, but like many clichés the expression of a valid insight, to suggest that, despite the majesty of *Paradise Lost,* the principal rival to Dante and the *Divine Comedy* in this category of theological epic may well be Goethe's *Faust.*

· Development of Doctrine

Although it is a distinctive characteristic of biblical faith that it is grounded in historical events such as the Exodus and the Crucifixion rather than in "timeless truths" that can be known apart from history, most Christian theology has encountered great difficulty in dealing with its own history. Because the God revealed in the history of salvation is affirmed to be beyond time and beyond change, that transcendence has been transferred also to the truth of salvation: "as it was in the beginning, is now, and ever shall be, world without end. Amen." It was HERESY that constantly changed, that was guilty of innovation, that did not stick to "the faith which God entrusted to his people once and for all" (Jude 3); orthodoxy was "always the same" (*semper eadem*).

That definition of unchangeable truth made Christian orthodoxy, whether Roman Catholic or Eastern Orthodox or Protestant, highly vulnerable to the attacks of the Enlightenment in the eighteenth and nineteenth centuries. Although the guiding principle for much of Enlightenment thought was the criterion of rationality, to which even the claims of revelation had to be subjected, the methodology for the use of that criterion was derived from critical history. Through the use of critical history, orthodoxy, as well as heresy, was seen as having been subject to historical change. For example, despite the elevation of the dogma of the Trinity to normative status as supposedly traditional doctrine by the Council of Nicea in 325, there was not a single Christian thinker East or West before Nicea who could qualify as consistently and impeccably orthodox. The conclusion that Enlightenment thinkers drew from this discovery was that all truth—except perhaps their own—had been historically conditioned and was therefore relative. The "Vincentian canon" represented an impossible idealization of the supposed doctrinal CONTINUITY of the Christian tradition. If that canon were to be applied as a statistical standard, no doctrine measured up, because the more information there was about what had actually been taught and believed, the greater the variety appeared to be. Historicism and relativism seemed to be the only alternative.

It was the historic achievement of the nineteenth century—primarily, though by no means solely, of JOHN HENRY NEWMAN—to stand this argument on its head. Newman's book of 1845, *An Essay on the Development of Christian Doctrine,* not only acknowledged the fact of change in the history of Christian doctrine; it embraced it. It was characteristic of all great ideas, Newman insisted, even of those propounded by "inspired teachers," that they were not laid down once and for all in their complete form; they grew from simple beginnings, through all kinds of vicissitudes, finally to emerge in mature form. In short, they developed. Thus a dynamic organic metaphor was substituted for a static mechanical one. Christ had indeed said to Peter: "On this rock I will build my church" (Matt. 16:18). But that church had gone on to acquire the name "body of Christ." A body is built by growth and development, by passing through times of crisis and trial yet preserving a continuity in which (in the poet's phrase) "the child is father of the man." Hence it should not be surprising to discover that even the most saintly of the early church fathers seemed confused about such fundamental articles of faith as the Trinity and original sin. It was to be expected, because they were participants in the ongoing development, not transmitters of an unalloyed and untouched patrimony.

Development of doctrine became a vital ECUMENICAL issue. As John Courtney Murray (1904–1967) once said, "I do not think that the first ecumenical question is, what think ye of the church? Or even, what think ye of Christ? The dialogue would rise out of the current confusion if the first question raised were, what think ye of the Nicene homoousion?"—the doctrine of the Trinity, which Protestants also accept. The difference between Protestantism and Catholicism, for Newman, was not, as earlier apologists had claimed, that Protestantism was constantly changing while Catholicism retained a continuity that could be equated with uniformity across the centuries, but the exact opposite: Protestantism remained stuck in the first century, like a fly in amber, while Catholicism affirmed development. Of course Newman recognized that not all development was a good thing—that cancer, too, was a growth. Therefore he closed the *Essay on Development* with a set of seven criteria by which to discern healthy from unhealthy development, truth from error; he worked on those criteria throughout his life, having decided, in the very year of the *Essay,* to become a Roman Catholic and having lived as a member of that church through the difficult times of the *Syllabus of Errors* and the First Vatican Council of 1869–1870.

But whatever the criteria and however debatable they might be, he remained convinced to the end that authentic orthodoxy had to accept the fact of development, for the church as a whole no less than for the individual. As he put it in the *Essay on Development,* it had to change "in order to remain the same. In a higher world it is otherwise, but here below to live is to change, and to be [mature] is to have changed often." That was true of Newman himself; yet he was sure that development was not only the law of human life, but also the law of divine truth.

▪ Dictionary

When the man of letters and lay theologian Dr. Samuel Johnson (1709–1784) in his *Dictionary* defined "lexicographer" as "a harmless drudge, that busies himself in tracing the original, and detailing the signification of words," that definition, as well as Dr. Johnson himself, turned out to be a kind of oxymoron; for only a lexicographer who was considerably more than a "harmless drudge" could have come up with it. That illustrates an important characteristic of all dictionaries, this one included, which it would be well for any user of the dictionary to keep constantly in mind: they appear to be as objective as the multiplication tables, antiseptically preserving a strictly alphabetical order, but in fact they reflect a highly individual and personal, perhaps even arbitrary, method both of selecting and of defining.

In the present context, it is not necessary to adhere to the distinction reflected in the *Oxford English Dictionary,* according to which "'lexicon' is the name usually given to dictionaries of Greek, Hebrew, Arabic, Syriac, Ethiopic, and some other literary languages," perhaps especially ancient ones, and "dictionary" to reference books dealing with the mother tongue, or at any rate with some living language. English usage has not observed it with any consistency, and "dictionary" remains the more common, as well as the more comprehensive term: every lexicon may acceptably be called a dictionary, although it would not be acceptable to use "lexicon" wherever "dictionary" appears. There are, in addition, dictionaries of quotations, as well as dictionaries of nonsense and dictionaries of the history of ideas, as well as Ambrose Bierce's *The Devil's Dictionary* (1906). But although Johann George Walch (1693–1775) published in 1733 a *Philosophisches Lexicon,* an equivalent work published in America by Charles Porterfield Krauth (1823–1883) in 1879 bore the title *A Vocabulary of the Philosophical Sciences.*

The study of theology has long depended on dictionaries of many kinds. The *Onomasticon* of the church historian Eusebius of Caesarea (ca. 260–ca. 340) was a geographical dictionary, which Jerome (ca. 342–420) revised and expanded in the process of translating it into Latin. From Jerome but also from many other sources, both classical and Christian, Isidore of Seville (ca. 560–636) prepared his *Etymologies,* which does indeed contain many etymologies but also summarizes a vast amount of other information; Isidore's *Etymologies* was the standard dictionary for many medieval writers. Its Byzantine counterpart was the *Lexicon* bearing the name of Suidas, which the eminent Byzantinist Franz Dölger (1879–1940) showed to be not the name of its supposed compiler, but a term for "fortress," as the dictionary was *ein' feste Burg* of reference data both philological and theological.

In modern times, Christian theology has not always fared well at the hands of dictionaries. The subtitle of this book reflects the process by which, through the work of the critic Pierre Bayle (1647–1706) entitled *Dictionnaire historique et critique,* "philosophical dictionary" became a standard term in English and in French for a work in which one or more of the *philosophes* propounded their alternatives to the Christian tradition. Yet this was not necessarily so: standing on a scholar's shelf, the thirty massive tomes of the *Dictionnaire de théologie catholique,* published between 1903 and 1950, are an assurance that there will almost always be something to say about most important topics. Its German Protestant counterpart, the *Realenzyklopädie für protestantische Theologie und Kirche* in several successive editions and revisions, performs much the same function. And the one-volume *Oxford Dictionary of the Christian Church,* which is revised and updated from time to time, is a desk-sized dictionary of definitions, identifications, and bibliography that manages, despite a gentle but unmistakable Oxonian and Anglican accent, to be both ecumenical and objective.

This "philosophical dictionary" does seek to be ecumenical but makes no pretense at being objective. Despite its adherence to the convention of an alphabetical sequence, it is quite candidly the expression of a particular scholarly and theological outlook; but it is a dictionary in which "both/and" is preferable to "either/or" and in which therefore the Terentian epigram *humani nil a me alienum puto* has been adopted as a motto.

▪ Dogma

Dogma is a term ordinarily used to designate the official doctrinal teaching of a Christian church. Although the Greek word *dogma* appears five (perhaps six) times in the New Testament, the only passage in which it has this connotation is Acts 16:4; and there it would seem to be primarily ethical and ceremonial decisions, rather than doctrinal ones, that the writer has in mind. In Ignatius of Antioch (ca. 35–ca. 107) the word begins to acquire its later meaning, which is also evident in Origen and other fathers. But only when the councils of the church actually began to formulate doctrine could the term begin to acquire the official, almost legal, significance it now possesses.

In the strictest sense, nothing less than the whole of the church is qualified to define dogma. Therefore the only dogmas in the most precise sense of the word are the dogmas of the TRINITY and of the INCARNATION, as these were defined in the first four (or seven) ecumenical councils. But like "Creed," the term is usually employed in a looser sense, to designate the particular doctrinal decisions of a church body. Its applicability varies with the degree of canonical status and the amount of enforcement that such decisions carry in the church body. For example, the formulations of the Cambridge Platform in Congregationalism or of the Thirty-Nine Articles in Anglicanism might be termed dogmas on the ground that they were officially promulgated by church bodies; but because in many parts of those church bodies they have become a dead letter, the term does not apply to them. On the other hand, the doctrine of the immaculate conception or, more recently, of the assumption can be called dogma, even though something less than the whole of the church was involved in their promulgation, because of the canonical status of these teachings and their enforcement on pain of excommunication.

In Protestant theology since the Enlightenment, the term "dogma" has carried a primarily historical connotation, being used especially in the study of the "history of dogma." The original function of that study during the eighteenth century was to demonstrate that the doctrines of the church had been conditioned in their formulation by the circumstances under which they arose. At the hands of its greatest practitioner, ADOLF VON HARNACK, the history of dogma became the discipline by which the continuing value and authority of ancient dogma were called into question. Concentrating his attention upon the ancient dogmas of the Trinity and the incarnation, Harnack sought to show that they were in considerable measure the products of the Hellenization of Christianity. Although his extreme attitude was reversed by the generation of theologians who followed him, the word "dogma" has not lost the opprobrium attached to it in common usage. It is noteworthy in this connection that even the most confessionally loyal among Lutheran theologians in Europe and America rarely use the term for the particular teachings of their own symbolical books, restricting it to the two dogmas of the ancient church and, in a polemical context, to the particular doctrinal promulgations of the Roman Catholic and Eastern Orthodox Churches.

The several Catholic churches continue to use "dogma" as a designation of their official teachings. For the Orthodox, it means the decisions of the seven ecumenical councils, as it also does for some Anglicans. Other Anglicans tend to include the decisions of subsequent Western councils until, but not including, the Council of Trent of 1545–1563. Roman Catholics mean the decisions of the ancient councils, the formulations of later Western councils until and including the Vatican Councils of 1869–1870 and 1962–1965, and the infallible declarations of the Pope *ex cathedra*. According to canon law it is required of Roman Catholic theologians, particularly since the Modernist controversy, to subject themselves to this dogma and to carry on their theological work within the limits set by it. It is therefore not permissible for a Roman Catholic New Testament scholar to come to any conclusions about the life of Jesus that would contradict the official dogma of the two natures in Christ.

Because the second half of the twentieth century has seen a deepening of the consciousness of the catholicity of the church in the Protestant churches, the possibility exists that dogma will begin to be accorded more status among them than it once had. But their central doctrinal concerns—like the atonement and justification by faith—are not part of dogma as it is usually interpreted. It would therefore seem that only through the reinterpretation of their own traditions and their connection with the Christian tradition as such will these churches be able to repossess the dogmas of the Christian past.

▪ Dostoevsky, Fyodor Mikhailovich (1821–1881)

Russian novelist and interpreter of Eastern Orthodox spirituality.

With the possible exception of GOETHE, no figure in modern literature has as much of a claim for inclusion in this dictionary. Although the detailed etiology of SIN, original and actual, was a phenomenon of Western theology, associated chiefly with the theology of Augustine and with the religious experience of Luther, perhaps its two most profound interpreters, Dostoevsky's sensitive grasp of the psychology of sin gave the doctrine concrete expression. Long before the rise of modern psychoanalysis, he described, in the crime committed by Raskolnikov in *Crime and Punishment,* how it is possible to rationalize a self-centered act by making the worse appear the better reason. And then, in his analysis of the process by which Raskolnikov eventually confesses his sin—the psychological process of toying with guilt as he is interviewed by the investigator Porfiry, and the spiritual power of a confrontation with innocence and holiness as Sonia reads to him the story of Lazarus from the Gospel—Dostoevsky's theology is unmatched by the work of any theologian.

Through a reading of *The Brothers Karamazov,* before the Slavophil theologians of nineteenth-century orthodoxy with their concepts of SOBORNOST' became so extensively known, it was possible to begin an inquiry into the distinctive meaning of Eastern Christianity within the overall history of Christian thought. As T. G. Masaryk (1850–1937) suggested in *The Spirit of Russia,* the monastic confessor and *starec* Father Zosima, who functions as the authoritative interpreter of the Eastern Orthodox tradition, is the central figure in the book. Combined as it was with a doctrine of sin that matched Luther's for religious power, this interpretation of Orthodoxy gives the lie to the conventional wisdom of Protestant theologians and historians that Eastern Christianity, both Greek and Slavic, has been too optimistic about human capacity and vague in its doctrine of grace. Therefore when the Cappadocians received fresh attention, Dostoevsky had prepared the way for an appreciation of their insights.

▪ Duty

The debasement of our linguistic coinage has affected every area of our common life, but none more gravely than religion and theology. "Pious" has a long and venerable history, going back to *pius Aeneas* in the *Aeneid,* but who would be willing to accept the characterization today? Despite literally hundreds of occurrences throughout the Old and New Testaments, "righteous" now almost automatically means "self-righteous"—which is the polar opposite of what it means everywhere in the Bible. If there is a need any longer to prove the existence of the devil, this ought to be proof enough. The term "duty" has not yet become a victim of the epidemic, but it is beginning to show troubling symptoms of being about to do so. When, for example, Florestan in Beethoven's *Fidelio* exclaims, *Süsser Trost in meinem Herzen, Meine Pflicht hab' ich gethan!* (Sweet is the consolation in my heart, That I have done my duty), sophisticated audiences have been heard to titter. The West Point motto of "Duty, Honor, Country" evokes similar reactions.

Whatever the long-range cultural and moral implications of this change, it has also negatively affected the capacity to understand the history of philosophy and theology, specifically that of the past two centuries. When the Enlightenment had called into question much of the foundation of supernaturalism and theism in the philosophy of the scholastics, and when in turn the critical philosophy propounded by David Hume (1711–1776) and above all by Immanuel Kant (1724–1804) had subjected Enlightenment rationalism to similar scrutiny, the sense of duty was pressed into service to assume much of the burden previously borne by the classic proofs for the existence of God. "Two things fill the mind with ever new and increasing admiration and awe," wrote Kant in the "Conclusion" to his *Critique of Practical Reason,* "the oftener and the more steadily we reflect on them: the starry heavens above and the moral law within." Kant took it for granted not only that there was such a "moral law within," but that a person could, without the aid of special revelation, be aware of it; he assumed, moreover, that there was some fundamental conformity between this moral law and the mystery present in "the starry heavens above." His younger English contemporary, the poet William Wordsworth (1770–1850), called duty "stern daughter of the voice of God," and Emerson could affirm:

> So nigh is grandeur to our dust,
> So near is God to man,
> When Duty whispers low, "Thou must,"
> The youth replies, "I can."

None of that, it would appear, may be regarded as self-evident any longer, and resort to this line of "proof" has largely, though not completely, disappeared from theological apologetics.

Apart from its endemic tendency to capitulate to the zeitgeist, contemporary theology has been abetted in its alienation from that tradition by the long-standing inability of many versions of Christian theology, beginning with the earliest forms of heresy in the second century and continuing to the present, to grasp the deepest implications of the meaning of law in the Hebrew Bible and in the faith of Israel. A one-sided reading of the theology of Paul—and on that basis, an equally one-sided reading of the theology of Luther—can lead to an interpretation of duty solely as a burden from which Christ came to bring salvation, and therefore to an idealization of spontaneity as the standard of the new life in Christ. Despite their obvious shortcomings as a summary of Christian theology, the philosophy of Kant and the poetry of Wordsworth and Emerson seem at this point to come much closer to the authentic spirit of the Bible and its religion.

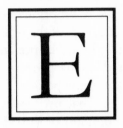

▪ Ecumenical

Derived from the Greek noun *oikoumenē*, which meant "the civilized world" (often equated with the Roman Empire or with Christendom), "ecumenical" has traditionally been a designation for certain forms and structures of AUTHORITY that extended beyond the local or regional church to claim some sort of acknowledged universal standing; in recent decades, it has gone on to acquire the additional (and sometimes contradictory) connotation of universal in the sense of interconfessional or transdenominational.

Of the five ancient episcopal sees to which the title "patriarch" attached itself—Rome, Byzantium or Constantinople, Jerusalem, Alexandria, and Antioch—it was the second, as "New Rome," that came to be known as "ecumenical." In a spirited correspondence, parts of which found their way into the compilations of medieval canon law, Pope Gregory I (590–604) disputed the right of the patriarch-archbishop of Constantinople to style himself by this title, by which "the peace of the whole church is being disturbed." Underlying this dispute over the right to be known as "ecumenical" was the growing difference over whether the primacy of the bishop of Rome had been derived from the status of Rome as the capital city of the Roman Empire as *oikoumenē;* for if it had, the transfer of the capital in 330 C.E. might seem to imply that the archbishop of the capital city, be it First Rome or Second Rome, was entitled to be designated as *oikoumenikos*. It may, however, be suggested that the very growth of Roman primacy—attended as it was by such changes of nomenclature as the assumption of the title of Supreme Pontiff and the gradual restriction of the title of Pope, once employed quite indiscriminately by other prelates, to the patriarch of the West—contributed to the process by which, conversely, the patriarch of Constantinople became, in a particular sense, the Ecumenical Patriarch. That process was probably also encouraged by the Muslim conquest of the other three Eastern patriarchates at Jerusalem, Antioch, and Alexandria during the seventh century. Because of his significance for the Eastern Orthodox churches among the SLAVS, the symbolic position of the universal (that is, universal-Eastern) patriarch of Constantinople, although not in any sense making him the Eastern counterpart of the Pope, did invest the title of Ecumenical Patriarch with special import.

Applied to church councils, the term "ecumenical" was involved in the disputes between Rome and Constantinople, but it also provoked special controversies of its own. Not only were all the great councils of the first several centuries, beginning with the Council of Nicea in 325, held in the East; but they were convoked by the Roman (namely, Byzantine) Emperor, not by the Roman Pope. It was possible to argue, therefore, that such a council, which spoke for the *oikoumenē*, was "ecumenical." Unfortunately, some of the gatherings that claimed to speak on behalf of the total Christian *oikoumenē* ended up taking positions on various Christian doctrines, above all on the incarnation, that were eventually condemned as HERESY. So it was, notoriously, at the synod held in Ephesus in 449 (to be distinguished from the Council of Ephesus in 431), which the bishop of Rome denounced as "the robber synod of Ephesus" (*latrocinium Ephesinum*) and which was superseded two years later by the Council of Chalcedon. Ephesus was not "ecumenical," but Chalcedon was: where was the difference? Roman apologists were quick to supply the answer that a synod was not an ecumenical council on *a priori* grounds, but only on *a posteriori* grounds, when, among other conditions, its ORTHODOXY stood beyond reproach and was so attested by Rome; "reception" of the council made it ecumenical. That leads to the definition: "a synod the decrees of which have found acceptance by the church in the whole world." By a strict application of the definition, according to which no council can qualify since the separation of the Eastern and Western Churches, there have been seven fully ecumenical councils: Nicea I in 325; Constantinople I in 381; Ephesus in 431; Chalcedon in 451; Constantinople II in 553; Constantinople III in 680–681; and Nicea II in 787.

In traditional Protestant usage since the Reformation, "ecumenical" is most often the term for three creeds: the Apostles', the Nicene, and the Athanasian. Those three names are, to be sure, all employed rather loosely. The Apostles' Creed was not composed by the apostles, as the legend transmitted by Rufinus of Aquileia (ca. 345–410) alleged, but evolved from earlier and shorter statements of faith, chiefly (despite its being Greek) in the West. What is now called the Nicene Creed and used as such in the liturgies of various churches is not the text adopted at the Council of Nicea I in 325, but probably a more ample creed affirmed at Constantinople I in 381. And Athanasius did not compose the Athanasian Creed—also known, from its opening words, as *"Quicunque vult"* (Whoever wishes to be saved)—which was written in Latin and therefore in the West, probably in the fifth century. Not only are all three of the names of the creeds less than precise; so is the designation of them as ecumenical. Both the Apostles' Creed and the Athanasian Creed are almost wholly Western, despite occasional acceptance of them in the East. The Nicene Creed is accepted by both East and West—but only without the Western addition of the FILIOQUE, by which even this creed was deprived of its fully ecumenical standing.

During the twentieth century, "ecumenical" has become the term for the effort to achieve—or, as its proponents have insisted, to discover—the unity of the church despite its obvious differences and divisions. As the Enlightenment strove to substitute historiography for polemics in the study of both heresy and orthodoxy, the complex pathology of those divisions and schisms came into view, and the absoluteness of the truth claims of competing denominations was challenged by a growing relativism about creed and dogma. Meanwhile, Christian individuals and groups found, above all in the mission field and under the pressure of war, that there was much more to bind them together than there was to separate them. The Faith and Order Movement, largely under Anglican auspices, was joined by Life and Work, whose guiding spirit was NATHAN SÖDERBLOM, to bring the churches and their theologians into meaningful dialogue, in which differences would not be glossed over—they seldom had been in denominational and confessional history—but in which, by contrast with most of denominational and confessional history, the existing unity could be affirmed. Initially a movement within Protestantism, ecumenism has reached out to Eastern Orthodoxy and, particularly since the Second World War and the Second Vatican Council, to Roman Catholicism. As most of the articles in this dictionary show, there is virtually no subject of theological and historical importance that has remained unaffected by this "great new fact" of Christian history.

· Emerson, Ralph Waldo (1803–1882)

Unitarian minister, essayist, theological nonconformist, and "the sage of Concord."

"Why should not we have a poetry and philosophy of insight and not of tradition, and a religion by revelation to us, and not the history of theirs?" That question appears at the very beginning of Emerson's first book, *Nature,* published anonymously in 1836. For a scholar whose entire lifework has been addressed to the understanding and vindication of tradition as an exposition of revelation, such a question must seem at best insensitive and at worst illiterate. From where except that very "tradition" is "insight" to come?

And yet, although he himself often provided sufficient grounds for his critics to accuse him repeatedly of such insensitivity and illiteracy, Emerson was of course fully conscious of the constructive role that tradition can play in the development of human thought, and he in fact devoted a substantial portion of his writings to a positive assessment of its place. In an essay entitled "Uses of Great Men," which serves as the introductory first chapter to his *Representative Men* of 1850, he observed that "the student of history is like a man going into a warehouse to buy cloths or carpets: he fancies he has a new article. If he go to the factory, he shall find that his new stuff still repeats the scrolls and rosettes which are found on the interior walls of the pyramids of Thebes." That introductory essay is followed by a series of six on individual "representative men": Plato, Swedenborg, Montaigne, Shakespeare, Napoleon, and Goethe.

Representative Men demonstrates that history (or historical biography) does not have to be dull, but that in order to be interesting it must receive the same care as any other literary work. Emerson was capable of turgid sentences and purple prose—already in *Nature,* he had burst out with the exclamation, "I become a transparent eyeball," which he could never quite manage to live down—but he had an abiding commitment to language of clarity and force. One major source of that commitment was surely his lifelong career as a lecturer and public speaker, which began, as such careers often have, in the pulpit. It is clear from the critical edition of his works, now in progress, that Emerson went on worrying over his writings even after they had appeared in print, working and reworking them for subsequent editions. As a result, he has won the respect of ever new generations. Just when a passage such as the following from his *Journal* for January 1842 seems to provide grounds for dismissing him as hopelessly optimistic or shallow—"The wealth of the universe is for me, everything is explicable and practicable for me"—that superficial impression is shattered by the very next paragraph: "And yet whilst I adore this ineffable life which is at my heart, it will not condescend to gossip with me . . . Moreover, whilst this Deity glows at the heart, and by his unlimited presentiments gives me all power, I know that tomorrow will be as this day: I am a dwarf, and I remain a dwarf." And so, as he wrote in conclusion, "I am defeated all the time; yet to victory I am born." Those words were wrung from Emerson upon the death of his son Waldo at the age of five. Passages like that mark him, despite superficial impressions, as an exponent of the APOPHATIC theology that has characterized orthodoxy at its best.

Emerson was an exception to many rules, including the generalization that a thinker tends to grow more conservative with age. Theologically at least, his odyssey appears to have carried him in the opposite direction. The point where that odyssey began was already a long way removed from the mainstream of Christian orthodoxy, whether Catholic or Protestant. There is much to be said in favor of the historical interpretation that sees the central point of New England Unitarianism as not its opposition to the traditional dogma of the Trinity in the name of the oneness of God (though this was certainly a major component of the polemical literature) but its rejection of the twin doctrines of sin and atonement as these had come to be taught within the Puritan version of Reformed Protestantism. In rejecting both the Augustinian scheme of salvation and the Athanasian picture of God, the early Unitarians insisted that they were restoring the authentic teaching of Scripture, which had been buried under the irrationality of later dogma, and they responded with defensive indignation to the orthodox allegation of a domino theory, by which this hostility to conventional ecclesiastical belief was said to lead inevitably to a weakening of the Christian allegiance to the uniqueness of the person and work of Jesus Christ.

When, therefore, Ralph Waldo Emerson seemed to have arrived at precisely such a weakening of allegiance, he was an embarrassment to the Unitarian cause. On 15 July 1838, at the invitation of the senior class, he spoke to the Harvard Divinity School. "Historical Christianity," he charged, "dwells with noxious exaggeration about the person of Jesus." It had imposed upon the human spirit the tyrannical demand: "You must subordinate your nature to Christ's nature." To the contrary, he asserted to the young men about to enter the ministry, "I think no man can go with his thoughts about him into one of our churches without feeling that what hold the public worship had on men is gone, or going." If they were ever to reverse this trend, they must break with a dead past—as Emerson himself had done: "Yourself a newborn bard of the Holy Ghost, cast behind you all conformity, and acquaint men at first hand with Deity." And by this means, he admonished, "let the breath of new life be breathed by you through the forms already existing."

For his part, Emerson would find, more and more as time went on, that the theological and liturgical "forms already existing" could not sustain him or his ministry. He resigned from the Unitarian ministry when he became convinced that he could not honestly profess even its minimalist doctrine of the Eucharist and keep his moral integrity. The lecture platform became his pulpit, the readers of his books and essays became his congregation, and the American commonwealth became his one holy catholic and apostolic church. As he crossed the country on his lecture tours, he would sometimes read his old sermons to his audience, pausing to look up from the manuscript and explain, "I don't believe that any more."

▪ Enlightenment

In a celebrated essay published in 1784, "Answer to the Question: 'What Is the Enlightenment?'" (*Beantwortung der Frage: "Was ist Aufklärung?"*) Immanuel Kant (1724–1804) proposed the definition: "Enlightenment is man's exodus from his self-incurred tutelage. Tutelage is the inability to use one's understanding without the guidance of another person. This tutelage is self-incurred if its cause lies not in any weakness of the understanding, but in indecision and lack of courage to use the mind without the guidance of another. 'Dare to know [*Sapere aude*]!' Have the courage to use your own understanding! This is the motto of the Enlightenment."

In the two centuries since that definition, the scholarly investigation of the Enlightenment (or, more accurately, of the Enlightenments) in various countries has complicated the picture considerably: it took drastically different forms in Protestant and in Roman Catholic cultures (not to mention what happened to it when it hit Russian Orthodoxy); it did not always have the same relation to the established political order; even its connection with modern science and philosophy was not uniform across Europe. At the same time, the experience of those two centuries, and especially of the last half-century, has modified the enthusiasm of many for the Enlightenment's exaltation of reason and rejection of the tutelage of tradition, as the power of demonic evil has manifested itself with unprecedented virulence among some of the most devoted and apparently rational of the children of the *Aufklärung*. Among theologians devoted to the recovery of orthodoxy, and even among many who, although finding such a recovery unacceptable, believe themselves to have gone beyond the celebration of reason to the rediscovery of will and of the irrational, it has in recent years become fashionable to dismiss the Enlightenment as intellectually and morally bankrupt.

Such celebrations of triumph seem to be in very poor grace coming from theologians who have been and continue to be the beneficiaries of the very movement they deplore. Far from representing the bankruptcy of the Enlightenment, the recognition that reason does not exhaust the range of meaning in human life is itself an accomplishment of reason. Even more important, the Enlightenment was a major force in establishing once and for all the methodological priority of HISTORIOGRAPHY as an instrument of liberation and a principle of interpretation. Although there were Enlightenment thinkers who were no less devoted than their orthodox adversaries to the quest for a timeless truth—an "essence" of universal wisdom and NATURAL THEOLOGY beyond the particularities of any historical form of religion—they began their pursuit by demonstrating the human, all too human quality of the orthodox tradition. In so doing, the Enlightenment impressed its devotion to the historical method on a broad range of thinkers throughout the eighteenth and nineteenth centuries. The very concept of DEVELOPMENT OF DOCTRINE, which exponents of orthodoxy have now embraced as an apologetic for the Christian tradition, came into being, as a study of Newman will show, specifically in relation to Enlightenment scholarship, and would not have "developed" without it.

· Erasmus, Desiderius (ca. 1469–1536)

Christian scholar, Renaissance humanist, pioneer student of the TEXT OF THE NEW TESTAMENT and of PATRISTICS.

In politics, according to the taxonomy propounded in *Iolanthe,*

> Nature always does contrive
> That every boy and every gal,
> That's born into the world alive,
> Is either a little Liberal,
> Or else a little Conservative.

Likewise, ever since the Reformation, theologians have been asked to choose between Erasmus and LUTHER, and very few have studied (much less followed) both. The experience—which is itself rather unusual—of having served as an editor for both of them puts that conventional antithesis into considerably different perspective.

The most permanent of the accomplishments of Erasmus lie in the area of "sacred philology." Many of the church fathers, Greek as well as Latin, owed the first printed editions of their writings to his tireless activity as scholar and publisher. Primary among his books is his *Novum instrumentum* of 1516, the first printed edition of the Greek New Testament. Although the humanistic prelate Cardinal Francisco Ximénez de Cisneros (1436–1517), archbishop of Toledo, had included an edition of the New Testament, printed in 1514, as part of his massive six-volume *Complutensian Polyglot,* which appeared between 1514 and 1517, the volume containing the Greek New Testament was not formally published until several years after Erasmus had published his. Nor is it simply chronological priority that makes the *Novum instrumentum* historic. Coming out as it did just one year before Luther's Ninety-Five Theses, it stimulated the interest of the Reformers in an exegesis based on the original text, and at the same time it capitalized on that interest. In one or another of its successive editions, this Greek text came to underlie the major translations into European vernaculars, such as Luther's German Bible, the Authorized Version (King James Bible) in English, and the *Biblia Kralická* in Czech. In publishing it, Erasmus was not only applying to the biblical text the same impulse to get back to the sources that was characteristic of Renaissance scholars in their use of the Greek and Latin classics, but was consciously (and often mercilessly) criticizing the dependence of the medieval church and of its scholastic theologians such as Thomas Aquinas on the Latin Vulgate, which was often defective in both text and translation.

Such uncritical acceptance of the Vulgate was, for Erasmus, symptomatic of a deep-seated malaise in the church. If, as most scholars are inclined to think, he is the author of the anonymous *Julius Exclusus,* a satire depicting the unsuccessful attempts of Pope Julius II (1503–1513) to get into heaven after his death, that is a measure of the vehemence with which Erasmus lampooned conditions in the church of his time. In many of the writings that did bear his name, he used his mordant wit and matchless command of language to draw a devastating contrast between the simplicity and poverty described in the Gospels as the Christian ideal and the luxury and vice that had infected the church in body and members. A special target of his ridicule was the monastic orders, which had become a caricature of the ideals of their founders and in which ignorance and gluttony reigned. The bishops of the institutional church, often up to and including the bishop of Rome himself, had grown rich by encouraging and exploiting the superstition of the common people. And the scholastic theologians, simultaneously victims and perpetrators of the Hellenization of theology, had been permitted, or even encouraged, to spin out dogmatic abstractions on such doctrines as the Eucharist for which there was no justification in the text of Scripture. As a corrective for these conditions, Erasmus called for a return to the clarity and power of the *philosophia Christi,* his slogan for a purified Christianity based on the New Testament, above all on the teachings of Jesus embodied in the Sermon on the Mount.

Although Erasmus was by no means alone in propounding the campaign for purification and biblical reform, the emergence of Luther faced him with serious problems. Luther himself was the first to acknowledge the superiority of his elder as a philologist and biblical scholar, recognizing his great debt to him for insights into the meaning of the New Testament. The enemies of both were sure that, as the saying ran, "Erasmus laid the egg but Luther hatched it." As Luther's individual viewpoint and activity grew into the Reformation movement, however, a fundamental alienation developed between the two men—a difference, no doubt, of personality, but also of theology and churchmanship. Although Erasmus yielded to none in his admiration for AUGUSTINE, whose works he was to edit in 1528–1529, he was increasingly dismayed at the direction, bordering on a fatalistic determinism, that Luther's version of the Augustinian doctrine of grace appeared to be taking; and in 1524 he published his *Diatribe on Free Will,* to which Luther replied in 1525. The exchange confirmed Luther in his suspicion that behind the sarcasm of Erasmus was a basic skepticism about central Christian teachings and an Epicureanism that cloaked itself in Gospel language but was in fact pagan. That picture, for which Erasmus himself had supplied more than enough material, became the standard portrait in Lutheran manuals of church history and dogmatics.

Another element in the caricature of "the frivolous humanist" has been the depiction of Erasmus as a coward who was unwilling to accept the consequences of his own reformatory intuitions and who pulled back into the sanctuary of Mother

Church when schism threatened. His writings against those whom he termed "pseudo-Evangelicals" after Luther's break with Rome pointed out that the new churches of the Protestant Reformation were encountering some of the very abuses they had denounced but that they had deprived themselves of such resources as the sacrament of penance for dealing with them, so that, as the Gospel said, "in the end the man's plight is worse than before" (Matt. 12:45). However corrupt the conditions in the church might be, the only hope for reforming them was to stay within the church's structures rather than attacking them from the outside.

During the last decade of his life, Erasmus was theologically and personally isolated from both (or all) of the parties. His books were placed on the *Index librorum prohibitorum* by successive popes, and the autonomous scholarship arising in Protestant centers of learning made Luther's followers less and less dependent on the biblical humanists. That isolation has continued during the centuries since his death. Only with the growing awareness of the historical ties between Renaissance and Reformation, and with the deepening recognition of Erasmus's anticipation of many insights of ecumenical theology, has his star once more begun to rise: the critical editions of his works appearing in Europe and in Canada express that new status and are bound to enhance it.

· Eschatology

Various observers have suggested that the nervous laugh is an infallible key to the deepest anxieties of any society. By that index, not merely death but all the major themes of eschatology—what Christian dogmatics calls "the last things" (*ta eschata* in Greek)—must be reckoned as unfinished business for many supposedly secularized moderns, for any public reference to them almost inevitably evokes a giggle. Modern Christians are no less embarrassed to be caught dealing seriously with eschatological questions.

The history of Christian theology provides considerable explanation for this embarrassment. On the pages of the New Testament, above all in such passages as the SERMON ON THE MOUNT, eschatological language seems to have sprung naturally from the lips of Jesus and of his early disciples. As twentieth-century scholarship on the GOSPELS has demonstrated repeatedly, the expectation of the end of all things is not some temporary aberration that may easily be excised from their message, so as to separate what is authentic and permanently relevant from what is spurious and transitory. On the contrary, the early Christian proclamation is permeated with the imagery of eschatology, even of apocalyptic; above all, the ethical content of that proclamation—which was the very part that modern readers wanted to rescue—is rooted in such imagery. "The ethics of the kingdom" meant the description and prescription of the kind of life appropriate to those who were looking for the coming of the Son of Man in the clouds of heaven. The early church stood on tiptoe as it listened to the message of the gospel.

The New Testament also contains evidence of what happened when the expectation began to meet with disappointment. When the first Christians died one by one, this precipitated a crisis, because Christ had not yet come to judgment. It became necessary for the apostle PAUL to explain that when their loved ones died Christians "should not grieve like the rest of men, who have no hope"; for "we who are left alive until the Lord comes shall not forestall those who have died" (1 Thess. 4:13-15). He himself continued to affirm that "we shall not all die, but we shall all be changed in a flash, in the twinkling of an eye, at the last trumpet-call" (1 Cor. 15:51). Yet he did die, and so did every one of the Thessalonians and Corinthians to whom he had written those words—and still the Lord had not returned and the last trumpet-call had not sounded. The mixture of disappointment and scoffery expressed itself in such questions as the one quoted in 2 Peter 3:4: "Where now is the promise of his coming? Our fathers have been laid to their rest, but still everything continues exactly as it has always been since the world began."

The outcome, evident already within the New Testament but especially during the second century of the Christian era, was a process to which German scholars have attached the mouth-filling title *Enteschatologisierung,* "de-eschatologization": as the original eschatological context of various statements and ideas began to make less sense, they were reinterpreted. For instance, the statement of Jesus that "the man who holds out to the end will be saved" (Matt. 10:22), which in the context clearly refers to the end of the world and of history, was individualized into a promise that by remaining faithful until the end of one's own life one would thus be saved. As has often been characteristic of the development of doctrine, however, this change did not reject the previous modality, but revised it to include an additional dimension. The long-promised end of the world, with the return of Christ to judgment, was permanently incorporated into the text of both the Apostles' and the Nicene Creeds as an article of faith which it was compulsory for all Christian believers to affirm.

Early Christian apocalyptic thus resembled a tape recording: it could remain on the shelf for years or even centuries, and yet could be replayed with all its original force and clarity whenever the *hora novissima, tempora pessima* seemed to warrant it. In the strict sense of the word dogma, then, the doctrines of eschatology remained constant: there will be an end, Christ "will come again with glory to judge the quick and the dead," those who believe and are baptized will be saved, but those who do not believe will be condemned (Mark 16:16). What could change, and did change, was the existential answer to the question, "Where now is the promise of his coming?" Over and over, under the stimulus of portents in nature or events in history or the visions of an apocalyptic seer, a particular generation of Christians at a particular place has come up with the answer, "It will be now." In the urgency of that answer they feel summoned to take action and to wait; and if the waiting is unfulfilled, perhaps precipitating a crisis in their own community, that does not deter others from concluding that although the answer "It will be now" had been mistaken, the eschatological doctrine as such is not. Officially at least, that has continued to be the state of the doctrine.

Yet like the shepherd boy who cried wolf in Aesop's well-known fable, the churches have repeatedly found that the doctrine itself has lost much or all of its credibility, and eschatology has been relegated to what was called by many theologians "that little chapter at the end" of a catechism or dogmatics. The presence of eschatological passages from the New Testament as the prescribed pericopes for the final Sundays of the church year may have made some attention to eschatological issues obligatory before and during Advent, but in many pulpits (and many pews) it became a dead letter. Its standing deteriorated further when biblical scholars concluded that such apocalyptic books of the Bible as Ezekiel, Daniel, and Revelation were themselves the products of particular historical conditions and therefore spoke of that time rather than of this time. Nevertheless, the experience of all the churches during the crisis of the Nazi period demonstrated that neither bourgeois lassitude nor historical skepsis had completely dampened the capacity for an eschatological perception of the crisis of one's own time: the last book of the Bible acquired a new voice and power, and despite the discomfiture it had caused an earlier generation of liberal theologians the "eschatological error" in the teachings of Jesus became the very means by which those teachings were lifted out of their own time and place and given universal relevance. If an earlier generation had been able to revise the CANON OF THE NEW TESTAMENT to eliminate the discomfiture, the later generation might have been denied access to the very resource it needed most. Thus development of doctrine, rather than constitutional amendment, has proved to be the process by which eschatology, as well as other articles of faith, have maintained continuity and simultaneously proved themselves open to continuing reinterpretation.

· Eucharist

It is one of the supreme ironies of Christian history, evident already in the New Testament (1 Cor. 11:17–34), that the Eucharist, intended to foster the unity of the church, has been a source of disunity and contention. But this must not be permitted to obscure the real areas of consensus among most Christians in the interpretation of the Eucharist.

All Christians would agree that the sacrament is a memorial action in which, by eating and drinking, the church calls to remembrance what Jesus Christ was, said, and did. There is also universal agreement among Christians that participation in the Eucharist enhances and deepens the communion of believers not only with Christ but also with one another. The breaking of the bread and the pouring out of the wine are recognized by every Christian denomination as the central symbols of the death of Jesus Christ on the cross. Augustine's designation of the SACRAMENTS as a "visible word" expresses the idea, shared by Roman Catholics, Eastern Orthodox, and Protestants, that the Eucharist communicates the same gospel that comes through the written and spoken forms of revelation. And most Christian traditions teach that Jesus Christ is present in the Eucharist in some special way, disagree though they do about the mode, the locus, and the time of that presence. In short, there is more of a consensus among Christians about the meaning of the Eucharist than would appear from the confessional debates over the sacramental presence, the effects of the Eucharist, and the auspices under which it may be celebrated.

According to the eucharistic doctrine of Roman Catholicism, the elements of the bread and wine are "transubstantiated" into the body and blood of Christ; that is, their whole substance is converted into the whole substance of the body and blood, although the outward appearances of the elements, their "accidents," remain. This eucharistic doctrine gives support to certain eucharistic practices and is supported by them in turn. For example, the adoration and reservation of the Host follow from the belief that the whole Christ is truly present in his body and blood under the forms of bread and wine. Similarly, the presence of the whole Christ in either of the consecrated species justifies the practice of distributing only the Host, not the chalice, to the laity. From the affirmation of the real presence comes substantiation for the sacrifice of the Mass: Christ sacrificed himself on Calvary once, but the Mass re-presents that sacrifice. By both asserting the doctrine of transubstantiation and redefining the meaning of the eucharistic sacrifice, the Council of Trent (1545–1563) continued the theological work of THOMAS AQUINAS and laid down the lines for further theological development. During the nineteenth and twentieth centuries the Roman Catholic liturgical movement put new emphasis on the frequency of communion, the participation of the entire congregation in the priestly service, and the real presence of Christ in the church as the fundamental presupposition for the real presence in the Eucharist. These were not new ideas, but they received new life through the issuance of *Mystici Corporis* in 1943 and *Mediator Dei* in 1947, both by Pope Pius XII (1939–1958), and above all through the decrees of the Second Vatican Council of 1962–1965.

The eucharistic beliefs and practices of Eastern Orthodoxy have much in common with those of Roman Catholicism. One of the differences in practice, the use of leavened rather than unleavened bread, is based on differing interpretations of when the Eucharist was instituted, whether on the last day of leavened bread or the first day of unleavened bread in the Jewish calendar. Eastern Orthodox faithful receive both of the consecrated elements in the Eucharist, but by the method of "intinction," the dipping of the consecrated bread in the cup. Whereas Roman Catholic theology maintains that the recitation of the words of institution constitutes the Eucharist as a sacrament, Eastern theology has taught that the invocation of the HOLY SPIRIT upon the elements (Greek *epiklēsis*) is the essential form of the Eucharist. In the area of eucharistic doctrine, Eastern Orthodox theology has not achieved the elaboration and precision of Western doctrine. There is a Greek term corresponding to transubstantiation, *metousiōsis,* but it is evident that the term was adopted by Eastern Orthodoxy in the course of theological discussions with the Western Church. As perhaps, together with the Trinity, the supreme example of the principle of *lex orandi lex credendi* in WORSHIP, the eucharistic liturgies of Eastern Christendom are a highly dramatic representation of the incarnation and resurrection of Christ as the transformation of the created world through the victory of life over death. It is probably accurate to say that the principal differences between Eastern Orthodoxy and Roman Catholicism on the Eucharist are in the areas of piety and liturgy rather than in doctrine.

Of the various theological tendencies in non–Roman Catholic Western Christendom, the two that adhere most closely to the traditions of Catholic eucharistic doctrine and practice, Eastern and Western, are the Anglican and the Lutheran. Early Anglican theology vigorously opposed Roman Catholic teaching on the sacraments, sometimes even identifying Anglican with Reformed theology. But from the beginning, and especially since Newman and the Oxford Movement of the nineteenth century, Anglican liturgical practice and eucharistic doctrine have kept, or recovered, more of the Catholic tradition than have Reformed practice and doctrine. The theology of Lutheranism in the sixteenth century unequivocally affirmed the real presence of the body and blood of Christ "in, with, and under" the bread and wine in the Eucharist. The term "consubstantiation," although not officially approved by Lutheran theologians, did summarize the Lutheran alternative to the idea of transubstantiation. In their liturgies, both Anglicanism and Lutheranism worked within the framework of the Western liturgy of the Mass, adopting certain elements and rejecting others; the liturgical movements in both communions during the nineteenth and twentieth centuries restored the eucharistic prayer and other elements of the tradition, even though the theological interpretation of the Lord's Supper continued to display great variety.

More radical in its rejection of traditional interpretations of the eucharistic presence and in its suspicion of traditional liturgical practices, Reformed Christianity replaced the altar with the communion table and subordinated the sacraments to the preached and written word of God. In the theology and practice of Ulrich Zwingli (1484–1531) the memorial aspect of the eucharistic celebration received new emphasis, overshadowing if not excluding other aspects. But the more characteristically Reformed doctrine was that of John Calvin (1509–1564), who taught a "real but spiritual presence" of the living Christ in the sacramental action rather than in the elements as such. The liturgical observance introduced by Calvin was intended to eliminate from the Lord's Supper what Calvin regarded as the superstitious practices of the Mass and to restore the simplicity of the Gospels. The doctrine of the Lord's Supper became the occasion for the most serious of the confessional debates between Reformed and Lutheran churches.

Other Free Church traditions have drawn upon Reformed thought and practice but have been even more thoroughgoing in their attempts to reform eucharistic doctrine and practice. The sacraments have become "ordinances," not channels of grace but expressions of the faith and obedience of the Christian community. Among Baptists the practice of "close communion" has restricted the ordinance to those who are baptized as adults upon a personal profession of faith. And the Society of Friends dropped the use of the Eucharist altogether, as well as the practice of baptism, in its reaction against formalism.

As a result of all this variety among the churches, the Eucharist has been a central issue in the discussions and deliberations of the ecumenical movement, whose discussions have led many to the conclusion that the various doctrines of the eucharistic presence may be complementary rather than antithetical and that each doctrine may need the others to rescue it from overemphasis and distortion.

· Evil

It is not playing with paradox to characterize Christian theology as a doctrine of "dualistic monotheism," for the New Testament describes the struggle against evil not only in moral but in cosmic terms, as a contest between light and darkness, in which a fallen humanity is simultaneously a willing participant and an unwilling victim. The Epistle to the Ephesians warns early believers: "Our fight is not against human foes, but against cosmic powers, against the authorities and potentates of this dark world, against the superhuman forces of evil in the heavens" (Eph. 6:12). The public ministry of Jesus is inaugurated by a confrontation with the Tempter (dramatized by Dostoevsky in the Legend of the Grand Inquisitor); it reaches its climax with his arrest and punishment, which he himself describes to his captors as "your moment—the hour when darkness reigns" (Luke 22:53); on his cross, according to the Epistle to the Colossians, "he discarded the cosmic powers and authorities like a garment, he made a public spectacle of them and led them as captives in his triumphal procession" (Col. 2:15); and the end of history is dramatized in the last book of the New Testament as the decisive battle of the cosmic war, in which "victory and glory and power belong to our God" (Rev. 19:2). Sometimes, indeed, the dualism gives the impression of having overwhelmed the monotheism, as when the apostle Paul refers to the Devil as "the god of this passing age" (2 Cor. 4:4), almost (but not quite) as though there were two gods just as there are two ages of history.

A faith at whose center stands the figure of crucified innocence had to find ways of coping with the presence of the power of darkness. To this assignment Christianity brought the resources of the Hebrew Bible: the Psalter with its refrain asking why the righteous should be permitted to suffer, and above all the Book of Job. The best-known Christian exposition of the latter is the *Moralia on the Book of Job* by Pope Gregory the Great

(590–604); but the depiction of the figure of Job desolate "among the ashes" (Job 2:8), in which they often combined Christ on the cross with the memory of Oedipus blinded and bleeding, was a familiar motif among other Christian theologians as well. Much of the consideration of the problem of evil in the history of the church has been pastoral rather than speculative, evoked by what Walter Rauschenbusch (1861–1918), the leading spokesman of the Social Gospel, once described as the heartbreak of children's funerals in Hell's Kitchen. Therefore there does not exist in Christian theological literature an unbroken succession of full-scale treatises on the question of "theodicy"—a term that seems not to have come into existence until the *Essais de théodicée sur la bonté de Dieu* of 1710 by Gottfried Wilhelm Leibniz (1646–1716). Rather, the problem has been dealt with primarily in other contexts, above all in connection with the doctrines of SIN and ATONEMENT.

The nature of evil has often been treated in highly personal and dramatic language, which subsequent Christian usage has sometimes modified. The concluding petition of the Lord's Prayer should probably read concretely, "Save us from the Evil One" (Matt. 6:13), and not abstractly, "Save us from evil." In the thought of the Cappadocians or of Luther, the genuine threat posed by the Devil, as a fallen angel, has decisively shaped the interpretation of how Christ saves through the cross: evil is the enemy, an entire kingdom, that holds dominion over its captives until its power is shattered by the greater power of God in the death and resurrection of Christ. A useful distinction proposed by several modern Swedish theologians is between an "ontological" and an "existential" dualism: in the "wondrous battle" (*mirabile duellum*) between Christ and the enemies, as in that between humanity and the enemies, the outcome of the conflict is genuinely in the balance, and God does not play with marked cards; but God is still God alone, so that the power of the enemies may challenge his dominion but cannot finally topple it. As various commentators on the Gospels have pointed out, the saying of Jesus in the Garden of Gethsemane, "This is your moment—the hour when darkness reigns," meant that darkness did indeed reign then and there, but only for that one awesome moment.

Dramatically powerful and pastorally comforting though such a distinction may have been, it has not proved very helpful in answering the unavoidable question, which, according to the church fathers, was constantly on the lips of all the Gnostic heretics: *Unde malum?* (Where, then, does evil come from?). As the history of theological speculation more than amply demonstrates, every answer to that question has been fraught with danger to one or another central affirmation of the Christian faith—or to several of them at the same time. Either the goodness of God or the omnipotence of God will seem impaired, either the freedom of human choice or the malignity of human transgression will be sold short. Schleiermacher divided the "natural heresies" in Christianity into those that made redemption unnecessary by minimizing the power of evil and those that made redemption impossible by maximizing it. It was as much an evasion as a solution when certain Christian theologians insisted on treating the problem of evil in the light of its outcome in redemption rather than in light of its origin; that could even lead, homiletically if not theologically, to the suggestion that evil had been arranged in order to manifest the goodness of God. As Arthur Lovejoy pointed out in a provocative essay, "Milton and the Paradox of the Fortunate Fall," this suggestion has repeatedly proved to be tempting, but has never proved to be satisfying.

Short of a full-blown theory of "the fortunate fall," such a treatment of the issue could produce, as it did in the early church father Irenaeus of Lyons (ca. 130–ca. 200), an elaboration of the providential view of evil. Whatever its origins may have been, evil has become, in the history of salvation, the occasion for God to lead the human race through the valley of the shadow to glory. This took place through the reenactment (Greek *anakephalaiōsis*) of the history of the First Adam in the life, death, and resurrection of Christ as the Second Adam. Evil, then, is not trivial, because it did make the cross necessary, but it is not ultimate either. When transposed to the area of Christian metaphysics, the problem of evil and of sin has been modulated by the formulation of the "meonic" (from the Greek *mē̄ ōn*, "non-being") definition of evil. Because, in Augustine's classic statement of the doctrine of creation, "being is good simply because it is being" (*esse qua esse bonum est*), by virtue of its participation in God as Being-Itself, it follows that whatever has being is, to that extent, good. Therefore the Fall, whether of Satan or of Adam and Eve, could not cancel their being and in that sense their goodness. Evil, consequently, could not have genuine being or reality, but had to be nonbeing and thus meonic. Yet the same Augustine who systematized that philosophical-theological doctrine as an ontological principle could also describe the existential power of evil in his *Confessions* as though it were very real indeed.

▪ Faith

The classic definition occurs in the Epistle to the Hebrews: "And what is faith? Faith gives substance to our hopes, and makes us certain of realities we do not see" (Heb. 11:1). Most of the other definitions in the history of Christian theology have been little more than variations upon this biblical formulation. Of the nearly 250 instances of the noun "faith" (Greek *pistis*) in the New Testament, more than half occur in the writings of the apostle PAUL. Pauline thought and usage, therefore, in addition to being the most prominent in the theological controversies over the meaning of faith and its connection with other themes of Christian doctrine and life such as GRACE and JUSTIFICATION, have had much to do with shaping Christian language about faith. The *Oxford English Dictionary* indicates that the earliest use of the term "faith" in English, whether as confidence or as assent or as the content of revelation, was the religious use, and only later was the term transferred to secular and purely human relations; this was the reverse of what had happened in earlier languages, especially in Greek and Latin.

In the Bible, "faith" has a variety of meanings. Its Hebrew root carries the connotations of trustworthiness, reliability, and loyalty, still suggested in the English adjective "faithful." Frequently in the Gospels and Epistles the idea of confidence or trust is suggested by the use of the noun "faith" and especially of the verb "to believe." Yet this confidence is not merely a subjective state of mind but an assurance or conviction "of realities we do not see." Faith is seen as a trust in that which is eternally real. There is only a short distance from this New Testament understanding of the objectivity of faith to the definition of faith by Thomas Aquinas as "the act of the intellect assenting to a divine truth because of a movement of the will, which is in turn moved by the grace of God." In reaction to what he regarded as the excessively intellectualistic cast of such a definition, Luther stressed the primacy of the element of trust, without, however, denying that faith as trust attached itself to what it knew to be true. John Calvin (1509–1564) called it "a firm and certain knowledge of God's benevolence toward us, founded upon the truth of the freely given promise in Christ, both revealed to our minds and sealed upon our hearts through the Holy Spirit," and Protestant orthodoxy eventually divided faith into knowledge, assent, and trust. Occasionally in the New Testament and much more regularly in the language of tradition, "the faith" is a technical term for the objective content of the Christian revelation, the CREED (from the Latin *credo*, "I believe") or what the Epistle of Jude called "the faith which God entrusted to his people once and for all" (Jude 3).

This distinction between the "objective" and the "subjective" does not, of course, appear in the New Testament; in fact, present-day usage is an almost complete reversal of what those two terms meant in scholastic and early modern philosophy. A traditional way of phrasing the distinction has been to speak of faith as "that which one believes" (*fides quae creditur*) and as "that by which one believes" (*fides qua creditur*). The correlate of faith is divine revelation: according to the Epistle to the Romans, "faith is awakened by the message, and the message that awakens it comes through the word of Christ" (Rom. 10:17). Where revelation has been understood principally as the disclosure of divine truth or sacred doctrine, faith has come to mean the acceptance, on authority, of what has been supernaturally disclosed. Where, by contrast, faith has been defined in more existential terms as an encounter, the element of trust has predominated over the elements of knowledge and assent.

It would be an oversimplification to designate these two

definitions as, respectively, Roman Catholic and Protestant; for in Eastern Orthodoxy and Roman Catholicism the mystical and Augustinian traditions have also emphasized the existential aspects of faith. On the other hand, the objectivity of revelation and the dependence of faith upon authority belong to an understanding of faith that characterizes both Roman Catholicism and orthodox Protestantism, although Protestant theology identifies this authority with the Bible alone whereas Roman Catholicism includes the teaching church past and present in its view of authority. Objective faith is "faith *that*" something is divine truth, historical fact, and authoritative dogma; it is, in the words of the First Vatican Council of 1869–1870, "a supernatural virtue by which we, with the aid and inspiration of the grace of God, believe that the things revealed by him are true, not because the intrinsic truth of the revealed things has been perceived by the natural light of reason, but because of the authority of God himself who reveals them." Subjective faith is "faith *in*" God as he is encountered in Christ; it is, in the words of Jacques Maritain (1882–1973) about Saint John of the Cross (1542–1591), a "faith that is one with the charity which informs it and the gifts that illumine it, a faith as it acts concretely in a holy soul—loving, wise, and fruitful."

The relation among faith, hope, and charity has long engaged the attention of Christian theology. If the meaning of faith were confined to the definition quoted from the Epistle to the Hebrews, the distinction between faith and hope would be difficult to specify. The distinction, according to Augustine, is that faith—in the sense of "faith that"—extended to many things, both good and evil, as for example to the existence of demons, and to things past, present, and future; "but hope deals only with good things, and only with those which lie in the future, and which pertain to the one who cherishes the hope." Although faith and hope have been more difficult to separate than have faith and charity, it is the relation between the latter two that has been the occasion for theological controversy. In a paraphrase of Galatians 5:6, Peter Lombard (ca. 1100–1160), and with him much of the medieval tradition, spoke of faith in its fullness as "faith formed by love" (*fides caritate formata*). Objecting to this formula as a denial of justification by faith without works, Luther asserted that it was faith alone that took hold of the righteousness of Christ and salvation, although love did follow of necessity. Although they differed about the definitions of faith and of the church, Roman Catholic and Protestant teaching agreed that faith, like hope and charity, required the community of the church for its proper nourishment and expression.

Both in the popular idiom and in philosophical writing, faith has frequently been equated with uncertainty: "I am not certain whether such and such is true, but I believe that it is." Traditional Christian theology has also distinguished faith from knowledge on the grounds that knowledge was based upon evidence whereas faith was based upon divine authority. But this did not mean that faith was less certain than knowledge; on the contrary, faith was taken to be free of the uncertainty caused by the fluctuations of knowledge and ignorance. Beset though it was by subjective difficulties and even doubts, it retained its objective certainty, the certainty of its object, which was God. With the rejection of the traditional proofs of the existence of God and with the loss of the authority of the church in Western culture, however, this understanding of the certainty of faith has been replaced in the thought of many Christians by other views: a theory of double truth (as in medieval Averroism), according to which something may be true religiously and false scientifically, or vice versa; or (as in Schleiermacher) by a definition of faith as "a feeling of utter dependence." Christian existentialism and the spirit of the age have both contributed to these redefinitions, but at the same time biblical study has uncovered the creedal elements in the New Testament and has thus recovered the "given" and objective character of Christian faith as faith in the word of God.

· Filioque

If there is a special circle of the inferno described by Dante
reserved for historians of theology, the principal homework
assigned to that subdivision of hell for at least the first several
eons of eternity may well be the thorough study of all the
treatises—in Latin, Greek, Church Slavonic, and various
modern languages—devoted to the inquiry: Does the HOLY
SPIRIT proceed from the Father only, as Eastern Christendom
contends, or from both the Father and the Son (*ex Patre Filioque*), as the Latin Church teaches? Futile or even presumptuous
though it may seem to pry into such arcane matters within the
inscrutable life of the Godhead, the problem of the Filioque or
"double procession," in the framework of the total doctrine of
the TRINITY, manages to touch on many of the most central
issues of theology and to display, more effectively than any other
of the "questions in dispute" (*quaestiones disputatae*), how fundamental and far-reaching are the differences between the
Orthodox Christian East and the West, whether Roman Catholic or Protestant.

To understand what is at stake in the Filioque controversy, it
is essential to grasp the basic distinction drawn by the Greek
church fathers between the concept of "economy" and the strict
sense of the word "theology": the former refers to the ways of
God to the world and to the human race within time and history; the latter to what God, through that "economy," has
revealed about the eternal mystery of the divine Being itself.
Although it was the indispensable presupposition for the Christian view of "economy" as the divine dispensation in history,
the dogma of the Trinity pertained to "theology" in the narrow
meaning. What was taken to be the heretical teaching of
Sabellianism—or, as it is usually known in modern histories of
dogma, "modalistic Monarchianism"—was the theory that Father, Son, and Holy Spirit were merely "economical," terms for
the successive manifestations of the one God within history that
did not have an eternal and ontological or "theological" status.

When applied to the procession of the Holy Spirit, the distinction meant to the Greeks that the Holy Spirit was indeed "sent" from both the Father and the Son "economically," in its descent upon the church at Pentecost and since, but that within the being of the Godhead only the Father was the one principle and source of being, from which both the Son and the Holy Spirit eternally "proceeded." The use of both terms in the saying of Jesus in John 15:26, "When your Advocate has come, whom I will send (Greek *pempsō*) you from the Father—the Spirit of truth that issues from (Greek *ekporeuetai*) the Father," was taken by Eastern theology as proof of that basic distinction between being sent and proceeding.

In the Latin West, it seems safe to say, that distinction, although not absent, did not play so decisive a role as it did in the East. Underlying these and other differences on the doctrine of the Trinity, however, were two quite distinct theological methodologies for safeguarding the doctrine of the unity of God. Despite some places in the writings of the CAPPADOCIANS that seem to incline toward the eventual Western position, the tenor of their trinitarian argumentation and many of their explicit statements make it evident that positing more than one "principle" (*archē*), as the doctrine of the Filioque seems to do, would threaten that unity: if there were more than one *archē*, each would have to be called God and the oneness of God would become a Platonic abstraction, "the fact of being God" (*auto to einai theon*) which the Three had in common. To Augustine in his treatise *On the Trinity*, on the other hand, the oneness could be taken for granted; but it was the equality and the distinction among Father, Son, and Holy Spirit as three "persons" in the Trinity that needed to be preserved against heresy. In the West during the eighth and ninth centuries, distinction was pitted against equality, by those who argued that if the Holy Spirit proceeded only from the Father and not from the Son, that made the Son less than the Father. The response was to assert that, in theology no less than in economy, the Spirit proceeded *ex Patre Filioque*.

Unfortunately, the formulators of the Nicene Creed had not

foreseen the crisis and had written concerning the Holy Spirit that "with the Father and the Son it is worshiped and glorified," but that it "proceeds from the Father." First at the local level in those regions of the West where it seemed necessary against the new heresy, but eventually throughout the West and finally with the approval of Rome, the Filioque became a part of the Nicene Creed. That unilateral revision by one part of the church became a doctrinal issue in its own right: Eastern theologians charged that even if the Filioque were orthodox (which it was not), Rome did not have the authority to insert it into a creed that, unlike many other regional creeds both Latin and Greek, was the common property of all of Christendom, and was the only truly ecumenical creed. It is important to recognize that the substantive trinitarian question and the procedural jurisdictional question were both doctrinal questions for both sides, all the more so because the dispute came to a head (as could have been anticipated) at the same time as the quarrel of East and West about other questions such as jurisdiction over the Slavs. Both sides went on citing the same passages of Scripture and quotations from the church fathers in support of their theories of the procession, but by now the question was a part of their deeper alienation over the nature of tradition and the very nature of the church.

Whenever East and West, under external threat from Islam or in a domestic crisis because of schism, have moved toward some measure of détente, ingenious compromise formulas on the Filioque have appeared. The most durable of these, incorporated in the Union of Florence in 1439 and reintroduced during the nineteenth and twentieth centuries as a result of the ecumenical movement, was the revision of trinitarian language to read: "who proceeds from the Father *through the Son.*" That seemed to satisfy the Eastern insistence on one principle, as well as the Western desire to have the Son participate ontologically in the procession of the Holy Spirit. Like many other doctrinal differences, the problem of the Filioque may be seen as rooted partly in the theory of DEVELOPMENT OF DOCTRINE, of which it represents an especially acute instance. Recognizing its extremely problematical character, Newman declared in one of his earliest statements of the theory, in 1843: "The doctrine of the Double Procession was no Catholic dogma in the first ages, though it was more or less clearly stated by individual fathers; yet if it is now to be received, as surely it must be, as part of the Creed, it was really held everywhere from the beginning, and therefore, in a measure, held as a mere religious impression, and perhaps an unconscious one." This puzzling formulation indicates that for historical scholarship no less than for ecumenical theology, the difficulties created by the Filioque on all sides remain formidable.

▪ Friendship

Although the primary function of this dictionary is to locate and describe some of the major themes of scholarship in the history of the Christian theological tradition, it should perhaps identify some themes that have been neglected. Despite the eternally touching story of David and Jonathan in the First Book of Samuel, Christian theology, and even Christian ethics, do not seem to have found an appropriate category for the meaning of friendship. Jesus is represented in the Gospel of John as declaring to his disciples during their last days together: "I call you servants no longer; a servant does not know what his master is about. I have called you friends, because I have disclosed to you everything that I heard from my Father" (John 15:15). Nevertheless, it would seem safe to say, even without the empirical evidence of a word count, that in manuals of theology and canon law references to disciples past and present as "servants" outnumber references to them as "friends" by a factor of fifty or a hundred. As a result, it is to the *De amicitia* of Cicero, rather than to theological works, that one is obliged to turn for a discussion of a topic that even the most fastidiously orthodox theologian would have to call "spiritual." Yet there certainly ought to be resources in the Christian theological tradition for probing this topic beyond the clichés that sometimes cling to it and, as with other themes in the relation of nature and grace, for going beyond "mere friendship" in order to understand friendship: Abraham not only is the exemplar for faith and therefore for justification (Rom. 4:3), but he also is referred to in an oracle from God to the prophet Isaiah as "Abraham my friend" (Isa. 41:8).

• Gibbon, Edward (1737–1794)

Historian of the Roman Empire, Enlightenment critic of orthodox theology, and master of English prose.

Like the Reformation, the fall of Rome has acquired the status of a historical test case: Tell me how you interpret this event, and I should be able to predict with some accuracy where you stand on an entire series of other historical—and, not incidentally, theological—questions. The fall of Rome already had this status as a consequence of the interpretations placed upon it by various Christian writers contemporary to the events such as Jerome (ca. 342–420), but above all through AUGUSTINE's *City of God,* which was evoked by pagan charges that Christianity, by alienating the Roman Empire from its ancient and traditional gods, had been responsible for the capture of Rome by Alaric and his Goths in 410 C.E.

The all but unquestioned authority of the *City of God* as an answer to the charge of a causal connection between Christianity and the fall of the Roman Empire came in for challenge from various philosophers, theologians, and historians of the Enlightenment. But none was more successful in that challenge than Edward Gibbon, whose *History of the Decline and Fall of the Roman Empire* has itself become something of a historical monument, a classic of the English language, and the starting point for reflection on a host of issues in the relation of Christianity and HISTORIOGRAPHY. Its fifteenth and sixteenth chapters, which he revised and abridged several times, are a capsule account of the rise of the early church, an explanation of its persecution by an otherwise tolerant Rome, and an analysis—set forth as objective and historical in intent, purportedly eschewing value judgments and theological explanations—of the reasons for its rapid and remarkable success in conquering the Roman world. These two chapters, understandably, have been most often singled out for attack, beginning in the author's lifetime; he replied to the attack in his *Vindication* of 1779. Yet NEWMAN expressed a judgment echoed by writers of every theological position when he observed in the introduction to his *Essay on the Development of Christian Doctrine*: "It is melancholy to say it, but the chief, perhaps the only English writer who has any claim to be considered an ecclesiastical historian is the unbeliever Gibbon."

In his *Autobiography* Gibbon left an oft-quoted account of the origins of his book: "It was at Rome, on the 15th of October 1764, as I sat musing amid the ruins of the Capitol, while the barefooted friars were singing vespers in the temple of Jupiter, that the idea of writing the decline and fall of the city first came to my mind." As many an author of a multivolume work of history has had reason to discover, the period from such an "idea of writing" to actual publication, even of Volume 1, can extend for a decade or more. Gibbon's first volume did not appear until 1776, the same year as Adam Smith's *Wealth of Nations* and the American Declaration of Independence, and the final volume was published in 1788. Upon completing that final volume, on 27 June 1787, Gibbon experienced "emotions of joy on recovery of my freedom, and perhaps the establishment of my fame," but these were soon mingled with the more "melancholy" sense that by finishing the work he "had taken an everlasting leave of an old and agreeable companion, and that whatsoever might be the future fate of my *History,* the life of the historian must be short and precarious." That "future fate" has turned out rather well, and the book seems never to have been out of print for the past two centuries.

Beyond an enormous plethora of narrative and biographical detail, the *Decline and Fall* is characterized by several unifying principles. One of these, enunciated in the third chapter, is the judgment that history "is, indeed, little more than the register of the crimes, follies, and misfortunes of mankind." Therefore crimes, follies, and misfortunes, especially those connected with the Roman Caesars, bulk large in Gibbon's account. They are often recited with sardonic wit and a prurient attention to sexual excesses, these latter usually documented in Latin or Greek; for in response to "the clamor that has been raised against the indecency of my last three volumes," in which many of these excesses, especially in the court of BYZANTIUM, had occupied him for pages at a time, with lengthy footnotes, he indignantly asserts: "My English is chaste, and all licentious passages are left in the obscurity of a learned language"—not, despite whatever suspicions one may have, as a result of collusion with the Latin masters of secondary schools, who, then as now, would resort to almost anything to make the young learn the classical languages. Yet these excesses of the emperors (and empresses) were only symptomatic of a deeper malaise, for "the decline of Rome was the natural and inevitable effect of immoderate greatness." The Roman Empire was in many ways the victim of its own success; "and, instead of inquiring why the Roman Empire was destroyed, we should rather be surprised that it had subsisted so long." For "as soon as time or accident had removed the artificial supports, the stupendous fabric yielded to the pressure of its own weight."

The role of Christianity in this demise of "the stupendous fabric" of the Roman Empire was, according to Gibbon's autopsy, difficult to determine. Despite such phrases as "the triumph of barbarism and religion," he recognized as well the positive contributions that the moral and even the spiritual vigor introduced by Christianity had made to Roman life. His chapters on the history of the doctrines of the Trinity and the incarnation are unsparing in their critique of the superstition and authoritarianism introduced in the name of the gospel, and he is relentless in exposing the hypocrisy of "Christian" emperors, of theologians and bishops—and above all of monks, for whom he seems to have had almost nothing but contempt, despite his own enormous dependence on the scholarly editions of the sources prepared by Benedictines and other members of religious orders during the seventeenth and eighteenth centuries. It is easy enough to point out the contradictions and absurdities in Gibbon's treatment of the church—in other words, to treat Gibbon the way he treated Christianity. But during the twentieth century a more sober and less defensive Christian historiography has on many specific historical points—such as persecution and martyrdom—found itself closer to his judgments than to those of his more orthodox critics.

Critics friendly and not so friendly have pointed out that overdosing on Gibbon's *Decline and Fall* while in one's teens can leave a permanent mark on both the style and the substance of a future historian's books. It can, however, have a positive effect as well. In an "Alexandrian" age of historical scholarship like our own, when the monograph, the review of the monograph, and the response to the review of the monograph sometimes threaten to swamp the learned literature, Gibbon's *Decline and Fall* can stand as a model of a work of history that has been willing to carve out one significant chunk of the human experience, to acquire such "mastery" of the primary sources in the several "learned languages" as a single "short and precarious" lifetime will permit, and to narrate the entire account with a beginning, a middle, and an end, in as lucid and forceful a prose as careful writing and rewriting can produce.

· Gifford Lectures

A series of lectures begun in 1888 at the universities of Scotland, designated by their founder, Lord (Adam) Gifford (1820–1887) "for promoting, advancing, teaching, and diffusing the study of natural theology, in the widest sense of that term, in other words, the knowledge of God." During the century of their existence, the Gifford Lectures have become the major forum for the philosophical, historical, scientific, psychological, and theological consideration of NATURAL THEOLOGY, giving rise to such classics as *The Varieties of Religious Experience* by William James (1842–1910), *The Living God* by NATHAN SÖDERBLOM, *Process and Reality* by Alfred North Whitehead (1861–1947), *The Spirit of Medieval Philosophy* by Étienne Gilson (1884–1978), and *The Nature and Destiny of Man* by Reinhold Niebuhr (1892–1971).

• Goethe, Johann Wolfgang von (1749–1832)

German poet and man of letters, statesman and scientist, philosopher of Nature and of life.

Theologians have long had some favorite "pagan" to whom they turned for wisdom, and for evidence that the cup of God's grace and truth runneth over. *Sancte Socrates, ora pro nobis!* (Holy Socrates, pray for us!) was the way Erasmus articulated the widely shared sense that this martyr (ca. 470–399 B.C.E.) had been a type of Christ; Dante's choice of Vergil (70–19 B.C.E.) as his guide through the underworld likewise expressed a long-standing Christian reverence.

But more than any other artistic or intellectual figure, Goethe represented for the generation of Christian intellectuals from Central Europe born during the half-century after his death—and, in many cases, also for their children and grandchildren—the summit of all that was attainable in the life of the mind and spirit. In part it was the sheer size and universality of his mind that fitted him for this role. "The Old Eternal Genius who built this world," according to Emerson, had "confided himself to this man more than to any other," so that Goethe had "said the best things about nature that ever were said." In each of the diverse fields of stagecraft, law, linguistics, optics, botany, and meteorology, he stood as a leading figure of his time. Nor were his interests in all of these disciplines the mere excursions of a dilettante or dabbler, for he meditated long and hard about the relations between them. "When we do natural science, we are pantheists," he observed in one of his many hundreds of *Maxims and Reflections*; "when we write poetry, we are polytheists; and when we reflect on morality, we are monotheists." He did all of these, and he was all of these: that was the source of both the admiration and the perplexity that he evoked from theologians.

The perplexity was reciprocated. The opening scene of Goethe's *Faust* presents the aged philosopher, who has gone through all the offerings in all the catalogues of all four faculties of the medieval university:

> I've studied now Philosophy
> And Jurisprudence, Medicine,—
> And even, alas! Theology . . .

Yet he is obliged to acknowledge that he knows no more than he had before taking all those higher degrees. "And even, alas! Theology" (*Und leider auch Theologie*) was an autobiographical description of the frustration Goethe described in his *Dichtung und Wahrheit* when he recalled his own years as a university student. For, to the dismay of the theologians of the nineteenth and twentieth centuries who attributed to his writings an almost deuterocanonical status, Goethe frequently spoke about theology, whether ecclesiastical or academic, with eloquent disrespect—and even, alas! contempt. Nor was the dismay relieved by the substitute theology to whose exposition Goethe's *Faust* was dedicated. Those to whom their critics referred as "Goethe-Christians" had to be reminded that it would not do to quote the words of the Almighty near the beginning of the play, "A human being will err so long as he aspires" (*Es irrt der Mensch solange er strebt*), to illustrate the Augustinian doctrine of sin, without recalling the basic denial of the orthodox Christian doctrine of grace that is chanted in the corresponding words of the angels near the end:

> This noble spirit now is free,
> And saved from evil scheming;
> Whoe'er aspires unweariedly
> Is not beyond redeeming

—as eloquent a statement of the Pelagian heresy as any that Augustine ever confronted and refuted. And the final lines of *Faust* about "the Eternal Feminine" (*das Ewig-Weibliche*), with their unavoidable echoes of the medieval doctrine of Mary, have aptly been termed "Catholicism minus Christianity."

Yet for all the objections that any Christian orthodoxy must raise about Goethe and about *Faust,* it is clear that Goethe could not leave theology alone. Faust, like every student of New Testament Greek before and after him, struggled with the meaning of the term *Logos* in the prologue to the Gospel of John (John 1:1–14), and he tried out several different translations without settling finally on any. The scene in Faust's study is also the source, at one and the same time, for one of the most unabashed statements of the supercilious "presentism" of many moderns in their treatment of tradition, including the Christian tradition, and for one of the most succinct formulations of the relation that this tradition, or any tradition so conceived and so dedicated, bears to the opportunity or obligation for responsible thought and action in the present.

Faust's amanuensis and research assistant, or *famulus,* Wagner (no relation to others of that name in the nineteenth century), seems to be Goethe's portrait of the would-be scholar, who does not know the difference between erudition and pedantry, but who is simply thrilled by propinquity to a world-class savant and is quite willing, even on Easter Eve, to stay up late (and to keep his master up late) if he can only pick up a few little crumbs of wisdom. Of the many fields of learning to which he was exposed through Doctor Faustus, history seems to hold a special fascination for Wagner:

a great delight is granted
When, in the spirit of the ages planted,
We mark how, ere our time, a sage has thought,
And then, how far his work, and grandly, we have brought.

Faust's response, "O yes, up to the stars at last!" is not only a rebuke for the smugness and condescension of the attitude that all past is prologue, but also a critique of a methodological naiveté that is unaware of the impenetrability of the historical record, which remains "a book with seven seals protected" and cannot be manipulated so as to document a simplistic theory of inevitable intellectual progress. It is the function of history, Goethe once said in another of the *Maxims and Reflections,* "to get the past off our backs," but that is not the way to do it.

Rather, in an epigram that is worthy of serving as the leitmotiv of the scholarly life, Faust declared:

What you have as heritage,
Take now as task;
For thus you will make it your own!

Was du ererbt von deinen Vätern hast,
Erwirb es, um es zu besitzen!

Goethe's debt to his own heritage—above all, as is visible in his aesthetics, to the classical heritage of Greece and Rome as interpreted by the Renaissance, but also to the Christian heritage both of the medieval culture upon which he drew in *Faust* and of the Reformation, to which all his life he maintained an ambivalent relation—became a "task" for him as well, which he reinterpreted for himself and for his own time. For that very reason, however, a similar reinterpretation of Goethe, even a reinterpretation that relates his "neopaganism" to its Christian roots, can be defended as a valid way of turning heritage into task and of thereby vindicating tradition.

▪ Gospel

Among the many languages in which the melody of theology has been sung, English is singularly blessed in having its own word for the Greek *euangelion,* the most distinctive of all terms for the Christian message. The Old English word *godspel* did not, regardless of what pious folk etymologies have supposed, refer to the name "God," but meant "good news," as does *euangelion.* Like the Greek original, the English term has been employed in several distinct senses, which it is helpful to sort out and identify.

The fundamental sense, to which all other uses of the term can be connected, is "the message of Jesus." But this means the message that was taught about him as well as the message that he brought. The duality implicit in that description comes through in the very first chapter of the Gospel of Mark, usually regarded as the earliest of the four Gospels. Its opening verse reads: "Here begins the gospel of Jesus Christ the Son of God." But a few verses later it continues: "After John had been arrested, Jesus came into Galilee proclaiming the gospel of God: 'The time has come; the kingdom of God is upon you; repent, and believe the gospel'" (Mark 1:14). Here Jesus proclaims the gospel and summons his hearers to believe it; but it is the entire story of his life, death, and resurrection—and not only the narrative summary of his proclamation—that is introduced as "the gospel of Jesus Christ the Son of God." From this it is natural to conclude that the followers of Jesus began very early to call both his teachings and their witness to his person "gospel," apparently with little or no need to make any such distinction. On the basis of the sermons in the early chapters of the Acts of the Apostles—for example, Peter's message at Pentecost (Acts 2:14–36)—it seems that the content of this gospel was a narrative of the miracles and other deeds of Jesus Christ, together with an identification of him, by means of a HERMENEUTIC of typology and fulfillment, as the Promised One of Hebrew prophecy, above all in his death on the cross and in his resurrection from the dead.

As far as we can tell, that primitive gospel circulated in a purely oral form; that supposition is confirmed by twentieth-century studies of how TRADITION is formed and transmitted. Throughout the Gospels, Jesus himself is described as having written only once—and that in a text of dubious manuscript provenance (John 8:6)—but as having always "taught with a note of authority" orally (Matt. 7:29). In the absence of reliable data about the process, New Testament scholars have been obliged, and have proved more than willing, to engage in speculative reconstruction of the process by which this oral gospel gradually became the written "Gospel" (or, rather, "Gospels") that we think of now when we hear the word. It cannot be emphasized too much that in the New Testament the word "gospel," like the word "doctrine," is always used in the singular when it refers to the authentic message; unlike "doctrine," moreover, which can be in the plural when those who "teach as doctrines the commandments of men" (Matt. 15:9) are being denounced, it appears in the singular even when "a different gospel" is being identified and attacked (Gal. 1:6; 2 Cor. 11:4). A nice sense of that usage would require, then, that the "Gospels of" Matthew, Mark, Luke, and John be rather called, as they generally are in ancient practice, "the Gospel according to" (Greek *to euangelion kata*) one or another of the evangelists: a single Gospel in several distinct (though not, of course, opposing) versions. Both from the evidence within the New Testament and from the long-lost manuscripts (especially in Coptic) that have surfaced in our own time we know that "many writers have undertaken to draw up an account of the events that have happened among us, following the [oral] traditions handed down to us by the original eyewitnesses and servants of the gospel" (Luke 1:1). Deciding among these was a major component of the process by which the CANON OF THE NEW TESTAMENT evolved.

The relations of the Gospels to one another, as well as the relation between the canonical four "Gospels" (plural) and "the gospel" (singular) were troublesome from the start. It is clear from the scholarly study of the TEXT OF THE NEW TESTAMENT that frequently the scribes would, intentionally or inadvertently, harmonize the language of one Gospel with that of another. Even more troubling are the problems of chronology raised by the form of the Gospels. Only the Gospel of John (in which the noun "gospel" does not appear, just as the noun "faith" does not), with its structure of Jewish holidays as the framework for narrating the life of Jesus, provided a warrant for extending the ministry of Jesus over a period of three years or so. "Harmonies of the Gospels"—the term itself comes from the sixteenth century, but the concern is ancient—arose partly in response to attacks like those of Origen's opponent Celsus against the historical credibility of the Gospel stories, and partly also for devotional, liturgical, and homiletical purposes. In the second century the Syrian heretic Tatian prepared the *Diatessaron* ("out of four"), which wove the narratives of the four Gospels into one. (Twentieth-century archeological findings indicate that it was probably prepared in Greek rather than in Syriac, as had been supposed because it was used in the Syriac Church as the only Gospel for several centuries.) But the most influential of these harmonies in the ancient Church was composed by Augustine; its title, *On the Agreement among the Evangelists* (*De consensu evangelistarum*), indicates its interest in demonstrating that disagreements among the several Gospels in matters of chronology, historical fact, or teaching were illusory.

In the usage of theologians, or at any rate of theologians in the tradition of the Protestant Reformation, the word "gospel" is probably employed most often in the sense it has in the writings of PAUL. "I am not ashamed of the gospel," he wrote (Rom. 1:16), which "is the saving power of God for everyone who has faith," namely, the message of the doctrine of justification. Although the word "gospel" with its derivatives appears in the Pauline writings literally dozens of times, he does not refer at all to the events of the life of Jesus narrated in the Gospels (except for the Passion story), quote any of the actions or miracles of Jesus (except for the resurrection), nor cite a single parable or other saying of Jesus (except for the words of institution of the Eucharist). To invoke a favorite Enlightenment distinction, by "my gospel" (Rom. 2:16) Paul would seem to have meant not the "religion of Jesus" but the "religion about Jesus," or, as he called it, "the facts which have been imparted to me" (1 Cor. 15:3–4) about the cross and resurrection. More specifically, he meant that which was believed by faith (Rom. 1:16–17), taught (1 Cor. 15:1–2), and confessed (2 Cor. 9:13)—which is how doctrine or even dogma has been defined. When leaders of the Protestant Reformation made "agreement on the doctrine of the gospel" (*consentire de doctrina evangelii*) a prerequisite for the unity of the church, therefore, they were echoing this Pauline usage, but were defining "doctrine" in a sense that brought it closer to the meaning of dogma; yet it is interesting to note that this Latin phrase in the Augsburg Confession had as its German counterpart "preaching in accordance with a pure understanding of the gospel."

In addition to the noun, the corresponding verb "to evangelize" (for which English has been obliged to fall back on the Greek word) has played an important role both in the history of Christian missions and in the development of the revival movement, as a result of which "evangelist" to many people has become the title for a twentieth-century preacher on radio or television rather than for the first-century writer of a Gospel.

· Grace

"The grace of God has dawned upon the world with healing for all mankind," the New Testament declares in a passage that was to become the standard epistle lesson for Christmas Day in the Western Church; "by it," the text continues, "we are disciplined to renounce godless ways" (Titus 2:11–12). Grace as healing (which in the Greek word *sōtēria,* and then in the Latin *salus,* is the root meaning of "salvation," already in pre-Christian usage) and grace as discipline have been the two principal aspects of its

definition in the history of Christian theology. Both in the vocabulary of the New Testament itself and in the language of
church theologians, the term "the grace of God" is closely related to "the love of God" and to "the mercy of God," so that it
is often difficult to distinguish among them; although the usage
is by no means consistent, it is helpful, within the general category of love, to define mercy as forgiving love and grace as
mediated mercy. Because of the centrality of the doctrine of
grace in the thought of AUGUSTINE, who came to be identified in
medieval theology by the sobriquet *Doctor gratiae,* his interpretations of the polarities between grace and other themes of the
Christian message have set the pattern for much of the subsequent discussion about grace in the Western Church and for the
DEVELOPMENT OF DOCTRINE.

Grace as healing meant grace as a gift. In the controversy
with Pelagianism, Augustine exploited the assonance between
gratia and *gratis* to urge that the idea of the grace of God *eo ipso*
excluded all notions of prior merit or worthiness in the recipient: if *gratia* was not given *gratis,* it simply could not be *gratia.*
Dangerous though it might appear to be for the moral imperative, the definition of grace as an unearned gift was, in the Augustinian system, indispensable to the meaning of the gospel,
which would otherwise be indistinguishable from paganism.
ORIGEN's pagan opponent, Celsus, recognized this with a clarity
that was not always shared by Christian theologians, when, in a
remarkable passage, he criticized the Christians for harping on
the centrality of the gift of grace. "Those who summon people
to the other mysteries," Celsus observed, "make this prelimi-
nary proclamation: 'Who has pure hands and a wise tongue.'"
By contrast with that universal stipulation of worthiness, he
continued, "let us hear what folk these Christians call. 'Whoever is a sinner,' they say, 'whoever is unwise, whoever is a child,
and, in a word, whoever is a wretch will be received by the
kingdom of God.'" The Augustinian term for this dimension
of grace was *favor Dei.* Grace was, in the first instance, something in God "to usward" (as the Elizabethan phrase of the
Authorized Version has it), not something in the recipient of the

grace; only as a consequence of that priority of the divine initiative could grace refer also to a quality of the human soul.

In this emphasis on the priority of the divine initiative Augustine was working with a fundamental distinction between grace and nature, which was to become the presupposition for most of Western theology. In his treatise *Nature and Grace (De natura et gratia)*, written in 415, he interprets nature on the basis of the words of Ephesians 2:3 as the capacity with which humanity was endowed by creation but which it lost through the sin of Adam and Eve, so that in this fallen state "nature" referred to incapacity rather than capacity. By contrast with nature in this sense, grace was the divine gift by which nature could be restored to the original condition intended by the Creator. As he was drawing such distinctions, however, Augustine was conscious—and was constantly being reminded by his opponents—of the danger that a distinction could be turned into a disjunction: the Manicheism to which he had adhered before becoming a Catholic Christian seemed to him to have separated nature and grace so radically as to make them ontological categories whose difference was too profound even for the saving action of God to bridge. Already in Augustine's own two-front war against Manicheism and Pelagianism the most sensitive issue was the relation of grace to free will, but the debate between Luther and Erasmus was to demonstrate that the Augustinian doctrine of the image of God continually needed to specify its opposition to Manicheism, not only to Pelagianism, on the relation of nature and grace. This it has done the most effectively in a formula shared by the *Summa Theologiae* of Thomas Aquinas and the *Commentary on Galatians* of Luther: "Grace does not abolish nature, but perfects it." This meant simultaneously that nature could not be perfected without grace, and that when it was perfected it did not have to be destroyed, because it was still God's good creature.

In the thought of Augustine during the final decade of his life, in the systems of late medieval Augustinians, in Luther's treatise of 1525 against Erasmus, and most powerfully of all in the theology of John Calvin (1509–1564), the emphasis on the free and sovereign grace of God led to a thoroughgoing doctrine of predestination. For if grace was not based in any way on the prior merit of the recipient, there was no alternative but to affirm that divine election alone decided who was to receive it. And because obviously not everyone did receive it, there appeared to be no alternative but to affirm, as a corollary, that likewise divine election alone decided who was *not* to receive it. Both Augustine and Luther had said as much at various points in their theological development, but each of them shrank from drawing the unambiguous conclusion of a predestination to damnation. Calvin and his followers saw no alternative to that conclusion, and they believed that thereby they were rescuing Augustine's doctrine of grace from the compromises into which it had fallen in the systems of the scholastics and even of Luther. At the same time their definition of grace as the unearned mercy of a personal God in Christ set this view of double predestination apart from the fatalisms of the deterministic philosophers. They claimed, moreover, that the doctrine of double predestination was vindicated whenever those who opposed it as unworthy of divine justice ended up attacking it also for being insensitive to human merit; for it was the very intent of the doctrine of predestination as double predestination to exclude every consideration of merit from the transaction of grace.

Conversely, many of the critics of the Calvinist doctrine of predestination argued that its one-sided interpretation of grace weakened the no less Augustinian insistence upon mediation through the "means of grace" in the word of God and the SACRAMENTS. Because the paradigm of the means of grace in the theology of Augustine had been the baptism of infants, there was no obvious conflict, but rather a preestablished consistency, between this principle of mediation and the stress upon the gratuitous quality of grace. But when, in the theology and church life of the Middle Ages, the paradigm was shifted from the passivity of infant baptism to those sacraments, such as penance and the Eucharist, in which participation was decisively dependent on the decision and action of the recipient, it proved difficult to avoid attaching at least some merit to such decision and action. And even when the official language of the church's dogma did avoid it, catechetical instruction and popular piety could speak as though the receiving or not receiving of the sacraments made the difference between those who were "in a state of grace" and those who were not. During the seventeenth century, Roman Catholic theology in France, Spain, and Italy was torn by conflict over the "aids to grace" (*auxilia gratiae*), by which a soul could prepare itself for a worthy reception of the gift of grace: those who emphasized such aids were accused of denying that grace was a gift, while those to whom this was the primary concern appeared to be neglecting the full implications of the doctrine of the means of grace.

Harnack, Adolf von (1851–1930)

Scholar of PATRISTICS, historian of DOGMA, and high priest of *Wissenschaft*.

Although he was, as the "von" indicates, knighted by the German Kaiser and was saluted on his seventieth birthday by the president of the Weimar Republic as "the bearer of German high culture" (*Träger deutscher Bildung*), Harnack was born not in Germany but in Estonia. His father, Theodosius Harnack (1816–1889), who had been born in Saint Petersburg and who later became a professor at the University of Erlangen and a distinguished student of the theology of Luther, taught theology at Dorpat (now Tartu). The Harnacks did not, moreover, have a purely German pedigree, but claimed to have been descended from émigrés who had come to Germany from Moravia (where their name meant, in its original form, something like "mountaineer").

The extent of Adolf Harnack's contribution to scholarship can be measured by anyone who has access to a reasonably well-stocked theological library, where there will almost certainly be scores, and conceivably hundreds, of cards in the catalogue under his name. He himself confessed, when presented with a bibliography of his published works for his seventy-fifth birthday, that he had "long since lost the rudder in the flow of the stream" and had not been able to keep track of his own publications. On each of several major subjects, his scholarship set the standards for decades to come: the history of early Christian literature, in the three volumes of his *Geschichte der altchrist-lichen Literatur bis auf Eusebius* (1893–1904); the history of *The Mission and Expansion of Christianity in the First Three Centuries* (in two volumes and five editions), also published in English; the series of writings of the Greek church fathers, *Die griechischen christlichen Schriftsteller der ersten drei Jahrhunderte,* founded and edited by him; the history of the Prussian Academy of Sciences; and, above all, the *Lehrbuch der Dogmengeschichte* (in three volumes, five editions, and an abridgment).

None of these works achieved the notoriety, or for that matter the circulation, of *What Is Christianity?* (*Das Wesen des Christentums*), public lectures he delivered at the University of Berlin in the winter semester of 1899–1900, which sold many tens of thousands of copies in German and in translation into most of the languages of Europe and other languages besides, and is still in print after nearly a century. In these lectures Harnack undertook to proceed "in a purely historical fashion" to identify the "essence of Christianity" within and behind the kaleidoscopic variety to which his research had been devoted. Despite his study of patristic theology—or, as he would have preferred to say, because of it—he could not find that essence where the church fathers had, in the doctrines of the Trinity and the incarnation, nor in any other doctrine or dogma at all. The Father and not the Son was the center of the preaching of Jesus; not the atonement but the Sermon on the Mount epitomized the essential meaning of Christ. Averse to controversy though he was, Harnack experienced vigorous attacks, and from both sides of the Atlantic, for the reductionism of *Das Wesen des Christentums,* and he was accused of being unable to understand the genuine "essence" as orthodoxy had formulated it. Yet even someone who finds the reductionism unacceptable must likewise find such an accusation unacceptable; for there are portions of the *History of Dogma* in which Harnack manifested a remarkable ear for the tonalities of an orthodox faith that he himself could not share. He was, in short, a better historian than he was a theologian.

Still, Harnack's interpretation of the history of Christian

doctrine does require fundamental revision, and that in several principal areas. In an appendix to the *History of Dogma* Harnack makes the shocking declaration that "the history of dogma in the first three centuries is not mirrored in the liturgy, as far as we know it, nor is the liturgy a clearly emerging basis of the dogmatics." This needs to be offset by a far greater recognition of the role that liturgy and the *lex orandi* of Christian WORSHIP have played in the development of doctrine as the *lex credendi*. An even greater shocker is his assertion: "To have rejected the Old Testament in the second century was a mistake that the main body of the church was correct in avoiding; to retain it in the sixteenth century was a historical fate that the Reformation was not yet in a position to escape; but to go on conserving it within Protestantism as a canonical authority after the nineteenth century is the consequence of a paralysis of religion and church." To the contrary, the historian of doctrine must devote much more positive and continuing attention to the role of ZION and of the Hebrew Bible in the development of Christian teaching. Harnack saw the condition of doctrine in Byzantium as "torpor" (*Erstarrung*), and its place in the Reformation as, in principle, the end of dogma. On both these scores, there is need to develop a new appreciation of the theological significance of the Christian East as well as a fresh emphasis on the continuity, and not only on the discontinuity, between the Protestant Reformation and the Catholic tradition.

On the other hand, such a preoccupation with the question of continuity makes it obligatory to look for a continuity with Harnack as well. He stands in a dialectical relation with JOHN HENRY NEWMAN, whose coat of arms bore the motto *Cor ad cor loquitur* ("Heart speaketh unto heart"), which complements the medieval inscription on Harnack's grave, *Veni Creator Spiritus* ("Come, Creator Spirit").

· Hellenization

"What has Athens to do with Jerusalem?" As formulated by the first significant Latin Christian writer, Tertullian (ca. 160–ca. 225), this question poses a disjunction whose earlier form appears already in the New Testament. "Jews call for miracles, Greeks look for wisdom," Paul wrote to Greek-speaking Christians in Corinth (1 Cor. 1:22–24), "but we proclaim Christ— yes, Christ nailed to the cross; and though this is a stumbling-block to Jews and folly to Greeks, yet to those who have heard his call, Jews and Greeks alike, he is the power of God and the wisdom of God." Together with the relation of Christian theology to ZION, then, its ties to Hellas have been a continuing issue, which has often taken the form of a debate over the problem of the alleged Hellenization of Christianity. It is necessary to speak of it as alleged because, more often than not, Hellenization is put forward not as a description but as an accusation. It has frequently appeared in theological polemics, including that of Luther, but is particularly identified with the historical and theological interpretations of ADOLF VON HARNACK and of the many twentieth-century critical theologians who have followed his lead.

Basically, what Hellenization implies is a question not of language but of Weltanschauung. The Gospel of Mark and the treatises of Pseudo-Dionysius the Areopagite on angels are both written in Greek, but that seems to be where the resemblance stops. To describe the contrast, critics often invoke such distinctions as those between dynamic and static, or between doing and being, or between history and metaphysics. The Jesus of the synoptic Gospels spoke in parables rather than in abstractions, making his distinctive identity known not in dogmatic formulas but in deeds of mercy and power. He frequently left it to his disciples or even to his enemies—and to the demons—to confess who and what he was. In his summons to his disciples, moreover, he was less interested in the correctness of their ideas and doctrines about him than in the quality of their lives: "Not everyone who calls me 'Lord, Lord' will enter the kingdom of Heaven," he warned in the Sermon on the Mount, "but only those who do the will of my heavenly Father" (Matt. 7:21). As the apostolic band was transformed into the Catholic Church, that imperative was transformed into an intellectualism for which "doing the will of the heavenly Father" was equated with calling him "Lord, Lord," and meaning by that Greek word *Kyrios* everything that the orthodox creed now confessed. Perhaps the most telling symbol of this process of Hellenization was the adoption by the Council of Nicea in 325 of the Greek neologism *homoousios,* "one in being," as the technical term for the metaphysical relation between the Father and the Son in the Trinity.

When it is diagnosed that way—which is not a distortion of Harnack's position, or at least is not intended to be one—Hellenization is usually viewed as a loss or mutilation of much that is essential in the Christian message. The substitution of correct teaching for faithful (or faith-full) living as the criterion of authentic Christianity drew a portentous distinction between doctrine as the possession of a learned caste of theologians and the implicit faith of the laity, whose duty it was to "believe what the church believes." In the development of the doctrine of the Eucharist and the formulation of the theory of transubstantiation, for example, philosophical categories such as "substance" and "accident" were viewed as a necessary component of such believing, and anyone who disagreed with the official party line of the church was guilty of heresy and liable to excommunication.

By refining the formulas ever more precisely, the official legislators of orthodoxy limited the scope of dissent and intellectual freedom, so that during the fourth-century debates over the doctrines of the Nicene Creed the distinction between *homoousios* and *homoiousios* began to make far more than "one iota of difference." The word of the Lord to Moses from the burning bush, "I am who I am" or "I will be what I will be" (Exod. 3:14), part of the summons for him to lead the children of Israel out of Egypt in the Exodus, became, in the standard interpretation of patristic, Byzantine, and scholastic theology, not a dynamic revelation of action divine and human, but what has been called "a metaphysic of the Book of Exodus," the divinely given answer to the ancient quest of the Greek philosophers for the true meaning of Being-Itself. In the process, God became the ultimate abstraction—in the phraseology of Blaise Pascal (1623–1662), "the God of the philosophers, not the God of Abraham, Isaac, and Jacob."

Yet the thought of Pascal itself provides ample evidence that Hellenization was not the catastrophe it has been supposed to be. If the history of Christian doctrine is read as more than the history of SACRED SCIENCE and of dogma—as it must be read if scholarship is to be historically responsible—the distinction between its "static" and its "dynamic" elements becomes much more ambiguous. For in its preaching, pastoral counseling, and catechetical instruction, above all in its WORSHIP, the church has always gone on translating the ontological formulas of its creedal *depositum fidei* into an existential "call to discipleship." Because of its crucial need for continuity, the dynamic of Christian doctrine has been obliged to find, or if need be to invent, static forms, practicing a kind of theological cryonics: the message of the gospel has been frozen in the categories invented by Hellenization, not in order to annihilate it but in order to make available to every generation the resources for a new life and a new faith, which are, nevertheless, very old. The very Eastern Orthodoxy which Harnack regarded as the ultimate cautionary tale of Hellenization has repeatedly found those resources precisely in its Hellenic tradition of ICONS, liturgy, mysticism, and patristic theology—and it has been able to do so during the twentieth century in part because of Harnack's achievements as historian of Christian literature and guiding spirit of the critical edition of the Greek fathers.

• Heresy

One of the monuments of the Enlightenment in the HISTORIOG-
RAPHY of Christian doctrine, the *Nonpartisan History of the
Church and of Heresy* of Gottfried Arnold (1666–1714), which
was published just as the eighteenth century was beginning,
was, as one manual has put it, "colossally partisan." Nevertheless it expressed a viewpoint that would enjoy wide support
within and especially beyond the field of ecclesiastical history:
that somehow the adherents of heresy were usually right, and
the orthodox opponents of heresy wrong. Caricature of a caricature though that summary of Arnold's thesis may be, it does
point to the skepticism or revulsion with which the concept of
heresy is often treated. It is, of course, a correlative of the attitude toward ORTHODOXY.

The objection to the concept of heresy is in reality an objection to the concept of orthodoxy. Short of a dogmatic AGNOSTIC
relativism about both doctrine and morality—which, as has
been pointed out hundreds of times, would, if consistently
maintained, undercut the passion and conviction with which
such relativism is usually held and espoused—it is difficult to
imagine a worldview in which there is no place for the concept
of heresy. Although the false teaching may be in the area of race
rather than of religion, a belief, for example, in the natural and
irremediable inferiority of one group of human beings, if perti-
naciously held and vigorously espoused, would not be regarded
by most thoughtful people today as merely an unfortunate
symptom of ignorance (like an inability to read Greek or an
incapacity to explain the Second Law of Thermodynamics), but
as—for want of a better word—heresy: "an error in matters
that pertain to [an article of] faith, and one that on the part of the
person in error implies pertinacity," to quote the standard definition employed by Thomas Aquinas. The Greek word *hairesis*
in the New Testament, as in classical Greek, basically means
"choice," and then "party" or "party spirit"; only by extrapolation, and only after the New Testament, did it come to refer

primarily to false doctrine and therefore to be distinguished from schism.

Historically, heresy has played a major role in defining orthodoxy. Although his disciple, W. G. Ward (1812–1882), *plus catholique que le pape,* saw the promulgation of dogma by an infallible church and papacy as a highly desirable way for doctrine to be formulated, Newman recognized that the ongoing process of worship and instruction, described by Roman Catholic theology as "the ordinary magisterium of the church," was the primary and normal bearer of continuity. Only when this was challenged, and with "pertinacity," was there the provocation and doctrinal controversy out of which formal definition of doctrine would eventually issue. "There must be heresies" (*Oportet haereses esse*), according to the Vulgate translation of a saying of Paul (1 Cor. 11:19) that dealt with party spirit rather than with doctrine; this has provided orthodox theologians of every period with the occasion to reflect on how the rise of false teaching had repeatedly compelled the church to address the ambiguity of its doctrinal language and conceptual framework and to come up with terminology that would make the meaning of the faith unequivocal. "Wherever there is a creed," according to a well-known bon mot of Alfred North Whitehead (1861–1947), "there is a heretic round the corner or in his grave."

The proliferation of heresies in the first centuries of the church's history was responsible for the invention of an entire genre of theological literature, the heresiology. Bearing a title such as *Philosophoumena* (*Exposition of Philosophical Tenets*) or *Panarion* (*Medicine Cabinet*) or simply *Adversus Haereses* (*Against Heresies*), such a book served as a doctrinal Baedeker-in-reverse, warning the unsuspecting theological traveler of the dangers to sound faith and pure morals that were waiting around every corner. Because it was standard procedure, upon the condemnation of a heretic, to destroy his offending books, historians owe to these heresiologies, and to the full-length refutations of individual heresiarchs by orthodox spokesmen, most of their knowledge about the doctrines of the condemned theologians.

Without such knowledge, the original meaning of many phrases of the creeds that have been recited for centuries would be inaccessible. Thus when the Nicene Creed says about the Son of God, "Whose kingdom shall have no end," it is condemning the teaching attributed to Marcellus of Ancyra (d. ca. 374), with echoes of the earlier doctrine of Origen on the basis of 1 Corinthians 15:28, that the end of the "economy" of world history would also be the end of the rule of Christ.

Because of these sources, it is often easier to document the history of heresy than the history of orthodoxy, which, because of its presumed continuity, was assumed not to have had a history. Conversely, a grasp of the significance of the DEVELOPMENT OF DOCTRINE depends upon knowing the history not only of orthodoxy but also of heresy. When Newman wrote his first book, *The Arians of the Fourth Century,* in 1833, he was still equating heresy with doctrinal novelty; but when, twelve years later, he published the *Essay on the Development of Christian Doctrine,* the patristic studies underlying that book and his translations of the church fathers made it possible for him to interpret the Arian heretics of the fourth century and the heretics of other centuries as catalysts for the development of orthodox doctrine.

• Hermeneutics

Until comparatively recent times, "hermeneutics" was a term restricted almost totally to theological usage, in which it refers to the methodological principles and rules by which Scripture is to be interpreted: when a university registrar discovered a course with the title "Introductory Hermeneutics" on an academic transcript from a theological seminary, it seemed rather quaint. But both the term and the problematics underlying the term have now been discovered by theoreticians among literary critics, with results that are often brilliant and sometimes baffling. Such has been the éclat of this theory that nowadays the use of the term for a branch of theology is sometimes dismissed by the uninformed as capitulation to a secular humanistic trend. It is, in fact, nothing more than the continuation of a discussion whose beginnings go back to the very beginnings of Christian theology—and, indeed, a great deal further than that, as do so many of the issues in Christian theology.

From the first, the Christian movement stood for a distinctive hermeneutical position: that in the person of Jesus of Nazareth the prophecies of the Hebrew Bible had found their fulfillment. In support of that position the early followers of Jesus assembled lists of biblical passages—from the familiar title of one such list, these compilations are now often called "testimonies"—to which the events of his life were said to correspond, from his birth at Bethlehem (Mic. 5:2; Matt. 2:5) and his flight to Egypt (Hos. 11:1; Matt. 2:15) to his dereliction and death on the cross (Ps. 22:1; Matt. 27:46) and his resurrection (Ps. 16:10; Acts 2:27). The origins of this hermeneutical method were traced back to Jesus himself. In a scene in the Gospels, he appears in the synagogue at Nazareth to read Isaiah 61:1–2. "'Today,' he said, 'in your very hearing this text has come true'" (Luke 4:21). It was to Jesus himself that the church attributed the hermeneutical novelty by which the Messianic king who is foreseen in the Hebrew Bible was equated with the suffering servant of God promised by the prophet Isaiah (Isa. 53). In his appearance to two of his disciples after the resurrection, as they recalled it, "he began with Moses and all the prophets, and explained to them the passages which referred to himself in every part of the scriptures" (Luke 24:25–27). That hermeneutic of prophecy and fulfillment pervades the entire New Testament, in which the Epistle to the Hebrews occupies a special place through its application of the details of Levitical worship to the *lex credendi* concerning the death of Christ.

Only occasionally, however—most notably in a single paragraph of Paul's Epistle to the Galatians (Gal. 4:21–27)—did the hermeneutic of the New Testament resort to the method of allegory, which had been practiced both in the Jewish exegesis of the Hebrew Bible and in the Greek interpretation of Homer and Hesiod. Once sanctioned by New Testament precedent, allegory soon established itself as not only legitimate but necessary. It served to explain away such shameful incidents as the polygamy of the patriarchs and the adultery of David, but it also enriched Christian preaching and poetry by enabling the interpreter to turn the most prosaic Old Testament passages into statements of profound spiritual meaning. Modern scholars often distinguish—more sharply, it must be admitted, than the church fathers themselves usually did—between allegory in general and typology, through which, for example, the flood of Noah was taken as an anticipation of Christian baptism, or the manna in the desert as a type of the Christian Eucharist. There were various attempts to codify the rules of allegorical interpretation, the most fundamental being a caution against any allegorization that would jeopardize the historicity of actual events narrated in Scripture: the allegorical sense was intended to go beyond such historicity, but it was not supposed to go around it.

The most widely circulated hermeneutical codification in the Latin Middle Ages was the doctrine of "the fourfold sense" (*sensus quadruplex*) of Scripture: literal, allegorical, tropological (moral), and anagogical (ESCHATOLOGICAL). A convenient mnemonic device for keeping these senses apart deserves to be quoted in its Latin original:

> Littera gesta docet,
> quid credas allegoria,
> Moralis quid agas,
> quo tendas anagogia.

As one translation renders it,

> The letter shows us what God and our fathers did;
> The allegory shows us where our faith is hid;
> The moral meaning gives us rules of daily life;
> The anagogy shows us where we end our strife.

Despite the insistence of Thomas Aquinas on the primacy of the literal sense among these four, it is probably fair to say that many medieval exegetes preferred the method of allegory. Perhaps the best-known biblical commentary of the Middle Ages was the book of *Sermons on the Song of Songs* by Bernard of Clairvaux (1091–1153); the Song of Solomon had long been the subject of allegory, also among some of the rabbis, and may indeed have been accepted as part of the CANON OF HEBREW SCRIPTURE on the strength of its allegorical interpretation, but the hermeneutical alchemy of Bernard transformed its erotic language into poetry of mystical rapture.

The new emphasis on biblical AUTHORITY in the Reformation, in combination with the new biblical study encouraged by Christian humanism in the Renaissance, set itself against this entire development of medieval hermeneutics, in the name of the "grammatical" or "literal" sense. To penetrate to that sense, knowledge of the biblical LANGUAGES was indispensable: more than ever before in the Latin West, New Testament Greek became the standard equipment of theology; more than ever before in East or West, Old Testament Hebrew was seen as no less necessary. On that basis Protestant scholars undertook an unprecedented campaign for the restoration of careful grammatical exegesis to a normative position. Yet their definition of the literal sense did not set them against the New Testament's view of prophecy and fulfillment. Where there was no explicit reference to a passage of the Old Testament in the New, there was room for asking what the passage meant within the Old Testament framework; but according to what Luther called "the literal prophetic sense," the primary meaning of the twenty-second Psalm or the fifty-third chapter of Isaiah, for example, was a description of the sufferings of Jesus Christ, because that was how the writers of the New Testament had read those passages.

Claiming to carry out the program of Reformation hermeneutics more consistently than the Reformers themselves had been able to do, the biblical scholarship of the Enlightenment also took up the search for the literal, historical, and grammatical sense of the text. Increasingly, however, that meant applying to the biblical text the same hermeneutical methods that would be appropriate for any ancient texts. Critical investigation of biblical history, moreover, required the interpreter to find parallels between the sacred text and other ancient texts, as well as to use source criticism in reexamining traditional assumptions about the authorship and literary integrity of the biblical books. In the process, the definition of biblical authority on the basis of a theory of the inspiration of Scripture was replaced by a historical-critical method that claimed to be free of presuppositions and theologically objective. Opposition to this hermeneutical method and to historical criticism in general helped to precipitate the rise of fundamentalism within various Protestant churches.

Nevertheless this same historical-critical method led to the Protestant rediscovery of the centrality of tradition in the development of the Bible. At the same time, the growing acceptance of the historical-critical method encouraged by the charter of modern Roman Catholic hermeneutics, the epoch-making encyclical *Divino afflante Spiritu* issued in 1943 by Pope Pius XII (1939–1958), has made its own contribution to the creation of the most complete hermeneutical convergence since the sixteenth century. *The Anchor Bible,* a major publication of modern biblical scholarship, is the joint production of scholars from all traditions—Jewish, Roman Catholic, and Protestant—representing both a fruit of the ecumenical movement and a resource for its future development.

▪ Historiography

As if to demonstrate that theologians have no monopoly on sectarianism, historians have been going at it again over problems of historiography and historical method, with charges such as "That's not real history!" (translate: Anyone who follows that method is not a real historian) or "That's nothing more than number-crunching!" (translate: Such quantification trivializes historical research) punctuating the polemics.

In part, the controversy over method is a function of the new and powerful instrumentation made available to historians by the computer, which enables one scholar to handle masses of data that previously lay completely beyond reach or that were at best accessible only to teams of scholars and research assistants: it is possible now to chart demographic trends, voting patterns, and commodity prices over decades and even centuries, and thereby to identify statistical relations that have not been visible until now. In part, the controversy is ideological, with the growing respectability of Marxist historiography even in such a field as the study of the Reformation compelling all sides to clarify, perhaps also to defend, presuppositions that they used to take for granted. Combining these two sources of dispute is the continuing schism between social history and intellectual history, which sometimes appears to be a generational struggle but which more fundamentally signifies a basic disagreement over the legitimacy of concentrating on the history of ideas and the development of systems of thought without explicitly and continually grounding them in the social, economic, and political movements of the period. Because Christianity in its history has been productive of a series of social, economic, and political movements, as well as of ideas and systems of thought, the issues in contention between social history and intellectual history—and also, by implication, the other points of historiographical controversy—affect how the history of Christian doctrine is to be studied, understood, and described.

Like any idea, the idea of "social history" is itself the outcome of developments in intellectual history. The social sciences as a distinct set of scholarly fields are a relatively recent phenomenon, having grown up under the auspices of philosophy and theology. William James (1842–1910) is a major figure in the history both of psychology and of the philosophy of religion, and his GIFFORD LECTURES of 1900–1902, *The Varieties of Religious Experience,* have decisively shaped both fields. Ernst Troeltsch (1865–1923) combined the perspectives of social science, theology, and philosophy, above all in his history of Christian social thought, *Die Soziallehren der christlichen Kirchen und*

Gruppen (*The Social Teachings of the Christian Churches and Groups*) of 1912. Despite the origin of their idea of history in the history of ideas, advocates of social history sometimes charge practitioners of intellectual history with treating ideas in a vacuum, disembodied from the "real world" of the society in which they arose. That charge is frequently based on the methodological assumption that doctrines and ideas (or "ideologies") come into being solely as an effort to understand or to justify particular social and political forces after the fact, rather than as beliefs grounded in such notions as revelation or authority. For example, the doctrine of the atonement systematized by Anselm of Canterbury (ca. 1033–1109), according to which the death of Christ was a means of rendering satisfaction to the justice of God that had been violated by human sin, would be interpreted as the extrapolation of the legal relation between suzerain and vassal developed by a feudal society.

At issue in such differences of opinion over historiography is the definition of what constitutes the proper context for the study of a theological system or doctrine. Therefore the case for treating the history of doctrine as a distinct field of scholarly endeavor rests in significant measure on the methodological presupposition that not only society but tradition defines context. To interpret the thought of the scholastics of the twelfth and thirteenth centuries, a scholar needs to understand the connections between institutional Western Christendom and feudal society, which enabled and required the spokesmen for medieval theology to carry out their public function simultaneously in the UNIVERSITY and in the church. Those connections are an indispensable part of the context for the theologies of Thomas Aquinas and Bonaventure (ca. 1217–1274). But so is the history of Christian doctrine in the Latin West during the centuries leading up to the thirteenth. In many respects, Augustine, who had died eight centuries earlier (thus longer ago in their past than they are in our past), is part of a more immediate context for the doctrines of Bonaventure or Thomas than is any emperor or pope contemporary to them. Yet because of the division of labor brought on by scholarly specialization, which among historians has tended to arrange itself by historical periods, few historians of the thirteenth century, even those who have concentrated on Thomas Aquinas, have been able to claim substantial firsthand knowledge of the writings of Augustine. Étienne Gilson (1884–1978) is an exception in this as in other respects.

It must be granted that decisions about periodization are themselves dependent on historiographic assumptions, in the history of doctrine no less than in other branches of historical study. If the history of Christian thought does have a legitimate scholarly autonomy, its periodization will not automatically correspond to the arrangement of the narrative for the history of the institutional church, any more than this in turn will necessarily be the same as it is for social, economic, or political history. Not all doctrines, moreover, have developed at the same speed during the same period: the doctrine of the Holy Spirit did not have much of a history for the first three centuries of the church, and then it suddenly moved to center stage, but held it only briefly. When historical theology has proceeded from an *ex professo* commitment to specific theological assumptions, its periodization has tended to rest on the theologian's view of where a particular current system of dogmatics (usually his own) has stood in the overall development of the church and its teaching. One of the most eminent of Protestant historians of doctrine in the nineteenth century, the Hegelian theologian Ferdinand Christian Baur (1792–1860) of Tübingen, felt able to divide the history of the doctrine of the atonement into three not quite equal periods: from the New Testament to the Reformation, about sixteen centuries; from the Reformation to Immanuel Kant (1724–1804), about three centuries; and since Kant— about three decades.

Perhaps a bit more subtle, but no less pervasive, is the influence exerted on the historiography of doctrine by each successive school of theological thought. Particularly since the Enlightenment, it has become customary for a work of dogmatics to locate itself within the history of theology, sometimes by opening with an overall historical introduction but also by prefacing its discussion of a specific doctrine with a miniature (or not so miniature) history of its earlier development. At the hands of an erudite and incisive theologian such as the Russian Orthodox student of patristic and Byzantine thought George V. Florovsky (1893–1979) and of others in his generation, this method has probably been responsible for more progress in the historiography of Christian doctrine during the twentieth century than has any work of the historians of doctrine themselves. As Florovsky's discussion of "The Predicament of the Christian Historian" makes clear, it has also raised with new piquancy all the old problems of historiography, just at a time when historians of every ideological stripe have been made acutely aware of such problems by the developments in their own field.

• Holy Spirit

Every time the baptismal formula (Matt. 28:19) is recited at BAPTISM, all those present are reminded that the Holy Spirit is, together with the Father and the Son, part of the "name" in which baptism takes place. The doctrine of the Holy Spirit was, from the beginnings of Christian theology, seen to belong to the doctrine of the TRINITY.

When it confessed that doctrine in its CREED, the Council of Nicea in 325, after declaring the faith of the church in the Father and in the Son at some length, continued with the phrase: "And [we believe in] the Holy Spirit"; but it said no more about what such belief in the Holy Spirit might imply. Not only was that enough to say in relation to the *status controversiae* on the question of the Holy Spirit, there having been very little doctrinal dispute over this question (by contrast with the question of Jesus Christ) during the preceding three centuries; but there had likewise been, during those same centuries, relatively little development of doctrine regarding the Holy Spirit. In the whole of extant ante-Nicene theological literature, there has not been preserved a single full-length treatise on the person of the Holy

Spirit. Then quite suddenly, almost exactly fifty years after Nicea, an entire doctrinal literature on the subject erupted in both Greek and Latin. Athanasius of Alexandria (ca. 296–373), the veteran of a half-century of bitter debates over the place of the Son of God in the Trinity, composed his four *Letters to Serapion* in 359 or 360, devoted to the place of the Holy Spirit in the Trinity. He was followed by the Cappadocians: Gregory of Nazianzus "the Theologian" devoted the fifth of his celebrated *Theological Orations* to this neglected topic, and the treatise *On the Holy Spirit* by Basil of Caesarea was written in about the year 375. So was the similarly titled treatise of Didymus "the Blind" (ca. 313–398), which now exists only in a Latin translation prepared by Jerome (ca. 342–420), the Greek original having been lost. Also bearing that title and also preserved in Latin—a work not of translation, but in the characteristically harsh opinion of critics such as Jerome, of virtual plagiarism from Basil—was the contribution of Ambrose of Milan (ca. 339–397) to the subject. In 381 the doctrine of the Holy Spirit was officially adjudicated at the Council of Constantinople, which amplified the creed of Nicea by expanding its brief statement on the doctrine into a full paragraph, which seems to have corresponded to its present-day form in what is now used in the liturgy of the Mass as the Nicene Creed—except, of course, for the later Western addition of the FILIOQUE clause.

So it came about that after more than three centuries of almost complete neglect, the dogma of the Holy Spirit had been placed on the doctrinal agenda of both East and West, debated by Greek and Latin theologians, and settled by an ecumenical council of the church in the capital city of the Roman Empire— all in the space of about two decades. Those who participated in these events were themselves conscious of what Gregory Nazianzus called "the special difficulty" of the controversy. Gregory explained the revelation of the doctrine of the Trinity in progressive terms, thereby propounding at least an inchoate theory of the development of doctrine: "The Old Testament proclaimed the Father manifestly, and the Son more hiddenly. The New [Testament] manifested the Son, and suggested the deity of the Spirit. Now the Spirit itself is resident among us, and is providing us with a clearer explanation of itself." Because it is in many ways an atypical example of doctrinal development, it does raise several fundamental questions.

It is not quite obvious why the dogma of the Holy Spirit should have been such a late bloomer, although the theory of progressive revelation suggested by Gregory Nazianzus may provide a significant part of the historical explanation. If the foundation of a Christian doctrine has always been some kind of historical revelation, and if therefore (to use the terminology of the Greek fathers) an exposition of theology, the doctrine of the eternal nature of God, has always been based on an interpretation of the divine "economy," the pattern of divine action within history, the successive stages of the economy have determined how the doctrine of the Trinity has developed. For the doctrine of God as Father, the history of Israel in the Old Testament, as read in the light of Christian presuppositions, provided the historical data. Then the history of the life, death, and resurrection of Jesus Christ in the Gospels came to supply similar data for the doctrine of God as Son to develop.

But neither in the Old Testament nor in the Gospels—nor for that matter in the rest of the New Testament—was there an analogous history of the Holy Spirit on the basis of which to formulate the dogma of the third person in the Trinity. Significantly, the closest the New Testament comes to providing such data is in the Acts of the Apostles, which is a historical narrative of the first generation of the church. What might be termed a set of Gospels about the history of the Holy Spirit, the necessary presupposition for the development of a doctrine of the Holy Spirit, did not come until the church itself had developed enough to have accumulated data for them. Persecution, conflict, the emergence of ecclesiastical structure, the conversion of the Gentiles, the peace of the church achieved in the Constantinian settlement—these were the history and economy of the Holy Spirit during the first four centuries. And at the end of the fourth century the church finally produced a theology and doctrine of the Holy Spirit to match that history.

When it did so, the model and even much of the vocabulary were derived from the doctrine of the Son, as hammered out in the many preceding controversies and councils. If the Son was "one in being (*homoousios*) with the Father," as the Council of Nicea had confessed, then the Spirit must be *homoousios,* too. If it was proper to refer to the relation between the Father and the Son (and even to the relation between the divine and the human natures in the Son) as one of "mutual interpenetration" (*per-ichōrēsis*), that terminology must suit the relation of the Holy Spirit with both the Father and Son. And then the right name not only for the Father or the Son, but for each of the divine Three, would have to be "person" (Latin *persona,* Greek *prosō-pon* or *hypostasis*). Even without loading this latter term with the freight carried by modern terms such as "personality," its use for the Holy Spirit was fraught with complications.

A "person" would, at the very least, seem to be defined as one who can be addressed in speech; hence a "divine person" would be defined as one who can be addressed in prayer. The existence of prayers to Jesus Christ in early Christian usage had been one of the clinching arguments for his coequality with the Father: either such prayers were being addressed to the true God, or they were idolatrous. In the Greek liturgical prayer of invocation called the *epiklēsis,* the church prayed for the Holy Spirit to descend upon the congregation as well as upon the elements in the Eucharist; but there were not, in public liturgy or private devotion, similar prayers *to* the Holy Spirit. These complications have been compounded across the various languages: *Spiritus* is masculine in Latin, as are *Geist* in German and *Duch* in the Slavic languages; but the original Greek for "the Holy Spirit" in the New Testament was *to Hagion Pneuma,* which is neuter. In a language like English, which is innocent of grammatical gender but not personal gender (and in which for that reason present-day advocates of "inclusive language" almost inevitably seem to confuse the issues), should one refer to the Spirit as "he" or as "it"? Throughout the history of English liturgical, hymnological, and theological usage both forms occur, often in the same author.

Dogmatically as well as liturgically, the complications of this development came to a head in the Filioque controversy; but whenever theological reflection has been obliged to come to terms with the nature of Christian experience, the underdeveloped state of the doctrine of the Holy Spirit has continued to manifest itself.

▪ Icons

The process by which a religion that had since its beginnings been reciting the Second Commandment of the Decalogue, "You shall not make a carved image for yourself nor the likeness of anything in the heavens above, or on the earth below, or in the waters under the earth"(Ex. 20:4), went on to produce one of the greatest explosions of religious art is a remarkable chapter in the history of PATRISTICS and BYZANTIUM. It pertains to art history, to the history of politics both secular and ecclesiastical—and to the history of theology as well, where it demonstrates how the shared major premises of a common orthodoxy could, by means of divergent minor premises, lead to radically different doctrinal and liturgical conclusions.

The shared major premises consisted of the dogmas of Trinity and incarnation as they had been formulated at the first six ecumenical councils between 315 and 681. Not long after the Third Council of Constantinople of 680–681, imperial prohibition and doctrinal denunciation of the use of images in the church converged when a series of critics, of whom the Byzantine emperor Constantine V (719–775) was the most important not only politically but also theologically, attacked the icons as idolatrous. Relying heavily on the criterion of continuity, they drew upon the standard interpretations of the well-known statement of Jesus, "God is spirit, and those who worship him must worship in spirit and in truth" (John 4:24), to argue, as for example ORIGEN had done against Celsus, that the difference between paganism and Christianity was to be found in the reliance of the former on the crude materialism of images but of the latter on the rational and spiritual worship of God in the mind and heart. In the presence of the body and blood of Christ in the Eucharist Christian believers had the authentic image, in fact the reality "in spirit and in truth," of God himself, and they did not need the poor substitutes for that true image provided by pictures. "Therefore," the iconoclasts said, "it is obviously not permitted to portray him in an image or to carry out a remembrance of him in any other way" than in the sacrament. As the controversy proceeded, the opponents of icons went on to rely ever more on an argument against images of Christ that was derived from the doctrine of the incarnation: such images could not portray both the divine and the human natures of Christ, because the divine nature was, by the familiar APOPHATIC definition, "beyond description"; from that it followed that the image was, at best, a depiction of only the human nature of Christ and thus a heretical rending of the single person of the Incarnate One.

Once introduced into the debate by the iconoclasts, however, the argument from the incarnation became the principal theological weapon of the defenders of images: the Byzantine theologian John of Damascus (ca. 675–ca. 749), Patriarch Nicephorus of Constantinople (ca. 758–829), and Abbot Theodore of Studios (759–826). The prohibition of images in the Ten Commandments, they maintained, had been valid and necessary in the history of Judaism because in the Old Testament era the divine revelation had been one of actions and words, but not one of a personal presence. With the incarnation of the Logos in the historical and human person of Jesus Christ, as affirmed in John 1:14, God himself had gone beyond the spirit and the letter of the Second Commandment by providing an image of his own very nature, the visible, personal Image in the flesh. To draw an image of the transcendent Deity had been and still was idolatrous, but now it had become possible to draw an image of the Image, which was not only no longer prohibited but had become commanded in obedience to the reality of the incarnation.

This was the very opposite of idolatry: worship paid to an icon of Christ was worship of Christ himself. And if it was legitimate to portray Christ in an icon, the Virgin Mary, Mother of God (Greek *Theotokos*) and the one who as the Second Eve had made the incarnation of the Logos possible, must be portrayed as well, and with her and her Son all the other saints, who had shared in his grace and who now communicated that grace to the faithful in the church. At the Second Council of Nicea in 787, the icons were officially restored to the church. The "Sunday of Orthodoxy" was decreed less than a century later to celebrate the event—ORTHODOXY in this liturgical designation, as elsewhere, referring at once to correct worship and to correct teaching.

Although the medieval West sometimes repeated these arguments for the use of images, the theological method remained alien even to Thomas Aquinas. Neither the Protestant Reformation nor the Enlightenment was able to resonate to it either, and therefore Western historiography, Protestant and even Roman Catholic, has experienced difficulty in interpreting the iconoclastic controversy. According to Adolf von Harnack, the case for the icons as presented by Theodore of Studios was "an amalgam of superstition, magic, and scholasticism." Nevertheless Harnack did recognize—and regret—that "all of orthodoxy is summarized in the cult of images." And it was also in the course of making the case for the icons that Patriarch Nicephorus spoke about the MELODY of theology.

· Image of God

The fundamental concept in the biblical understanding of what it means to be human is the doctrine of creation in the image of God. Despite the obvious analogies between human anatomy or physiology and those of other creatures—recognized long before the theory of evolution was proposed—both Judaism and Christianity have affirmed that there is an even more basic and profound analogy between human existence and the very being of the living God. They have founded this affirmation on the words of the Hebrew Bible in Genesis 1:26–27: "And God said, 'Let us make man in our image and likeness.' So God created man in his own image; in the image of God he created him; male and female he created them."

For Hellenistic Jews like Philo of Alexandria (ca. 20 B.C.E.–50 C.E.) and Hellenistic Christians like ORIGEN OF ALEX- ANDRIA, moreover, the recognition of the divine image was not dependent on acceptance of the specifically biblical confession about the mystery of God, but could be known, and had been known, also by those to whom the biblical revelation had not been given, and particularly by Platonic philosophers. The doctrine of the image of God became one of the principal links between biblical faith and various kinds of idealism ancient and modern, and orthodox Christianity went on supposing that acceptance of its doctrine of the Trinity was not necessary for grasping the doctrine of creation in the image of God. One of the most vocal of eighteenth-century Enlightenment critics of the orthodox doctrine of the Trinity penned perhaps the most widely circulated secular version of the doctrine of *imago Dei:* "We hold these truths to be self-evident, that all men are created equal; that they are endowed by their Creator with certain inalienable rights; that among these are life, liberty, and the pursuit of happiness."

Curiously, for a doctrine as central to biblical faith as this, the biblical data for the concept of the image of God are remarkably skimpy.

> He that sheds the blood of a man,
> for that man his blood shall be shed;
> for in the image of God
> has God made man.

This warning of the divine revenge threatening the murderer (Gen. 9:6) is explicitly grounded in the image of God, but it does not make the content of that image specific, declaring *that* it is without explaining *what* it is. The content has had to come from elsewhere. An obvious source is the biblical picture of God. Those divine attributes spoken of in the Bible that appeared to be communicable to a creature could become part of the image. Four such attributes appeared in the language of the Bible itself to represent analogies between God and the image of God. When the Psalmist, speaking in the name of God, admonished, "Do not behave like horse or mule, unreasoning creatures" (Ps. 32:9), that appeared to assign to the human image the same rationality that was preeminently characteristic of the divine prototype. When the Sermon on the Mount urged, "There must be no limit to your goodness, as your heavenly Father's goodness knows no bounds" (Matt. 5:48), that likewise ascribed to human life the capacity to mirror forth in some immanent but nevertheless distinct fashion the transcendent goodness of the heavenly Father. When the First Epistle of John asserted that "God is love" and went on to urge that "he who dwells in love is dwelling in God" (1 John 4:16), that, too, was a declaration that the ultimate mystery of the divine being—which was neither eternity nor omnipotence nor even divine justice, but love—had its counterpart in the human capacity, mysterious in its own right, to give love and to respond to love. And when the Gospels called God "Father," they were saying—as Athanasius (ca. 296–373) and after him Karl Barth (1886–1968) insisted on the basis of Ephesians 3:14–15—that human parenthood was patterned after its divine model, rather than saying that God the Father was a projection of someone's need for a father figure. The concept of human personality, therefore, was part of the image of God, reflecting the personal quality of a God to whom it was possible to pray as Father.

Much of this represents common ground between Judaism and Christianity, both of which affirm creation in the image of God on the basis of the first chapter of the Bible they have in common, which Christians call the Old Testament. But the Christian version of the concept has been distinctively and decisively affected by those passages in the New Testament where Jesus Christ, as Son of God and Son of Man, is described as the image of God in a unique personal sense. Because the First Adam on the other side of the Fall is hidden from our eyes by the mists of sin and death, we are authorized to fill in the content of the image of God granted at the creation of the First Adam from what has been revealed at the epiphany of the Second Adam: Christ is thus not only the revelation of God to man, but the revelation of man to man—of man as God had intended man to be and as God planned for man to become again. The history of the Christian doctrine of the image of God, therefore, is the application to the human condition of the ideal humanity (*Urbild,* "primal image," is the highly loaded German term for it) now manifested through the INCARNATION in the person of Jesus Christ.

The tension between "image of God" as the universal content of authentic humanity, present also outside the state of grace and knowable also outside revelation, and "image of God" as the special gift both of revelation and of grace as conferred in Christ, led such early Christian teachers as Irenaeus of Lyons (ca. 130–ca. 200) within a century after the New Testament era to posit a distinction Genesis seemed to make when it had God say, "Let us make man in our image and likeness (Latin *similitudo*)" (Gen. 1:26). Most biblical scholars would probably agree that this was not meant as a distinction but as the familiar biblical device of parallelism; when the Virgin MARY sings in the Magnificat, "Tell out, my soul, the greatness of the Lord, rejoice, rejoice, my spirit, in God my saviour" (Luke 1:46–47), it would violate the fundamental tenet of biblical monotheism to deduce from that (as apparently some kinds of heresy did in the second century) a distinction between "the Lord" and "God my saviour." Nevertheless, the use of the two terms "image" and "similitude" in the Creation account provided a convenient device for distinguishing between those qualities of the original creation that continue to be present, albeit in diminished force, in all the descendants of Adam and Eve (such as rationality), and those qualities that had been a special gift of grace to Adam and Eve and that were consequently lost in the Fall, not to be present in human existence until they were restored in Christ (such as eternal bliss); the first set of these were "image," the second "similitude." Despite its shaky exegetical grounding, the distinction made it possible to hold together the universal and the particular in the way the Scriptures spoke about the meaning of being human.

The content of the Christian doctrine of the "image of God" did not come only from the doctrine of the person of Christ. Taking off from the language in Genesis, "Let us make man in our image," Augustine repeated the standard argument of most early Christian teachers that these plurals were proof for the doctrine of the Trinity in the very first narrative of the Bible; he went on to add his own brilliant codicil to the argument by suggesting that the plurals were an indication that the "image of God" was itself trinitarian. Therefore he devoted the second half of his *On the Trinity* (*De Trinitate*) to a review of possible "footprints of the Trinity" (*vestigia Trinitatis*) in the human soul. Although these vestiges could not represent a perfect correspondence between Creator and creature, the triad of love, reason, and memory came close: each of these three was distinct from the other two, and yet together they made one single mind. That made the human mind an image of the Trinity: of the Father, who not only has love but "is love," according to 1 John 4:16; of the Son, who is reason or *logos,* according to the first verses of the Gospel of John (John 1:1–14); and of the Holy Spirit, whose distinct function, according to that same Gospel, is to "call to mind all that I have told you" (John 14:26). These three were distinct "persons" and yet remained one single Godhead.

The doctrine of the image of God has been a major force in the development of characteristically Western ways of looking at the meaning and promise of human life, and as such it deserves the serious attention of anyone seeking to interpret the value systems that have shaped us. If the doctrine of the image is lost, it is difficult to provide alternative grounding for the ethical norms that are derived from it. For the historian of Christian doctrine, it is also one of the most intriguing of case studies in the DEVELOPMENT OF DOCTRINE by which, from a relatively modest beginning in the few explicit passages about it in the Bible (all of which could be copied onto one index card), it became a full-blown article of faith—and then went beyond the faith to become a part of the philosophy of secular humanism of the Enlightenment and of nineteenth-century idealism. The link between the Christian and the philosophical versions is probably to be sought in the blend of Christian humanism and secular idealism in the thought of the Renaissance, which is the source for so many of the other theological concepts that have found their way into our general thought and language.

• Incarnation

Although the doctrine of the Trinity as formulated by the Councils of Nicea in 325 and of Constantinople in 381 had been aimed at defining the question of the relation between Jesus Christ and God, by declaring that the divine in him was "one in being (*homoousios*) with the Father," these definitions made necessary and possible a further definition of the relation, within Jesus Christ, between the divine and the human. That relation was the content of the doctrine of the incarnation, as stated in the climactic closing sentence of the prologue to the Gospel of John: "So the Word became flesh (*kai ho Logos sarx egeneto*); he came to dwell among us, and we saw his glory, such glory as befits God's only Son, full of grace and truth"(John 1:14).

By excluding several extreme positions from the circle of orthodoxy, the formulation of the trinitarian DOGMA determined the course of subsequent discussion about the incarnation. It also provided the terminology for that discussion, because fifth-century theologians were able to describe the relation between the divine and the human in Christ by analogy to the relation between the Father and the Son in the Trinity. The word that was found to express this relation in Christ was the term "nature" (Greek *physis*). There were three divine "persons" in one divine "essence" or "nature": such was the outcome of the

doctrine of the Trinity. But there were also two natures, one of
them divine and the other human, in the one person of Jesus
Christ. Over the relation between these two natures the controversy on the incarnation was carried on. The abstract questions with which the controversy dealt, some of them almost
unintelligible to a modern mind, must not be permitted to obscure the central and abiding issue of the Christian faith that was
at stake: How could Jesus Christ be said to possess that identity
with God which he had to have to be the Savior of humanity,
and yet be called the Brother of humanity, as he truly had to be
to make that salvation available?

During the half-century between the Council of Constantinople in 381 and the Council of Ephesus in 431, several major
points of emphasis developed in the doctrine of the incarnation;
significantly, these are usually defined by the episcopal see that
espoused them. There was a way of talking about the incarnation that was characteristic of the see at Alexandria. It stressed
the divine quality of all that Jesus Christ had been and done, but
its enemies accused it of absorbing the humanity of Christ into
his divinity. The mode of thought and language employed at
Antioch, on the other hand, emphasized the true humanity of
Christ; but its opponents maintained that in so doing it had split
Christ into two persons, each maintaining an individual self-
hood while they acted in concert. Shaped as it was by the
thought and vocabulary of Augustine, Western theology, whose
spokesman especially in the fifth century was the bishop of
Rome, Leo I (440–461), was not as abstract as either of these
alternatives. Its central emphasis in the doctrine of the incarnation was a practical concern for human salvation and for the
preservation of unity through as irenic a settlement of the Chris-
tological conflict as was possible without sacrificing that
concern.

As often in Christian history, the doctrine of Mary was the
question on which the conflict between Alexandria and Antioch
over the incarnation came to a head. Nestorius (d. ca. 451), who
was patriarch of Constantinople from 428 to 431, took exception to the use of the title *Theotokos* (Mother of God) for

Mary, insisting that she was only *Christotokos* (Mother of Christ). In this insistence the Antiochene emphasis upon the distinction between the two natures in Christ made itself heard throughout the church. The Alexandrian theologians responded by charging that Nestorius was dividing the person of Christ, which they represented as so completely united that, in the famous phrase of Cyril of Alexandria (d. 444), there was "one nature of the Logos which became incarnate" (*mia physis tou Logou sesarkomenē*). By this he meant that there was only one nature, the divine, before the incarnation, but that after the incarnation there were two natures indissolubly joined in one person; Christ's human nature had never had an independent existence. There were times when Cyril appeared to be saying that there was "one nature of the incarnate Logos" (*mia physis tou Logou sesarkomenou*) even after the incarnation, but his most precise formulations avoided this language. The Council of Ephesus in 431 condemned Nestorius and proclaimed Mary to be *Theotokos*.

But the actual settlement of the doctrine of the incarnation was not accomplished until the calling of the Council of Chalcedon in 451. The basis of that settlement was the Western understanding of the two natures in Christ, as formulated in the *Tome* of Pope Leo I. Chalcedon declared: "We all unanimously teach . . . one and the same Son, our Lord Jesus Christ, perfect in deity and perfect in humanity . . . in two natures [a textual variant read: *from* two natures], without being mixed, transmuted, divided, or separated. The distinction of the two natures is by no means done away with through the union, but rather the identity of each nature is preserved and comes together into one person and being." This formula expressed emphases from both Alexandria and Antioch; both the unity of the person and the distinction of the natures after the incarnation were affirmed. Therefore the decision of the Council of Chalcedon has, ever since 451, been the basic statement of the doctrine of the incarnation for most of the church—Eastern Orthodox, Roman Catholic, and Protestant. The Western part of the church went on to give further attention to the doctrine of the ATONEMENT.

In the Eastern part of the church the Alexandrians and Antiochenes continued the controversies that had preceded Chalcedon; but, as has been the pattern of orthodoxy, they now clashed over how to interpret Chalcedon. The controversies over the Monophysite and Monothelite heresies in the sixth and seventh centuries were efforts to clarify the interpretation of Chalcedon, with the result that the extremes of the Alexandrian position were condemned just as the extremes of the Antiochene had been. Then in the eighth and ninth centuries the theology of Byzantium found justification in the doctrine of the incarnation for the place of icons in the worship and teaching of the church.

Emerging from all this theological discussion was an interpretation of the doctrine of the incarnation that affirmed the oneness of Jesus Christ with God and his oneness with humanity, while maintaining at the same time the oneness of his person. It is a vindication of the principle of worship as *lex orandi lex credendi* to note that the liturgies of the church had already been maintaining this sense of the incarnation at a time when the theologians of the church were still struggling for clarity about it; and the final formula can be seen as a scientifically precise restatement of what had been present germinally in the liturgical piety of the church. In the language of the Council of Chalcedon that solution finally found the framework of concepts and vocabulary that it needed to become intellectually consistent.

In one sense, therefore, what Chalcedon formulated was the tradition of what Christians had been believing from the beginning; the council affirmed and maintained the continuity of doctrine. In another sense, however, Chalcedon represented a development of doctrine from the earlier stages of Christian thought. This makes the history of the doctrine of the incarnation a prime illustration of both the principle of continuity and the principle of development of doctrine—and of the tension between them.

▪ Justification by Faith

The doctrine of justification by faith was labeled by the theological descendants of the Protestant REFORMATION, in the phrase of John Calvin (1509–1564), as "the main hinge on which religion turns" and, as others put it, "the doctrine by which the church stands or falls" (*articulus stantis aut cadentis ecclesiae*); and it was seen by them as well as by their Roman Catholic adversaries before and after the Council of Trent (1545–1563) as the principal, and finally non-negotiable, point of separation between them.

To their consternation, both sides in the Reformation disputes discovered upon closer inspection not only that a doctrine which appeared to be so central had never achieved the formal status of a dogma, but also that during much of Christian history it had not even engaged the serious and sustained attention of theologians. The terminology of "justification" had been used loosely if at all, without the degree of conceptual specificity that had been achieved in the debates over the incarnation and even, though more recently, in reflection on the atonement. As during the controversy of Augustine over the genealogy of his doctrine of original sin, he and his defenders in the next generation had been compelled to vindicate their continuity by an appeal to the criterion of worship as *lex orandi lex credendi,* so the Protestant Reformers saw in the prayers of the saints for mercy an admission that they had no merit of their own on which to base their relation with God, but had to cast themselves on sheer GRACE, whose undeserved gift was the justification of the sinner. In keeping with their affirmation of the sole authority of Scripture, they appealed to the biblical doctrine of justification. Except for a single appearance in the Gospels, in the parable of the Pharisee and the Publican (Luke 18:14), the verb "to justify" was largely confined to the Epistles of Paul, and within these chiefly to Romans and Galatians; it also appeared in the Epistle of James.

It was in his confrontation as *Doctor in Biblia* with the texts of the Epistles to the Romans and to the Galatians (together with the Psalms, read in that light) that MARTIN LUTHER came to the discovery of justification by faith as the essential meaning of the gospel. *Justitia enim Dei in eo [sc. evangelio] revelatur ex fide in fidem; sicut scriptum est: 'Justus autem ex fide vivit'* ('The righteousness [or justice] of God is revealed in it [namely, the gospel], in a way that starts from faith and ends in faith; as it is written, "The righteous one shall live by faith"'). These words of the Vulgate in Romans 1:17, with their quotation from the Hebrew Bible (Hab. 2:4), appeared self-contradictory, for they declared that the REVELATION given in the gospel was the reality of the *justitia Dei,* the awesome truth that the Almighty, as a just judge, rewarded the innocent but punished the guilty. To a man as deeply troubled by sin as Luther was, that revelation did not seem to be much of a gospel. Nor was it evident to him from the text just how and why all of this should "start from faith and end in faith." His predicament, exegetical as well as existential, was resolved when he saw that the genitive in *justitia Dei* was not passive but active: not the "justice" by which God is a just judge, but the "righteousness" by which the defendant, who stands before the judge and in total trust throws himself on the mercy of the court, is pronounced innocent. With that discovery, he would recall thirty years later, "the gates of Paradise were opened" to him, and so were the text of Scripture and the fundamental meaning of the gospel. In that first chapter of the Epistle to the Romans, Paul had already announced the conclusion to be summarized later (Rom. 3:28): "Our argument is that a man is justified by faith quite apart from success in keeping the law."

The antithesis of justification by faith was justification by works, the system of merit and reward, which had some disquietingly strong support not only in tradition and in the moral implications of the Christian idea of duty, but in the New Testament itself. In the Sermon on the Mount Jesus spoke of "a rich reward in heaven" (Matt. 5:12), warned that "to make a show of religion before men" meant that "no reward awaits you in your Father's house in heaven" (Matt. 6:1), and promised that if his followers would "pray to your Father who is there in a secret place" the outcome would be that "your Father who sees what is secret will reward you [openly]" (Matt. 6:6). Still more explicit was the Epistle of James. Arguing, as Paul did in the Epistle to the Romans, on the basis of the faith of Abraham as described and praised in the Book of Genesis (Gen. 15:6), James seemed to come to opposite conclusions: "Was it not by his action, in offering his son Isaac upon the altar, that our father Abraham was justified?" and therefore "You see then that a man is justified by deeds and not by faith in itself" (James 2:21, 24). Luther resolved the contradiction by calling James an "epistle of straw," although its place in the canon of the New Testament compelled him to keep it in his translations of the Bible. Other statements of Lutheran doctrine, including the Apology of the Augsburg Confession of 1530–1531, sought instead to harmonize Paul and James by interpreting James as speaking of faith in terms of its results, namely, works, rather than in terms of its objects, namely, grace and the atonement, which were apprehended by faith alone.

The Council of Trent (1545–1563), in its own reaction to Luther's doctrine of justification, explained justification by faith to mean that "faith is the beginning of human salvation, the foundation and root of all justification," and therefore "we are said to be justified gratuitously, because none of those things that precede justification, whether faith or works, merit the grace of justification." But that was the beginning of an entire process, "not only a remission of sins but also the sanctification and renewal of the inner man through the voluntary reception of the grace and gifts whereby an unrighteous man becomes righteous"; and not only the beginning but the process was properly called "justification," which consequently was not by faith alone, but by faith and works. In the pursuit of historical scholarship and with an ecumenical interest, several Roman Catholic scholars in the twentieth century have interpreted the language of Trent to harmonize with, or at any rate complement, Luther's doctrine, which in turn they have striven to harmonize with that of Thomas Aquinas.

The lack of a verifiable continuity for the doctrine of justification by faith, then, was seen to be a theological resource. Viewed in the light of tradition and of development of doctrine, the doctrine of justification required clarification by reference to its historical position and theological context. As the medieval doctrine of the atonement emerged as the consequence of a previously developed patristic doctrine of the incarnation, which was in turn based on the Nicene dogma of the Trinity, so the Reformation discussion of justification came out of the preceding speculation about redemption. To call it "the doctrine by which the church stands or falls" apart from this historical position and theological context was to misinterpret the place of the Reformation in the ecumenical history of the church, to which it continued to pledge its allegiance.

▪ Languages

"If you have many languages," an impish European professor remarked some time ago, "you are a polyglot; if you have only two, you are bilingual; but if you have only one, you must be an American!" In view of the studied refusal of many Europeans, at any rate of those who already speak a *Weltsprache,* to learn any other language, the remark is gratuitous. Yet in view of the linguistic capabilities of many who belong to linguistic minorities—Danes, Hungarians, or Ukrainians, for example—it does raise questions that are culturally troubling. The questions become theologically troubling when the footnotes and bibliographies, and often the contents, of books that pass for serious SCHOLARSHIP in the study of the Christian faith demonstrate that the author is unencumbered with a mastery of any language, modern and especially ancient, save the mother tongue. Yet it can be useful to put this question, too, in historical perspective (even if it requires some knowledge of languages to do so).

The supreme example of linguistic illiteracy among Christians, and one with far-reaching consequences, is the inability of most of the theologians in most of the centuries of the history of the church to read the Hebrew Bible in the only language in which, according to most of those theologians, it was inspired by the Holy Spirit. Studies of the quotations from the Old Testament in the writings of Paul suggest that although he sometimes quoted directly from the Septuagint, he did not rely on that translation by Hellenistic Jews but could also supply a Greek translation or paraphrase of his own when it suited his argument. But Paul was a Jew, and he felt deeply the burden and glory of the special place of the people of Israel in the plan of God. A study of patristics, by contrast, is a study of works by Gentiles, most of whom did not know Hebrew and did not sense much need to learn it. In the first century or so after the New Testament, Origen stands as the great exception; for, as Jerome (ca. 342–420) said of him, he studied Hebrew, "in opposition to the spirit of his time and of his people." But the history of Christian hermeneutics is dominated by an indifference to the original language and text of the Old Testament; or, to put it more sharply, most of Christian dogma developed without the benefit of any knowledge of Hebrew. And so, when Justin Martyr (ca. 100–ca. 165), in his *Dialogue with Trypho the Jew,* spoke of the Hebrew Bible as "your Scripture, or rather, ours," he meant the Septuagint. We know now, thanks to recent studies, that there were serious efforts from time to time throughout the medieval period to learn and to teach Hebrew. Yet it was only with the Renaissance and the Reformation that it came to be required of a large body of Christian scholars. In all charity one must add that it did not help this situation when the Council of Trent (1545–1563) made the text of the Latin Vulgate normative.

That action appeared to minimize the value not only of Hebrew but of Greek, and most theologians would agree that being able to read the New Testament in the original is even more important for the Christian theologian than being able to read biblical Hebrew. The gravity of the Western neglect of this resource is therefore difficult to exaggerate. Peter Brown has pointed out that Augustine was "the only Latin philosopher in antiquity to be virtually ignorant of Greek," which cut him off from the *ipsissima verba* not only of Plato and of Plotinus, but also of Paul and of the Cappadocians. It is a testimony to his speculative and exegetical genius that both in his *On the Trinity* and in his commentaries on the New Testament Augustine nevertheless penetrated to the meaning of Scripture as have very few others before or since: his *Tractates on the Gospel of John* may well be the most important exposition of the Fourth Gospel ever written.

But the role of the FILIOQUE in dividing East and West, as well as Augustine's place in its rise, does compel the question of how the development of doctrine, and specifically of the doctrine of the Trinity, might have been different if Augustine had not, as he himself acknowledged in *De Trinitate,* found incomprehensible some of the most fundamental distinctions of Greek trinitarianism. A further question, and an even more ambiguous one, is how Augustine's idiosyncratic doctrine of sin was affected by his belief, on the basis of the Vulgate's rendering of Romans 5:12 as *in quo [sc. in Adamo] omnes peccaverunt,* that all had sinned "in Adam," when the argument of the text was, as the *New English Bible* correctly renders the prepositional phrase, that "death pervaded the human race, *inasmuch as* all men have sinned." (On the other hand, it is salutary to remember that the recovery of New Testament Greek by Protestant theologians did not prevent them from repeating the Augustinian version of this doctrine.)

A keen observer once acknowledged that he found it "disquieting to reflect that the variety of the languages, so interesting in itself, is bound, to a certain extent, to keep human culture shut up in compartments." For Christian doctrine, such compartments have often been an obstacle to realizing the catholicity of the church. The liturgical status of Latin and its theological use have sometimes worked toward unification. That this does not happen automatically will be clear to anyone who recalls that in the sixteenth century not only the adversaries of the Reformation but also its leaders wrote in Latin; to borrow a celebrated bon mot about the Americans and the British, the Protestants and the Roman Catholics were kept apart by a common language. Liturgically, the dominance of Latin before the Second Vatican Council was often taken as evidence of the universality of the church, beyond nation and language, and it was; but there was also more than mere wit in the comment that the use of Latin guaranteed that wherever Roman Catholics went in the world they would be sure to understand the Mass as little as they did at home. Culturally, the Latin of the Mass could also serve as an introduction to the Latin of ancient Rome and to the resources of pre-Christian antiquity. Whereas the missionary policy of Eastern Orthodoxy enriched the nations whom it converted, and above all the SLAVS, by translating the Bible and the liturgy into their languages, it did not provide similar access to pre-Christian Hellenic antiquity.

These examples suggest that beyond the ignorance of languages and its theological consequences, the special qualities of each language have also been factors in the history of theology. Both in Latin and in the Slavic languages, for example, it is necessary to get along without definite and indefinite articles—an inadequacy for which the languages descended from Latin, as well as late Latin itself, compensated by pressing demonstrative pronouns and the adjective "one" into service. This lack of articles enabled Latin to evade making a decision in a case such as the saying of the centurion at the cross in Matthew 27:54, rendered in the *New English Bible* by "Truly this man was a son of God," but with the footnote "Or 'the Son of God'"; the Vulgate could get by with *Vere filius Dei erat iste,* which could mean either "a son of God" or "the Son of God." But this quality also hindered Latin theological writers from considering the specificity in the definite article, or the lack of it in the indefinite article, as the basis for an interpretation: the saying of Jesus to the Samaritan woman in John 4:24, "Spiritus est Deus," rendered a Greek sentence in which "God" (*theos*) had an article but "Spirit" (*pneuma*) did not, so that it was probably unwarranted to quote these words as specific proof for the divinity of the Holy Spirit (even though such proofs were hard to come by).

English as a theological language has a problem bequeathed to it by its Germanic and Latin-Norman ancestors, as the doctrine of justification strikingly illustrates. The Germanic ancestor gave it the adjective "righteous" (Old English *rihtwis*), which has in English a corresponding noun but no corresponding verb; that had to come from the Latin *justificare* (justify).

This leads to the anomaly of saying in English that "justification" means, etymologically, "making righteous," which it does in almost every other language, including of course New Testament Greek. On the other hand, among the special qualities of theological English is its possession of two rich central terms. In most languages, some variant of the Greek *leitourgia* or of the Latin *cultus,* or at best, as in Russian or German, some translation of "the service of God," is used to describe an activity for which English has the matchless word "worship." And whereas most languages—Romance, Germanic, and Slavic alike—have similarly been obliged to transliterate the Greek *euangelion,* English is able to use (for all its ambiguity) the native term "gospel."

• Libraries

The natural habitat of SCHOLARSHIP is the library. Like every habitat, it is more fragile than its inhabitants sometimes suppose, but without it theology as SACRED SCIENCE in the historic sense of the word would have been impossible, as several episodes from the history of this interaction between libraries and theology amply document.

The contribution of libraries to the intellectual and doctrinal development of the Middle Ages is an important chapter in the history of ideas and of learning. At the Sixth Ecumenical Council, held at Constantinople in 680–681, the most burning issue on the theological agenda, the question of the correct doctrine about the relation of the divine nature and the human nature in the incarnation, came down, as such issues have so often, to the question of tradition. The several parties to the dispute all claimed the authority of tradition and all charged their opponents not only with misinterpreting the meaning of the ancient texts, but also with corrupting the text of the manuscripts. The quotations cited by the heretics as tradition, declared the *Acta* of that council, were "plastic and false." Authentic copies of the crucial texts were collected in a single volume in the library of the Holy See in ROME—the ancestor of what today we call the Vatican Library—and sent under seal to Constantinople, where they were collated with the manuscripts in the library of the Ecumenical Patriarchate. There they were read out to the fathers of the council by the *chartophylax,* which literally means "guard of the manuscripts" and today would be rendered "rare-book librarian." This massive authority carried the day, and Adolf von Harnack is probably right in calling the Third Council of Constantinople "the council of antiquarians and paleographers."

A century or so later, in the Latin West—which during this period was usually at least a century or so behind Byzantium in many scholarly fields, and especially in this one—the libraries once more came to the rescue of theology. Among the claims and counterclaims in the controversies of the Carolingian period, the outcome sometimes turned on such arcane codicological issues as whether the Latin passive verb "is adopted" in a text from the manuscripts of Hilary of Poitiers (ca. 315–367) should be read as a subjunctive (*adoptetur*) or as a simple indicative (*adoptatur*). In another of the controversies of the ninth century, over grace and predestination, the positions on the doctrinal questions often corresponded with the literary question of the authenticity of certain writings attributed—wrongly, as has now become clear—to Augustine. Sometimes it seemed that every theologian had become his own librarian, literary critic, and textual scholar. Nevertheless, the high standards of fidelity set for the libraries and the scriptoria of the Carolingian period—to which, as the introductions to modern critical editions of the church fathers and even of the pre-Christian classics still attest, we owe many of the most indispensable Latin manuscripts—served to assure the preservation of the text, even when the textual variant best attested by the evidence seemed to oppose the orthodox view.

Yet perhaps the most dramatic incident in the history of the impact of libraries on theology came in the twentieth century, as part of the upsurge of scholarly and theological interest in the thought of MARTIN LUTHER. Probably the decisive event in bringing about this upsurge was the discovery of his *Lectures on Romans,* which he had delivered during the crucial years of 1515 and 1516. In the nearest thing to an autobiography he ever wrote, the lengthy foreword to the first volume of his Latin works, published in 1545, just a year before his death, Luther himself spoke of these lectures as a turning point in his spiritual and theological odyssey. Yet they were never published. The various collected editions of Luther's works from the sixteenth to the nineteenth century did not include the *Lectures on Romans,* and it was widely (though by no means universally) assumed that the work had been lost. Then, early in the twentieth century, a copy of the manuscript was found, providing the basis for a provocative reinterpretation of the beginnings of the Reformation, *Luther und Luthertum in der ersten Entwicklung,* published in 1904 by a historian of medieval university education, the German Dominican Heinrich Denifle (1844–1905). This priceless copy of the charter of Protestantism had turned up in the Vatican Library, as part of the *Bibliotheca Palatina* that had come to Rome during the Thirty Years' War.

These episodes from the history of doctrine suggest that as a repository of tradition, the library, more than any other agency of theology or the church, stands as proof of the heterogeneity of our common past, and above all of the pluralism of theology. In the novel *1984* by George Orwell (1903–1950), whenever the totalitarian régime changed its mind on some question or other, it would dispatch its "truth squads" to the libraries and archives to doctor all the historical records in conformity with the new policy. The epigram that Aristotle in the sixth book of his *Nicomachean Ethics* ascribes to the Greek poet Agathon of the fifth century B.C.E., that "even God cannot change the past," can be contradicted when an authoritarian system—be it political, ecclesiastical, scientific, literary, or academic (or all of the above)—attempts to iron out the contradictions in its heritage and to achieve a *Gleichschaltung* that reinforces its control by homogenizing the past. It is not enough to capture the contemporary media of communication (thereby determining the present) and the agencies of education (thereby rigging the future): the past, with its rich and varied layers of experience, must also be bent into shape. And if the church has been more guilty of this assault on libraries than have other institutions in the society, that is all the more tragic—not only because the moral posture of the church is so fundamentally compromised by such dishonesty, but also because it is from the libraries, and sometimes from the libraries alone, that renaissance, reformation, and enlightenment (with or without capital letters) have come.

Therefore the ancient library of Alexandria is said to have borne on its portal an inscription, which has been adopted by the Carolina Rediviva, the library of the University of Uppsala: *Psychēs iatreion* (A hospital for the soul).

· Luther, Martin (1483–1546)

Doctor in Biblia, university professor, reformer of the church and of its theology.

It has often been said, difficult though it may be to substantiate, that more is published about Luther each year than about any other figure in the history of the church except Jesus Christ. It certainly is noteworthy that interest in the many ancient Christian writers East and West brings scholars to an International Conference on Patristic Studies at Oxford every four years, but the International Congress for Luther Research, which meets in a different country every five years or so, is devoted exclusively to this one historical figure. "Luther at Worms," declared the Roman Catholic historian Lord Acton (1834–1902), "is the most pregnant and momentous fact in our history."

During the nineteenth and twentieth centuries the interest in Luther and his theology, which has never flagged since the sixteenth century, has experienced a quantum leap so great as to have earned the name "the Luther renaissance." This should probably be dated from the quadricentennial of his birth in

1883, which was the occasion for launching the first truly critical edition of his works, published at Weimar. (Its index volumes are still in the process of appearing, which means that Luther's editors have devoted more than twice as many years to producing the Weimar Edition as Luther himself devoted to composing the works that have gone into it—a comparison that will seem astounding only to someone who has never undertaken to edit Luther.) For both scholarship and theology, a high point of the Luther renaissance came in 1917, at the four-hundredth anniversary of the event from which the REFORMATION is usually dated, the Ninety-Five Theses of 31 October 1517: at the public observance of that event, with the shadow of impending defeat in the First World War hanging over Germany, Karl Holl (1866–1926), professor at the University of Berlin, delivered a lecture under the title *Was verstand Luther unter Religion?* (What did Luther mean by religion?), which charted Luther's inner development as a means of measuring his significance for Christian history. Meanwhile, under the inspiration of Nathan Söderblom and others, Sweden was experiencing a Luther renaissance of its own; and in the years after the Second World War the scholarship of the United States and England, stimulated by such Reformation scholars as Wilhelm Pauck (1901–1981), who had studied under both Karl Holl and Adolf Harnack, emerged from its years of tutelage to make a distinctive contribution to Luther research. The loving care of Luther's contemporaries and followers and the industry of modern Luther research have now made it possible to trace the development of his thought.

Among Luther's very early writings, his *Lectures on Romans* of 1515–1516 have attracted a great deal of attention, and properly so. For in these lectures, discovered in various LIBRARIES and published only in the twentieth century, there is evidence of his growing insight, as well as testimony to his keen interest in the problems of individual and social ethics. Like the lectures on Romans, those on the Epistle to the Hebrews of 1517 show the prominence of ESCHATOLOGY in the theology of the young Luther. As they stand, the Ninety-Five Theses of 1517 do not seem very radical, for they contain little or nothing that could not have been said by other critics of the church; but in the context of his entire development they became a turning point. By 1519 Luther's thought about such central questions as JUSTIFICATION and AUTHORITY had progressed considerably. That progress is reflected particularly in his *Commentary on Galatians* of that year, which documents his incisive analysis of the question of law and gospel and his interpretation of the atonement as the victorious liberation from law and sin. This commentary was reworked in 1523, and a longer one appeared in 1535.

Perhaps the best known of Luther's works is the trilogy that appeared in 1520—*To the Christian Nobility, The Babylonian Captivity of the Church,* and *On Christian Liberty.* The first of these was directed against three basic assumptions of the medieval church: the supremacy of spiritual over secular government; the absolute right of the pope to interpret Scripture; and the exclusive authority of the pope to convoke an ecumenical council. Closely associated with these assumptions were the sacerdotalism and sacramentalism which Luther subjected to serious scrutiny in his essay on the Babylonian Captivity. And against the entire authoritarian structure of the church, Luther's treatise on Christian liberty asserted the freedom of the Christian from any heteronomous authority, as well as the bondage of the Christian through the lordship of Christ to be "the servant of all." That freedom was not to be construed as a freedom in relation to God, and in his polemic of 1525 against ERASMUS entitled *De servo arbitrio (On the Bondage of the Will)* Luther came down decisively on the side of the sovereignty of GRACE, even at the price of surrendering free will. In later years, however, Luther warned that he had not meant this treatise to be understood as an essay in metaphysics.

For the old Luther, probably no work is as revealing as his massive *Lectures on Genesis,* delivered from 1535 to 1545. Despite the insistence of his theoretical hermeneutics upon the literal meaning of the sacred text, Luther frequently goes far beyond either its explicit or its implicit significance. Nevertheless—or, perhaps, therefore—the Genesis commentary leaves very few theological problems untouched. During the time that he was lecturing on Genesis, he took time off to compose an essay *On the Councils and the Church* (1539), in anticipation of a reform council, which was not in fact convoked until just before his death. This work of profound historical and theological scholarship is also revelatory of Luther's thought on the nature of the church, providing the clearest and most systematic definition we have from his pen of the distinction and the connection between the empirical church and the hidden or, as it was later called by Protestants, the "invisible" church.

In these writings, in the many volumes of his sermons, and in his letters and *Table Talk,* the theology of Luther the *Doctor in Biblia* (a title he received as an academic degree in 1512) is completely intertwined with the experience of Luther the believer and doubter, as it is in Paul and in Augustine. Like those spiritual ancestors of his, therefore, Luther has been relevant to an astonishing variety of theologians.

▪ Mary

Out of the sparse details of the life of the mother of Jesus as portrayed in the GOSPELS, Christian piety and theology have constructed a picture that fulfills the prediction ascribed to her in the Magnificat: "From this day forth, all generations will count me blessed" (Luke 1:48). Surely, neither the maid of Nazareth nor the writer of the Third Gospel could have foreseen how, through the development of doctrine, that prophecy has been fulfilled. Nor could they have anticipated that she was, as the prophet Simeon said of her Son, "destined to be a sign which men reject" (Luke 2:34). At each successive stage in the history of the Christian picture of Mary faith and doctrine have gone different ways in different portions of Christendom.

Probably the earliest allusion to Mary in Christian literature is the reference to Jesus in Galatians 4:4 as "born of a woman." As parallels in Old and New Testament (not to forget *Macbeth*) suggest, the phrase is a Hebraic way of speaking about the essential humanity of a person. When applied to Jesus, it was intended to assert that he was truly human, in opposition to the attempt, later seen in the Docetists, to deny that he had a completely human life. Therefore the phrase made of Mary the guarantee of the reality of the INCARNATION. That insistence has been the irreducible minimum in all the theories about Mary that have appeared in Christian history. Those who deny the virgin birth usually claim to do so in the name of this insistence upon true humanity. Those who defend the virgin birth usually maintain that the true humanity was made possible when the Virgin accepted her role as the guarantee of the incarnation: "I am the Lord's servant; as you have spoken, so be it" (Luke 1:38). This is the original source of the title "coredemptress" assigned to Mary in Roman Catholic theology, though the term has come to connote a more active participation by the Virgin in the redemption of mankind.

By far the most voluminous narratives about Mary in the New Testament are the infancy stories in Matthew and Luke. In their present form, both accounts make a point of asserting that Jesus was conceived in the womb of Mary without any human father (Matt. 1:18–25; Luke 1:34–37). The most voluminous discussions of Mary in postbiblical literature have also been those dealing with her virginity. On the basis of those narratives, it was the unanimous teaching of all the orthodox fathers of the church that Mary conceived her Son with her virginity unimpaired, a teaching enshrined in the Apostles' Creed and concurred in by the classical Reformers as well as by most Protestant believers since the Reformation. Only with the rise of Protestant theological liberalism did this teaching begin to lose the universal support it had enjoyed. One of the major points in the attack by fundamentalism upon this liberalism is the insistence on the literal accuracy of all the miracle stories in the Bible, especially those dealing with the miraculous conception of Jesus.

The first major theological controversy over Mary had to do with the propriety of applying to her the title of *Theotokos,* "God-bearer" or "Mother of God." The title itself was a logical development of doctrine from the dogma of the full deity of Christ as this was established during the fourth century, and those who defended that dogma were also the ones to draw the deduction. By the end of the fourth century the title had successfully established itself in various sections of the church, and at the Council of Ephesus in 431 it was formally approved. In the devotion of Eastern Christendom the *Theotokos* (Russian *Bogorodica*) has played a major role, also becoming one of the favorite subjects for ICON painters. Through its incorporation in the Ave

Maria, the title "Mother of God" has been circulated throughout Western Catholicism. By the approval it received in both Lutheran and Reformed confessions during the period of the Reformation, the title assured itself a place in the theology, though not in the piety, of orthodox Protestantism.

One corollary that could be deduced from the New Testament assertion of Mary's virginity in the conception was the doctrine of her perpetual virginity, not only "before birth" but "in birth and after birth," to use the usual phrases. The Apostles' Creed appears to teach at least her virginity "in birth" when it says "born of the Virgin Mary." The doctrine of the perpetual virginity has no explicit warrant in the New Testament, and in addition posed two problems of biblical interpretation, both of which were discussed in detail by defenders of the perpetual virginity, from Jerome to Luther. To the argument, on the basis of such a biblical title for Jesus as "first-born" (Luke 2:6), that Mary must have borne further children, these defenders replied that an only child is a first-born child no less than is the eldest of several. The other biblical problem was that of the "brothers" of Jesus referred to several times in the New Testament. Defenders of the perpetual virginity explained these either as kinsmen or as children of Joseph by a previous marriage. Partly because of these problems, the doctrine of *Semper Virgo* has not enjoyed unanimous support, despite its official dogmatic status.

As the doctrine of perpetual virginity implied an integral purity of body and soul, so in the opinion of many early theologians Mary was also free of other sins. In a discussion aimed at proving the universality of sin, Augustine spoke for the Western Church when he wrote: "We must except the holy Virgin Mary. Out of respect for the Lord I do not intend to raise a single question on the subject of sin. After all, how do we know what abundance of grace was granted to her who had the merit to conceive and bring forth Him who was unquestionably without sin?" But it was the distinction between original and actual sin, firmly established in Western theology by the same Augustine, that eventually compelled a further clarification of what the sinlessness of Mary meant. Was she free of original sin? And if so, how? Thomas Aquinas took a representative position when he taught that her conception was tarnished, but that God suppressed and ultimately extinguished original sin in her, apparently before she was born; but this position was opposed by the doctrine of the immaculate conception, systematized by Duns Scotus (ca. 1265–1308) and finally defined as Roman Catholic dogma in 1854 by Pope Pius IX (1846–1878). According to this dogma, Mary not only was pure in her life and in her birth, but also "at the first instant of her conception was preserved immaculate from all stain of original sin, by the singular grace and privilege granted her by Almighty God, through the merits of Christ Jesus, Savior of mankind."

When the immaculate conception was promulgated, petitions began coming to the Vatican for a definition regarding the assumption of the Virgin into heaven, as believed by most Roman Catholics and celebrated in the Feast of the Assumption: the *lex orandi* of worship, they requested, should become *lex credendi*. During the century that followed, more than eight million persons signed such petitions; yet Rome hesitated, the doctrine being difficult to define on the basis of either Scripture or tradition. No account of the place and circumstances of Mary's death was generally accepted in the early church, no burial place acknowledged, and no miracles credited to relics of her dead body. But such arguments from silence did not suffice to establish dogma, and even the earliest doctrinal and liturgical tradition appeared relatively late in history. Pope Pius XII (1939–1958) made the dogma official in 1950, declaring that "the immaculate Mother of God, the ever Virgin Mary, when the course of her earthly life was run, was assumed in body and in soul to heavenly glory." As it was formulated, the dogma left open the question of Mary's death.

Even those churches which have most vigorously criticized the Mariolatry they claim to find in Eastern Orthodoxy and Roman Catholicism have hailed her as (in the words of a widely used Protestant hymn) "higher than the cherubim, more glorious than the seraphim." As she had prophesied, from that day forth, all generations have counted her blessed.

• Medieval

It is almost a cliché to point out that those who lived in the Middle Ages did not know that this was பе "middle" period of Western history, between the "ancient" and the "modern." As we use it now, "medieval" is a term bequeathed to us by the humanist thinkers of the RENAISSANCE, for whom it was primarily a term of opprobrium. To the extent that they believed themselves to be engaged in the revival of classical antiquity, symbolized for example by the purification of Latin usage and perhaps above all by the recovery of Greek, they could interpret the intervening centuries as the middle between the normative golden age of Greece and Rome and their own age. Like "Gothic," the term "medieval" often carried at least some connotation of barbarian.

Yet those same middle centuries, whether barbarian or not, were also, for better or worse, the age of the Christianization of the West and, in that sense, of "the birth of Europe" (to borrow the title of an influential and incisive account of medieval history by Robert S. Lopez). Consequently, any evaluation of the Middle Ages will inevitably involve taking some position on the question of that process of Christianization. If, as some have felt obliged to assert in the name of a secular worldview, that process suppressed much of what was noble and rational in life and society, the medieval experiment must be counted a tragedy, if not a disaster. Conversely, if one holds, with the Reformation and its heirs, that the Christianization was incomplete and imperfect not only in medieval society and its culture but above all in the medieval church and its theology, then, too, such terms as "tragedy" and "disaster" would not seem inappropriate.

During the twentieth century, scholarly research into the history of medieval culture, and in particular medieval philosophy and theology, has gone far beyond such antitheses. Pope Leo XIII (1878–1903) gave medieval studies a new charter in his encyclical *Aeterni Patris* of 1879: because the study of philosophy was a legitimate and necessary object of research for Christian scholars, the thought of the scholastics deserved special consideration, and within it the philosophy and theology of THOMAS AQUINAS as "by far the preeminent leader and master of them all" (*omnium princeps et magister*). This was in keeping with the assumption, widely held among both Roman Catholic and Protestant theologians of the nineteenth and twentieth centuries, that the presuppositions of philosophy were the decisive factor in the shaping of a theology. As a result, in the words of Étienne Gilson (1884–1978), who was himself a historian of philosophy rather than of theology, "the general tendency among historians of medieval thought has been to imagine the Middle Ages as peopled by philosophers rather than theologians." Gilson's complaint, which can be verified by examining almost any bibliography of medieval intellectual history, reflects the evolution of his own scholarly work, which came increasingly to emphasize the patristic and theological significance of medieval thought even when it dealt with questions that appeared to be primarily philosophical. That can be seen in a special way in his Gifford Lectures, *The Spirit of Medieval Philosophy*.

Although the problem of periodization must be central in any consideration of methodology in historiography, both the *terminus a quo* and the *terminus ad quem* in the very definition of "medieval" raise special questions for the historian of Christian doctrine. "Constantine sitting among the Christian bishops at the ecumenical council of Nicea," the historian of BYZANTIUM N. H. Baynes suggested, "is in his own person the beginning of Europe's Middle Age"; but the Middle Ages do not begin—or end—at the same time for historians of politics, architecture, jurisprudence, national literature, philosophy, and theology.

Because of the undoubted importance of philosophy in the development of the systems of the scholastics, one possible line of demarcation is suggested by the use of classical thought. The Middle Ages may be said to have begun when the majority of theologians were acquainted with Greek and Roman thinkers, not at firsthand, but chiefly through their incorporation into Christian writers. Plato was known in the medieval West principally as the author of the *Timaeus,* which had been translated by Chalcidius, and Aristotle as the author of the logical writings of the *Organon;* the Renaissance was, among many other things, the rediscovery of classical antiquity on its own terms. But in keeping with the need to stress the specifically theological factors in medieval development, a better criterion might be derived from the history of the doctrine of the SACRAMENTS. In the first several centuries of the church, partly because of its missionary posture, the definition of "sacrament" was derived principally from baptism, as the writings of Augustine amply document. But at some point the Eucharist, seen not only as "communion" but as "sacrifice," came to dominate sacramental practice and sacramental thought, and it continued to do so throughout the Middle Ages. Yet another way of viewing and defining the history of medieval theology is to locate it in the development of the doctrine of the INCARNATION. Most of the history of the doctrine of Christ took place in the Greek-speaking Eastern part of the church, and most of it was addressed explicitly to the formulation of the doctrine of the person of Christ and the Incarnation. The Middle Ages may be defined as the period when the theology of the Latin West took up the doctrine of the work of Christ and formulated, in the work of Anselm of Canterbury (ca. 1033–1109), the doctrine of the ATONEMENT as the central content of the gospel.

However it is defined, the history of medieval theology has established itself as an indispensable component in the study of any aspect of the Middle Ages. When a historian of medieval architecture seeks to understand why a depiction of the manna from heaven appears on the left wall of a church opposite the depiction of the Eucharist, it is the typological use of the Hebrew Bible in medieval hermeneutics that supplies the answer. If the reader of DANTE wants to go beyond metaphors and classical allusions, Dante's version of the doctrine of the Trinity is an indispensable literary resource, perhaps even (as some Dante scholars have suggested) for the very idea of the terza rima of the *Divine Comedy.* For all of its attention to problems of logic and of language, medieval philosophy wanted to be seen also as a prolegomenon to the systematic consideration of Christian theology as sacred science and it is being misunderstood if that dimension is ignored. Historians of theology have illumined the development of the Middle Ages in ways that have, among other results, also fundamentally revised the study of the Reformation, by concentrating on its continuities and discontinuities with the later Middle Ages. Instead of emphasizing only the novelty of Luther, current scholarship seeks to place him into the contexts of nominalism, mysticism, and medieval reform movements. Above all, however, medieval doctrine has earned the right to be considered on its own merits, as yet another variation on the melodic themes of theology.

▪ Melody

Of all the arts, the one that has had the most continuous positive relation with Christian faith and theology is music. Christian architecture changed forever the landscapes of Europe and the New World, but there was no Christian architecture to speak of until the fourth century and the Constantinian "peace of the church." The ICONS are a monument in the history of Christian art, but they established themselves only after a vigorous conflict during the iconoclastic controversies. With drama the church has had an even more tenuous connection: although Greek tragedy manifested evident analogies with the gospel of the cross, it played a minor role in the apologetics addressed by the early Christian fathers to the pagan world; but in the development of the miracle plays and mystery plays of the Middle Ages there did emerge a positive and constructive tie to the dramatic art. Even by comparison with drama, dance has had an uneasy place in the Christian system; except for certain traditions like that of the Coptic Church and some highly effective modern experiments, dance has been a stepchild, despite its similarities with processions and other liturgical motions.

But there has never been a time, since Jesus and his disciples sang the Passover Hymn in the upper room on the night of his betrayal (Matt. 26:30), that music and verse did not figure prominently in Christian life and worship. The Epistle to the Ephesians admonished the early Christians: "Let the Holy Spirit fill you: speak to one another in psalms, hymns, and songs; sing and make music in your hearts to the Lord; and in the name of our Lord Jesus Christ give thanks every day for everything to our God and Father" (Eph. 5:18–20). One of the earliest extant non-Christian documents about the early Christians, a letter from Pliny the Younger (62–113) to Emperor Trajan (ca. 52–117) early in the second century C.E., gives this account of their gatherings: "They declared that the sum of their guilt or error had amounted only to this, that on an appointed day they had been accustomed to meet before daybreak and to recite a hymn antiphonally to Christ, as to a god"(*carmen . . . dicere secum invicem Christo quasi deo*). The music itself has been lost, but modern biblical scholars have identified the words of such hymns in various passages of the New Testament, including the words in 1 Timothy 3:16 about the mystery that had been disclosed in the incarnation. Although the scarcity of existing sources and the apparent secretiveness of the early Christians about the details of their liturgy have resulted in the preservation of only a small number of these early hymns, the evidence collected by patristic scholars such as Johannes Quasten confirms the usual opinion that the church has always been hospitable to music.

That music has, however, manifested great variety of form and style. Perhaps the most familiar is the liturgical plainchant, wedded to the text of the Latin Vulgate, above all to its Psalter, and cultivated in the monasteries and churches of the medieval West. It was only later that polyphonic music acquired a place in liturgical usage. With it came the possibility for individual creativity on the part of composer and performer, hence also the temptation to substitute performance for worship as its primary function, calling forth from the twenty-second session of the Council of Trent in 1562 strict legislation about the kinds of music to be permitted as part of the celebration of the Mass.

Meanwhile the Protestant REFORMATION made the music of worship a central element of its redefinition of worship. Believing that "the devil should not have all the pretty tunes to himself," Luther adapted various medieval hymns and wrote others, publishing them in his several hymnals. The musical inspiration produced by the Reformation was to lead to the flowering of Christian music in the seventeenth and eighteenth centuries, of which that of Johann Sebastian Bach (1685–1750) was, in the judgment of many, the richest and most profound, earning for him the title "the fifth evangelist."

Beyond these specifics, however, music has made its special contribution not only to liturgy, but also to the metaphors of theology. On the basis of the musical heritage of Byzantium the defender of the legitimacy of icons in Christian worship, Patriarch Nicephorus of Constantinople (ca. 758–829)—commenting on the Trisagion, the "Holy, Holy, Holy" sung by the angels appearing to Isaiah in his inaugural vision (Isa. 6:3)—spoke of the "theological knowledge" conveyed by the images. They were, he said, "expressive of the silence of God, exhibiting in themselves the ineffability of a mystery that transcends being. Without ceasing and without silence, they praise the goodness of God, in that venerable and thrice-illumined melody of theology." Almost exactly a thousand years later, Schleiermacher wrote in the second of his *Addresses:* "The virtuosity (or special calling) of a person is at the same time the melody of that person's life, and it remains a simple, meager series of notes unless religion, with its endlessly rich variety, accompanies it with all notes and raises the simple song to a full-voiced, glorious harmony."

▪ Mystery

Mystery is usually thought of as the quantity of the unknown: a mystery story is one in which the detective identifies the culprit (or "alleged perpetrator," in the current argot of the police) and thus solves the mystery. When theology has accepted this definition of mystery, as it has throughout much of its history, it has tended to lay claim to the territory of the unknown as the realm of mystery, and hence as the appropriate content of a divine REVELATION. Thereby it has also opened itself to the possibility—which, in the period since the Enlightenment, has been a high probability—that acquisition of further knowledge about the subject would reduce the mystery and reduce the necessity for revelation. Even apart from the problem of authority as it applied to the Bible, the mystery of creation has appeared to be under threat from the discoveries of the natural sciences. Together with miracle and authority, mystery was the theme of the Tempter's questions to Christ in the Legend of the Grand Inquisitor that forms the best-known chapter of *The Brothers Karamazov* by F. M. Dostoevsky.

Both in the usage of the New Testament and in the language of the church, however, "mystery" has referred not only to the quantity of the known but also to the quality of the known, and thus to awe rather than merely to ignorance. Perhaps the most striking illustration of this usage in the New Testament is the application of the Greek word *mystērion* to marriage in Ephesians 5:32. Certainly the union between a man and a woman has always been part of the quantity of the unknown for a child and is in that sense a mystery, but it has remained a genuine mystery also for an adult who participates in such a union. Beginning with the early chapters of the Book of Genesis (Gen. 4:1), the use of the verb "to know" as a euphemism for the sex act has been taken by both Jewish and Christian exegetes as evidence that the acquisition of such knowledge did not dissipate the mystery, but only deepened it. In the context in which the term appears in Ephesians, it is invoked as a way of speaking about the relation between the incarnation and the church, which, the writer appears to be saying, is a "mystery" to those outside the community of faith, who are uninformed about the nature of the special relation between the life of Jesus Christ and the common life shared with him in the church, but which remains an even deeper mystery to those who do share in it and which becomes ever more mysterious as the sharing deepens. "I for my part refer it to Christ and the church," the text in Ephesians concludes, identifying these two realities, as well as the relation between them, as special instances of divine mystery.

The incarnation has long been, in ecclesiastical as well as in biblical language, a primary locus of mystery. "Great beyond all question," the New Testament (1 Tim. 3:16) affirms, probably quoting an early hymn, "is the mystery of our religion":

"He who was manifested in the body,
vindicated in the spirit,
seen by angels;
who was proclaimed among the nations,
believed in throughout the world,
glorified in high heaven."

This, too, has sometimes been taken to refer to the quantity of the unknown: "seen by angels" and not by mere mortals, "glorified in high heaven" but not here below. But the principal tenor of the passage is in the opposite direction: this is a mystery that is "manifested" and "proclaimed among the nations." Such New Testament statements as that of Luke, that he had carried out research and had "gone over the whole course of these events in detail" in preparation for writing his "connected narrative" (Luke 1:3–4), suggest that the events of the life of Jesus are an appropriate subject for historical research, by whatever are the appropriate methods, and that such research could reduce the amount of unknown information about him. But in the deepest sense of "mystery," no amount of such research could make the life of Jesus any less mysterious to the eyes of FAITH, for which "the mystery of our religion" is above all the divine dimension of that which has been "manifested in the body" and "believed in throughout the world."

By derivation, the church itself came to be called a mystery; perhaps the most systematic formulation of this concept of the church as mystery came in the encyclical of Pope Pius XII (1939–1958), *Mystici corporis* of 1943, but the idea itself was very

old. The author of the Gospel of Luke continued his account of
the life of Jesus by writing an account of the early church in the
Acts of the Apostles. Even more than the data of the life of
Jesus, the data of the life of the church have been seen ever since
as an appropriate object of historical research; beginning with
the *Ecclesiastical History* of Eusebius of Caesarea (ca. 260–
ca. 340) and continuing with such works as the *History of the
English People and Church* of the Venerable Bede (ca. 673–735),
scholars have long applied whatever were regarded as the
proper methods of critical historiography to those data. What
was MYSTICAL or "mysterious" about the church to the eyes of
faith was not the result of ignorance about these names and
events, but the result of the reality of the HOLY SPIRIT "mysteri-
ously" at work in and through the ambiguities of those names
and events. A lifetime of research into the facts and events, even
into the facts and events of theological reflection on the
meaning of revelation, is not an easy avenue to understanding
(or accepting) this *mysterium Ecclesiae;* conversely, it does not
make such acceptance impossible either.

Within the church, it is the SACRAMENTS to which the word
"mystery" has most often been applied; *mystērion* became the
technical term for them in Greek theology. (No instance of the
term in the New Testament, neither the reference to matrimony
as a *mystērion* in Ephesians 5:32 nor the designation of the apostles in 1 Corinthians 4:1 as stewards of the mysteries of God,
seems to have implied this technical sense.) What made
the sacraments mysterious was that within and beyond—"in,
with, and under," to use the phraseology of Luther's Small
Catechism—an empirical reality such as water or bread or oil
there was at work a divine reality of grace that could not be
empirically verified. The evolution of sacramental theology,
above all the medieval Western development of the doctrine
of the real presence in the Eucharist, has frequently emphasized the quantity of the unknown as the mysterious component
in the sacrament; but the language of Eastern theology, for
which the presence was simultaneously "mysterious" and
"real" and neither of these without the other, reflected more

faithfully (if less precisely) the patristic approach both to the sacraments themselves and to all the other mysteries.

• Mystical

The mystical can be defined as the immediate experience of oneness with Ultimate Reality. At first examination nothing seems further from this mystical spirit than the prophetic tradition of biblical religion. Nevertheless, the mystical has flourished in the Judeo-Christian tradition, not merely as an example of Hellenization but as an authentic expression of the faith of Israel and of the church. Exegetes are sharply divided on the question of whether there are mystical elements in the New Testament itself. There are unmistakable parallels between mystical language and such statements as that of Paul in Galatians 2:20, "The life I now live is not my life, but the life which Christ lives in me," or of Jesus himself according to the Gospel of John (15:5), "I am the vine, and you are the branches. He who dwells in me, as I dwell in him, bears much fruit." It certainly is true that the idea of a mystical technique for the attainment of unity with God, which figures so prominently in the history of mysticism, is absent from the New Testament and alien to its spirit, and that there remains an essential qualitative distinction between the pantheistic yearning for oneness with an impersonal All and the response of FAITH to the life, death, and resurrection of a historical person.

This fundamental distinction marks all subsequent Christian mysticism, despite its obvious borrowing from Greek, and especially Neoplatonic, thought. Both the distinction and the borrowing are evident in the earliest Christian thinkers to whom the title "mystical" may be applied. When Origen described the stages of the spiritual ascent of the soul toward Christlike perfection, he did employ Greek language about the contemplative life, but not at the expense of illumination through divine grace.

Bringing the thought of Origen more closely into alignment with orthodox dogma, the Cappadocians propounded an APO-PHATIC theory of Christian mysticism whose goal was the vision of God, attained by the denial of lesser goods and the purification of the soul through asceticism and devotion. In the West, AUGUSTINE also found Neoplatonic language congenial for describing the return of the soul to rest in God after the estrangement of SIN. Those various mystical strains of early Christianity continued to be audible in the Byzantine, the medieval, and the Reformation versions of mystical theology.

Many of them were caught up and synthesized for the Byzantine Church by Dionysius the Areopagite, known especially for his treatment of the doctrine of ANGELS. His *Mystical Theology* described the threefold path of "deification" (Greek *theōsis*) as purification, illumination, and union: the soul was to put both the empirical and the rational world behind; by this "way of negation" it would find union with God and, in the words of the New Testament, "come to share in the very being of God" (2 Pet. 1:4). Writing around a century later, John Climacus (ca. 570–ca. 649) combined mystical and ascetic themes in his *Ladder of Paradise* (sometimes also called *Ladder of Virtues*), which outlined thirty steps to perfection, one for each of the mysterious years of Christ before his public ministry. Even more dependent on Pseudo-Dionysius, Maximus the Confessor (ca. 580–662) took over the Dionysian idea of mystical ecstasy, which, however, in the words of his leading American interpreter, "is not used here in the full Dionysian sense of an irrational suprarational estrangement of the mind in the divine darkness." The most thoroughgoing systematization of both mystical theory and mystical technique in the history of Byzantine spirituality came in the thought of Gregory Palamas (1296–1359) and the movement called Hesychasm. The aim of mystical devotion was "serenity" (Greek *hēsychia*). To achieve it, the mystical hesychast strove for control of bodily actions, even of breath, and recited the name of Jesus in one continuous prayer. The significance of Hesychasm for Christian mysticism lies in its influence upon most of Eastern Orthodoxy, especially

Russian Orthodoxy, and in its divergence even from the Dionysian forms of the Western mystical tradition.

In that Western tradition the Dionysian strains were blended
with the Augustinian, most notably in its best-known medieval
expression, the Christ-mysticism of Bernard of Clairvaux
(1090–1153). His mystical *Sermons on the Song of Songs,* a monument
in the history of both hermeneutics and mystical spirituality, is
probably the best-known Christian exposition of this book of
the Bible, on which the monks composed more commentaries
than on any other. Here the soul ascended from penance ("kissing the feet of Christ") through imitation of Christ ("kissing his
hands") to mystical rapture ("kissing his mouth"). Bernard's
treatise *On Loving God* gave a theological foundation for his
mystical teaching. Although in modern times the mystical is
often set over against the theological and is said to be more
authentic or more subjective or simply more dithyrambic, the
two forms of religious thought can in fact exist side-by-side in
the same person, as they did in Bernard and in Thomas Aquinas
and in many of the other scholastics.

During the later Middle Ages, Catholic mystical thought
moved in several contrasting or even contradictory directions.
The most widely read book in the history of Christian mystical
literature, and probably the most widely circulated book in
Christian history except the Bible, is *The Imitation of Christ,* attributed to Thomas à Kempis (ca. 1380–1471). The mystical
devotion of the *Imitation* is practical, nonspeculative, simple—
so much so that some scholars have refused to call it "mystical"
at all. A different line of development runs from Meister Eckhart (ca. 1260–1327) through Johann Tauler (ca. 1300–1361) to
the "friends of God" (German *Gottesfreunde*). Although it is
inaccurate to depict Eckhart as a pantheistic opponent of the
orthodox doctrinal tradition, as was the fashion in the nineteenth century, his mystical speculations about the nature of
God did go well beyond traditional dogma. The *Theologia Germanica,* an anonymous treatise from the late fourteenth century,
summarized much of this German mysticism.

The importance of the *Theologia Germanica* stems from the

circumstance that its first printed edition was prepared by Luther in 1518. In the opinion of many historians, it was at least in part from this source that Luther drew his stress upon the passivity of the soul in its reception of grace, which was in turn part of the presupposition for his doctrine of justification by faith. Nevertheless, the principal places to look for the mystical theology of the Reformation are the Radical Reformation and the Catholic Reformation. The attacks of the magisterial Reformers on the Catholic conception of the sacraments enabled radical Reformers to break with the tradition of mediated revelation more drastically than the Dominican mystical tradition of the late Middle Ages had dared to do. Caspar von Schwenckfeld (1490–1561) drew upon that tradition but carried it much further, coming to an interpretation of the union of the believer with Christ that was condemned by both Protestants and Roman Catholics. In Spain, the Catholic Reformation produced an exquisitely wrought but thoroughly orthodox mysticism, whose chief exponents were Teresa of Avila (1515–1582) and John of the Cross (1542–1591). Teresa attempted to identify the "prayer of quiet" and the "prayer of union" as stages between ordinary prayer and the spiritual marriage of the soul with Christ, in which the will of the mystic and the will of God become one. John of the Cross was successful in schematizing the steps of mystical ascent, because he combined a poetic sensitivity to the nuances of mystical experience with a theological and philosophical precision shaped by a study of Thomas Aquinas. His best-known work, *The Dark Night of the Soul,* described the process by which the soul sheds its attachment to all things created and eventually passes through a personal experience of the cross to the incandescent union of fire with Fire.

In short, neither Byzantine nor medieval nor Reformation theology makes sense without its mystical voices.

Natural Theology

The natural knowledge of God is the knowledge of God apart from REVELATION. According to the New Testament, the apostle Paul addressed both to Athens and to Rome appeals based on the natural recognition of the divine presence as well as the supernatural revelation of that presence. To the Athenians (Acts 17:18–34) he argued from "an altar bearing the inscription 'To an Unknown God,' " from "some of your own poets," and from the evidence of the created world and of history; to the Romans he asserted what "God himself has disclosed," namely, that "his invisible attributes, that is to say, his everlasting power and deity, have been visible, ever since the world began, to the eye of reason" (Rom. 1:19–20).

Those two passages of the New Testament, together with the standard proof text about the atheist as "impious fool" (Ps. 14:1), have provided much of the biblical warrant for including in the audience of theology those whom Schleiermacher called "the cultured among the despisers" of religion. A large part of the Greek and Latin theological literature of the first four centuries of the Christian era was devoted to that apologetic enterprise. It was, from the beginning, caught in the tension between striving to credit as much as possible to natural knowledge in order to leave Gentile as well as Jew "with no defense" (Greek *anapologētos*) (Rom. 2:1) and demonstrating the inadequacy of natural theology in order to leave as much room as possible for revelation. In various sources from pagan literature, some of them (like the Sibylline oracles) doctored to suit the Christian case and others (like the Fourth Eclogue of Vergil) appropriated for its purposes, the apologists found verification for the existence of a natural theology. Above all, such verification came from Greco-Roman philosophy, to which at least some exponents of natural theology were prepared to assign a function in Gentile history analogous to the function of the law in Jewish history, as "a kind of tutor in charge of us until Christ should come, when we should be justified through faith; and now that faith has come, the tutor's charge is at an end" (Gal. 3:24–25).

Less obvious but in many ways more significant for the history of Christian doctrine itself than apologetics was the function of natural theology as a source of presuppositions for the affirmations of church teaching. For example, in his apologetic treatise *Against the Heathen,* Athanasius (ca. 296–373) maintained, as a "principle of natural philosophy" and as "an admitted truth," teachings about the absoluteness and transcendence of the divine nature that became, in his polemical treatises *Against the Arians,* the foundation for his defense of the doctrine of the TRINITY. Reading such presuppositions from natural theology into the language of the Bible, the spokesmen for dogma could take these for granted in their expositions of the revelation in Scripture. When the presuppositions changed as a result of shifts in philosophical or scientific assumptions, it became the task of later generations, as heirs of the conclusion that had been drawn from such presuppositions, to justify it now in the light of a new natural theology. That process became evident in the conflicts within medieval philosophical theology, between an interpretation of Augustine that had carried the presuppositions of Neoplatonic natural theology and a Thomism that strove to employ Aristotelian philosophy to "correct Augustine in the name of Augustine." Much of the documentation for the accusation of a HELLENIZATION of Christianity, as set forth by Harnack and other critics, comes from the natural theology in this hidden agenda of the dogmaticians.

Applied to the history of Christian doctrine before the Enlightenment, the term "natural theology" usually refers to the proofs for the existence of God in the theological prolegomena of the scholastics. During the first millennium of its development, the theology of the church did not make much use of such proofs, although it was confronting not only heathen but ATHEIST/AGNOSTIC systems of thought. Only after the church had established its political hold over secular society and had put the truth claims of its dogma into a privileged position beyond challenge did it go on to ask whether it was possible to establish some of those truth claims also without the aid of revelation. In addition to his importance for the history of the doctrine of the atonement, Anselm of Canterbury (ca. 1033–1109) was the Western thinker who first made the demonstrability of the existence of God a central issue. His Augustinian solution of the issue, the "ontological argument" that the very capacity to conceive of a Being "than which nothing greater can be thought" made the existence of such a Being "necessary," did not gain general support among theologians. But the question, once asked, could no longer be dismissed. For the Anselmic ontological argument Thomas Aquinas substituted "five ways," which proved the existence of God from motion, causality, possibility, "the gradation to be found in things," and "the governance of things." The position of these "five ways" at the very beginning of the *Summa Theologiae* was taken to be an indication that, as Thomas said about the doctrine of grace, "the theology of revelation does not abolish natural theology, but perfects it."

Although the Reformation did not primarily affect natural theology, both the philosophical theology of the Enlightenment and the philosophical criticism of that theology in the thought of David Hume (1711–1776) and Immanuel Kant (1724–1804) claimed to be carrying out the implications of Reformation teaching. The theologians of the Enlightenment retained the traditional distinction between natural and revealed theology, but to the eyes of the defenders of the church's teachings they appeared to assign to revealed theology a steadily diminishing share of truth about God, freedom, and immortality. When Kant's *Critique of Pure Reason* put these three issues beyond the capacity of natural reason to prove or disprove, that appeared to be the end of natural theology as either a philosophical or a theological enterprise. Kant did go on to affirm the validity of a "moral proof" for the existence of God from the presence of the sense of duty, but not in the sense in which the Thomistic "five ways" had claimed to be able to prove it. In much of Protestantism during the century after Kant, natural theology was in a state of disarray; within Roman Catholicism the First Vatican Council of 1869–1870 sought to reinforce it by giving the demonstrability of the existence of God by reason the status of an article of faith. A special chapter, or series of chapters, in the history of natural theology was provided by the establishment in 1888 of the GIFFORD LECTURES. Yet the variety of both methodologies and conclusions evident in the Gifford Lectures demonstrates the impossibility of arriving at a common definition of natural theology as well as the necessity of not surrendering the enterprise.

· Newman, John Henry (1801–1890)

Philosopher of education, discoverer of the DEVELOPMENT OF DOCTRINE, Roman Catholic apologist, and cardinal of the church.

In 1946 it was possible to obtain the B.D. degree from a venerable Lutheran theological seminary and to receive the Ph.D. degree in historical theology from a distinguished university divinity school without ever being obliged to read a single page of John Henry Newman. Also at many Roman Catholic seminaries of that time, locked in as they were to a particular version of Thomism (if not to much study of Thomas Aquinas himself), his thought remained a puzzle even while he himself was, for apologetic purposes, celebrated as a convert and Catholic intellectual.

Then as now, Newman is perhaps best known for his book

The Idea of a University Defined and Illustrated. It has been said, with only slight exaggeration, that "modern thinking on university education is a series of footnotes to Newman's lectures and essays." The crises in the UNIVERSITY precipitated by the political, social, educational, and intellectual convulsions of modern times gave *The Idea of a University* a new relevance during the second third of the twentieth century, and Newman's formulation of some of the most fundamental issues is so clearly defined—and so eloquently stated—that he became the obvious starting point for the discussion. Above all, his identification of the centrality of "general education" in the mission of the university spoke forcefully to the new awareness of the problems created by overspecialization and professionalism in university education. Under the title "Discourses on the Scope and Nature of University Education, Addressed to the Catholics of Dublin," Newman presented his thoughts in preparation for his appointment as rector of the projected Catholic university there. In the event (to use one of his own favorite phrases), Newman's career as a university administrator turned out to be unsuccessful—not only, and perhaps even not primarily, by his own fault.

It is ironic that *The Idea of a University,* for all its power as an essay in the philosophy of higher education, is the documentation of a brilliant failure. It is no less ironic that the most influential theme of the essay should have turned out to be his eloquent insistence on the nontheological, humanistic component in university education; for this insistence was, in his own mind, a corollary of his no less eloquent formulation of the place of theology as another essential component, a theme that has received far less attention in twentieth-century debates over university education. Just as he wanted nothing to do with a theology that did not learn from the liberal arts and sciences, so he wanted theology to take its place among them in the university curriculum. This interrelation between theology and the liberal arts in his own education and religious development is one of the major themes of Newman's *Apologia pro vita sua,* the history of his religious opinions and of the path by which they had brought him to his conversion to Roman Catholicism in 1845. As its title suggests, the *Apologia* is also a statement of the apologetic case for the Christian faith, and specifically for the dogmas of the Catholic faith. Written in conscious dependence on the *Confessions* of AUGUSTINE, it follows its model in being simultaneously a highly subjective account of a personal crisis and a public affirmation of a theological position professedly objective in its validity and universal in its implications. For the subjective account, a valuable supplement to the *Apologia* is Newman's roman à clef of 1848, *Loss and Gain,* in which "Charles Reding" gradually moves from Anglicanism to Roman Catholicism.

Most Newman scholars would probably agree that his most profound and original work of theology is *An Essay in Aid of a Grammar of Assent,* first published in 1870. That was the year of the First Vatican Council, a coincidence that adds piquancy to Newman's analysis of the nature of religious knowledge and affirmation. In its defense of the true faith against modern attack, the council reaffirmed the intellectualism of Thomas Aquinas, which had proceeded deductively from premise to conclusion and from demonstration to certainty. Without confronting Thomism head-on, Newman's *Grammar of Assent* accepted the positive function of doubt as a means of moving toward faith, and it elevated "probability" to the status occupied by "certainty" in earlier systems. For any such epistemology, psychology and experience necessarily became prominent; in this respect as in others, Newman manifested more affinities with Augustine than with the scholastics. "Conscience," he said, "is nearer to me than any other means of knowledge," and "considered as our guide, is fully furnished for its office." Neither the "objectivism" of official church theology nor the "subjectivism" of its critics was satisfactory to Newman; neither camp was satisfied with his position either. But written as it was by the most celebrated convert to Roman Catholicism in the nineteenth century, who was to be elevated to the status of cardinal less than a decade after its publication, the *Grammar of Assent* became a classic in the philosophy and the psychology of religion, one whose importance would grow as the theology of the church deepened in its appreciation of the very factors that had made the *Grammar* unacceptable to much of the conventional orthodoxy of his own time.

Within the program of this "philosophical dictionary," Newman's *Essay on the Development of Christian Doctrine,* published in 1845 and revised in 1878, must be accorded pride of place, for it added development of doctrine to the theological and scholarly vocabulary. Read in the light of his own development, it looks in both directions: toward his first book, published in 1833, *The Arians of the Fourth Century,* and the scholarly work in which he had been engaged as a student of patristics, which had raised for him the problems of continuity and authority; and toward the decision he made, while the book was in press, to be received into the Roman Catholic Church. He saw the question of development as both a descriptive-analytic tool and a normative-theological issue. But read in the light of subsequent development in the almost one hundred years since his death, the *Essay on Development* has proved to be the seminal work for the thought of theologians and historians—and, above all, of historians of theology, who, even if they have been obliged to disagree with its methods or its conclusions, have been no less obliged to accept its formulation of the central problem. Not only to his latter-day disciples, therefore, but to many of those who have drawn other conclusions from his insights, John Henry Newman has become the most important theological thinker of modern times.

▪ Origen of Alexandria (ca. 185–ca. 254)

Scholar, apologist, speculative thinker, and fountainhead of subsequent doctrinal and spiritual development.

"Every kind of greatness met in one man, and that man was a Christian"—this epigram was originally spoken about Blaise Pascal (1623–1662), but it has been fittingly applied to Origen as well. From the miniature biography of him we have in Book 6 of the *Ecclesiastical History* of Eusebius of Caesarea (ca. 260–ca. 340), from the often reverential tone with which his pupils and other contemporaries spoke of him, and from those of his own writings that have survived, it is possible to construct a partial portrait of his person and thought; but the loss of many sources and the mistranslations in others, combined with the almost unparalleled rancor of the posthumous attacks upon him, make a complete account impossible. For the past two centuries or so, however, the polemic of the heresiologists has been giving way, even among many orthodox theologians, to profound sympathy with his spirit and intentions, in spite of continuing disapproval of his ideas, or at any rate of the version of his ideas that has been transmitted. Although he may never be formally canonized, it would not be going too far to say that for many in the twentieth century he has become, more so even than Jerome (ca. 342–420), the patron saint of Christian theological SCHOLARSHIP.

Probably the most widely read of his many writings throughout the centuries was his *Contra Celsum,* an apologetic work evoked by the attacks of one of the ablest pagan critics of Christianity (about whom, however, no more is known for certain than what Origen himself tells us). The paucity of extant source material from that period on intramural church teaching—due in considerable measure to the reluctance of early Christians to write down the mysteries of the faith for general public circulation—has made it necessary for historians of doctrine to attempt reconstructions on the basis of the apologetic literature, which is an extremely hazardous procedure, because the defenses usually address only the specific points under challenge. Origen's treatise has the advantage over most other early Christian apologetics of managing to touch on almost all the salient points of doctrine and ethics. Thanks to this, it provides invaluable insight both into what a highly sophisticated interpreter of the gospel born less than a century after the apostolic age took to be its meaning and into the impression it was making on (to use Schleiermacher's phrase) "the cultured among its despisers" in the Greco-Roman world. It has been said, with only slight exaggeration, that from antiquity to the Enlightenment every major argument against Christianity had been anticipated by Celsus. With equal appropriateness it can be said that most major defenses of Christianity were anticipated by Origen.

If *Contra Celsum* is the work of Origen's that readers have known best, *De Principiis* (*On First Principles*) is the one that has given him the most trouble with orthodox critics. Just how much of that trouble was actually deserved is difficult to say, because the work as a whole is available today only in a Latin translation by Rufinus of Aquileia (ca. 345–410), which may be "partial" in the sense of being fragmentary but which is certainly "partial" in the sense of being partisan. In the controversial preface to *De Principiis,* Origen (and/or his translator) distinguished between those teachings on which the church had spoken definitively, which it was therefore illegitimate to question, and those that were still left open, on which it was permissible for believers to disagree and to speculate. Armed with that license, Origen felt free to speculate, not only by applying his version of Platonism to theological questions but also by looking for ways to resolve inconsistencies between doctrines as well as contradictions between various statements of Scripture. Out of his speculations came such ideas, later declared to be heresy, as the eternity of the world (which denied the doctrine of creation as this eventually came to be confessed) and the subordination of the Son to the Father (in opposition to the orthodox dogma of the Trinity). It was the first attempt ever to organize Christian doctrine into a systematic whole, so that in many ways the history of theology as SACRED SCIENCE and as an intellectual discipline does begin with Origen and with *De Principiis*.

Measured by the amount of time and energy he invested or by sheer volume, Origen's principal work was in the field of biblical exegesis and text criticism. His *Hexapla* is a monumental collation of the original Hebrew text of the Bible, a transliteration of the Hebrew words, and four (sometimes more) Greek translations, copied side by side to provide a basis for determining the authentic words of the Old Testament. It is a work so thorough and painstaking as to be said to have no peer in ancient scholarship—pagan, Jewish, or Christian. Yet it does seem puzzling that all of this meticulous textual criticism was intended to serve as the basis for an allegorical hermeneutics so extravagant as to earn for Origen the reputation of slighting the historicity of biblical events in the interests of the "spiritual sense" of Scripture, which turned out to be identical with some Neoplatonic notion. That reputation is considerably unjust, certainly on the basis of Origen's interpretations of the New Testament; even in dealing with the Old Testament, moreover, he would appear in his treatment of many passages to be taking the literal sense for granted, as obvious enough to be ignored rather than as always simply false.

Through it all, Origen was—or, at any rate, wanted to be, and wanted to be known as—what he himself termed "a man of the church." His pagan contemporaries were amazed that a Neoplatonic intellectual of his obvious genius should be wasting a decade and a half of his life compiling the various Greek versions of the Hebrew Bible, but he did so in the service of the

Christian proclamation. His manner of life was simple and ascetic, although there is some reason to doubt the report that at least once he interpreted a biblical passage literalistically, by becoming a "eunuch for the Kingdom of God's sake" (Matt. 19:12). He did come into conflict with his bishop, but he was neither the first nor the last theologian in Christian history to do so. Twentieth-century research on Origen has laid new emphasis on his profound spirituality, which some have called MYSTICAL. In a small gem of a treatise, *On Prayer,* which is an exposition of the Lord's Prayer, this spirituality and his exegetical skill produced a handbook of Christian devotion that was to serve as a model for later generations.

Those later generations have returned a mixed verdict on Origen. Origen did not choose his enemies wisely: Justinian I (483–565), Roman Emperor and accomplished lay theologian, led the charge against him, before and after the fifth ecumenical council, held at Constantinople in 553. Throughout the medieval period, it was standard for catalogues of false doctrine both Greek and Latin to include an entry on "Origenism," but no less standard for biblical commentaries in both East and West to go on quoting him as an authority. Those who condemned him and those who defended him both drew from him much of their insight, inspiration, and vocabulary; the ORTHODOXY of the Cappadocians is no less his descendant than is HERESY, and both the Arian heresy and the Council of Nicea had learned from Origen. Modern critical scholarship has led to great historical caution about ascribing to Origen himself all the doctrines lumped under "Origenism," so that it is more accurate to speak about "the condemnation of Origenism" than about "the condemnation of Origen." There is a lingering hope that somewhere in the Middle East someone may still unearth manuscripts for the many lost Greek originals of his writings, and with that hope the unexpressed conviction that these would lead to his vindication as "a man of the church." Short of such vindication, his place in history is nonetheless assured.

▪ Orthodoxy

Despite the impression usually held by its detractors—and, somewhat less often, given by its defenders—orthodoxy is not a synonym for obscurantism and repression. Nor, despite the clever distinction attributed to the Anglican bishop of Gloucester, William Warburton (1698–1779), according to which "orthodoxy is my doxy, heterodoxy is another man's doxy," is it a completely arbitrary decision about what someone else ought to believe and teach.

No enormous amount of historical research is required to discover why orthodoxy has acquired such a reputation. Many of those who have been victims of a heresy hunt, whether in a Christian denomination or in the Communist Party or in an anti-Communist investigation, have described in detail the equation of some party line or other with the ultimate nature of things and the consequent enforcement of that party line as a truth that stands beyond question or investigation. Most of the thinkers who have taken forward steps in the history of natural science or of scholarship generally, not only Galileo (1564–1642) or Charles Darwin (1809–1882) but Thomas Aquinas as well, have been resisted by some theologian or prelate as threats to Christian orthodoxy—even though, as in the case of Thomas Aquinas, they have sometimes gone on to become part of a new orthodoxy that had to be defended in turn against some new challenge. When, beginning in the fourth century, the church has been able to invoke the police power of the state to monitor the belief and doctrine of its members, orthodoxy has become a means of preserving public order as well as theological conformity. Dostoevsky's Legend of the Grand Inquisitor in *The Brothers Karamazov* put into words the deep-seated suspicion that the enforcers of orthodoxy have often been men who themselves believed very little of the "true faith" they were sworn to uphold, and that if they had their way they would, in the name of doctrinal purity, take the necessary steps to silence Christ himself.

The historic meaning of "orthodoxy" has included both correct doctrine and correct worship, each in accordance with the other; that was the intention behind the formula for the doctrinal authority of WORSHIP, *lex orandi lex credendi*. "Correct" (Greek *orthon*) doctrine or DOGMA, therefore, meant doctrine that corresponded to the prescribed system of giving "praise" (Greek *doxa*) to God. In their defense of the doctrine of the Trinity, orthodox theologians such as the Cappadocians took for granted the patterns of worship that both they and their opponents had inherited from the early church. In those patterns of worship, when there was as yet no dogma and when the creed was still unclear in many particulars, it had already been standard "from the beginning" to sing and speak about the Son of God as "Lord" and "God." The dispute was not primarily about the propriety of such worshiping, but over the form of sound doctrine that would do justice to it. What emerged as trinitarian orthodoxy out of the controversies of the fourth century, in the Niceno-Constantinopolitan Creed and its normative interpretations, was a statement of the necessary implications of a worship that was already "trinitarian." Once affirmed as dogma, this orthodoxy was in turn declared to be—and to have always been—the doctrinal presupposition, not merely the logical implication, of such worship.

Sometimes the movement of orthodoxy has followed in the opposite direction, from *lex credendi* to *lex orandi*. That was, at least in part, the direction taken by the doctrine of the Holy Spirit. Although in the argumentation of the Cappadocians it was said to be the doctrine consistent with the worship practice of the church as stated by Christ himself in the baptismal formula (Matt. 28:19), its codification as orthodox dogma prepared the way for further development of orthodox worship. The medieval Western hymns to the Holy Spirit, most of them variations on the theme *Veni Creator Spiritus,* had not been in existence during the dogmatic debates and therefore could not be used for doctrinal proof as the hymns to Christ had been; but now they could become a part of correct worship. In the East there was an even more dramatic illustration of the movement from correct teaching to correct worship. During the eighth and ninth centuries, the theological vindication of the use of icons in worship as "orthodox" was based on the "orthodox" doctrine of the incarnation that had been formulated by the councils of the church during the fifth, sixth, and seventh centuries. Once achieved on this basis, the restoration of the icons has been celebrated in Eastern Orthodox churches ever since 843 on the First Sunday of Lent (or of "Great Lent," as it is called to distinguish it from what the West calls "Advent"). The celebration is called the "Feast of Orthodoxy," which here implies primarily—in the Russian word *pravoslavie* (*pravo* means "correct," *slava* means "praise" or "glory") as well as in the Greek word *orthodoxia*—correct worship, and therefore also correct teaching.

Each of those cases illustrates as well the complex relation of orthodoxy to the freedom of theology and of the theologian. During much of the history of the church, those who continued to oppose orthodox doctrine were routinely deposed from office, regularly sent into exile, and not infrequently mutilated or executed. Viewed in historical perspective, however, these extreme measures to guarantee orthodoxy have not been successful in quashing free inquiry. The history of the doctrine of the incarnation provides the longest continuing evidence for the thesis that whenever a dogma has been defined, the schools of theology whose controversy had helped to provoke it went on to regroup themselves in response to it and within its boundaries: Alexandrian and Antiochene theologians did not lay down their arms after the councils of Ephesus in 431 and of Chalcedon in 451 had condemned as HERESY the extremes of both of their respective positions, but they now articulated their distinctive emphases within the framework, and if possible in the terminology, of those ecumenical councils. By drawing the boundary line of orthodoxy, the church has in effect declared the difference between a theological fair ball and a theological foul ball, but it has still left a vast space within which a ball is in play.

As a statement of faith about the eternal and living God, orthodox doctrine has been tempted to ignore its APOPHATIC character and to proceed as though it, too, were eternal and timeless. When it has done so, it has made itself vulnerable to the kind of critical historiography that has subjected the doctrines of the Christian message, one by one, to historical scrutiny and shown them to be not bits of timeless truth in hermeneutically sealed packages, but the conditioned products of particular times and places. An orthodoxy that refuses to take into its definition of itself the dimension of time and history cannot be expected to endure very long. On the other hand, the speedy and total demise of orthodoxy, as predicted by historical relativists since the Enlightenment, has likewise not occurred. The apologia for orthodoxy expounded by John Henry Newman showed the necessity of embodying within the very definition of orthodoxy and of TRADITION a careful statement of the DEVELOPMENT OF DOCTRINE.

• Patristics

In a revision of his *Decline and Fall* that was never completed, Edward Gibbon spoke about undertaking to describe "the decline and fall of the empire of Rome, of whose language, religion, and laws the impression will be long preserved in our own and the neighboring countries of Europe." The fall of Rome, he seemed to be suggesting, had helped to make Latin a world language.

The texts that achieved this status for Latin, however, were not the *Gallic War* and the *Aeneid* but the Vulgate and the Latin Mass. With a touch of academic malice, therefore, patristics could be defined as a study of the period during which Latin was becoming a world language—a period that did not begin until after the end of the historical period with which most departments of classics concern themselves. Similarly, the bad press accorded to Byzantium (for which Gibbon must bear a considerable portion of the blame, at least in the English-speaking world, though he had help from many scholars and theologians) has made those same classics departments indifferent or even hostile to the development of Greek thought and literature, pagan as well as Christian, during (and especially after) the Hellenistic period, when they were imprinting upon our culture much of the image of the tradition of Greece that it still bears. If the presence of a DICTIONARY indicates the status of a particular scholarly discipline, it bears noting here that only in the 1960s did *A Patristic Greek Lexicon* appear, and that for the Latin fathers it is necessary for patristic scholars to make do with Alexander Souter's *Glossary of Later Latin,* the Blaise-Chirat *Dictionnaire latin-français des auteurs chrétiens,* and the lexico-graphical supplement to the *Corpus Christianorum.*

No one scholar can be an expert in all the disciplines that properly belong to so complex a field as patristics, for work on early Christian literature calls for an entire cluster of scholarly skills. The investigator of patristic theology who personally lacks adequate technical preparation in languages or text, as many do, is forced to rely on the work of others; on the other hand, a philological scholar of great erudition such as Eduard Schwartz (1858–1940), whose editions and monographs have become indispensable to the field, also exhibits the limitations of a philological approach whose judgments are shaped by a certain hostility to the theological enterprise. Because so much of the basic research on the period has been preoccupied with the New Testament, a patristic scholar needs to acquire a more than cursory grasp of the current methods and results of biblical study—without, it may perhaps be added, falling victim to its repeated epidemics of trendiness. But because so many of the church fathers, notably those such as ORIGEN OF ALEXANDRIA and the CAPPADOCIANS who undertook the apologetic task against Greco-Roman thought, were perforce more heavily in-volved with Hellenistic philosophy than any of the writers of the New Testament had been, it is indispensable to know such movements as Middle Platonism, later Stoicism, and the various eclectic philosophical combinations that engaged the attention of the church fathers.

Modern theological scholars are not in a position to cast the first stone at their colleagues in the humanities over the neglect of patristics. With their backgrounds in liberal Protestant theol-ogy, graduate divinity schools at most American universities have not been much more hospitable to the study of ancient Christian writers than have their colleagues in classics, and young doctoral candidates with an initial interest in patristic or Byzantine studies have sometimes been compelled to move, by default, into other periods and fields, such as the considerably more popular age of the Reformation. The result, even for Reformation study, has been a scholarship that connects theology more directly with the development of critical Protestant thought in the nineteenth century than with its patristic and medieval roots. Contending, in an extensive memorandum of 1888, that "only a scholar who commands ancient church history has a right to be a church historian," Adolf von Harnack maintained that those who "one-sidedly cultivate the history of the Reformation or of the Middle Ages and when it comes to the history of the ancient church can express only a kind of 'common sense'" (the English phrase is his) could not understand either the Reformation or the Middle Ages properly. In his own mind, therefore, the very model of a modern Reformation scholar was his student Karl Holl (1866–1926), whose scrupulous scholarly work on the critical edition of the Greek church father Epiphanius of Salamis (ca. 315–403) had prepared him for the study of other periods. Holl's eventual achievement in helping to set the pattern for the modern study of the life and theology of Luther was to bear out Harnack's judgment, but very few Protestant Reformation scholars since Holl have brought his kind of preparation to their research.

As the state of medieval studies suggests, the performance of Roman Catholic students of Thomas Aquinas has not been significantly better on this score. The reason for his preeminence, according to the encyclical *Aeterni Patris* of Pope Leo XIII (1878–1903), who was quoting the sixteenth-century Thomist scholar Cajetan (1469–1534), was that Thomas had "supreme veneration" for the ancient fathers of the church; not merely his individual achievement as a thinker, but his constructive use of the patristic tradition gave him his special position. As a leading twentieth-century student of Thomas Aquinas, Martin Grabmann (1875–1949), once put it, it must be acknowledged that neo-Thomism did not pay sufficient attention to this emphasis of *Aeterni Patris,* devoting far more attention to how Thomas used the newly available Latin translations of the metaphysical writings of Aristotle than to how his continued study of Augustine shaped his theological development, through his critique of the remnants of Neoplatonism in Augustine's thought but also through his continually deepening grasp of the dogmatic tradition out of which Augustine came. How different in its theological approach and apologetic style a patristic avenue to Roman Catholic doctrine and spirituality could be, was made evident by the thought of a man whom the same Pope Leo XIII made a cardinal of the Roman Catholic Church, John Henry Newman.

There is perhaps no topic in theology and church history to which patristic scholarship can make a greater contribution than the relation between the Eastern and the Western Churches. For both of them, tradition is constitutive of the life and teaching of the church and is seen to consist of the orthodox dogmas of the Trinity, the incarnation, and the like. Yet beneath and behind this consensus lie profound differences not only on the formal question of AUTHORITY, but on substantive issues, as even a superficial comparison between the Cappadocians and Augustine on those same doctrines of ORTHODOXY will document; from these two sources, in turn, sprang distinctive traditions of theology and spirituality associated respectively with Eastern Orthodoxy and Roman Catholicism. Nevertheless, these church fathers on both sides believed themselves to be members of one church and to stand in a discernible CONTINUITY with their theological ancestors in both East and West. Only through patristic study is it possible to penetrate to their understanding of the catholicity of the church and to inquire about its historical foundation.

▪ Paul the Apostle (d. ca. 65)

Citizen of Tarsus, convert from Judaism to the church, apostle to the Gentiles, and supposed author of approximately half the books in the CANON OF THE NEW TESTAMENT.

If the biographical sketch incorporated into the Acts of the Apostles is accepted as historically trustworthy and if the autobiographical information provided, usually *en passant,* in the Epistles bearing his name is taken at face value—and if all of these data can be harmonized—then the career and thought of the apostle Paul are more fully documented in the New Testament than those of anyone else, including Jesus of Nazareth. Fascinating though these issues are for the historian and exegete of the New Testament, for the purposes of this dictionary they are secondary to the role of Paul and of his theology in the ongoing history of Christian thought and interpretation: not what he actually taught, but what it was thought he taught, is primary here, in the case of Paul as in the case of the Sermon on the Mount, even if several Epistles were attributed to him that he did not actually write. And unless the New Testament exegete is convinced (as some seem to be) that the history of all hitherto existing Pauline scholarship is the history of misunderstanding, the place of Paul in TRADITION is itself a topic of theological significance.

The oft-quoted apophthegm of the radical theologian and historian Franz Overbeck (1837–1905), that in the second century there was only one theologian who understood Paul and he misunderstood him—a reference to the Paulinism of Marcion of Pontus (d. ca. 160), condemned as heresy by the mainstream of Catholic orthodoxy—raises in hyperbolic fashion the historical question of the interpretation of Paul in the first two or three centuries after his death. So closely has Pauline theology been identified with the teachings of the Protestant Reformation, above all of Luther, that scholars have found it difficult not to measure the ante-Nicene church and its teachings by this later authority—by which the Catholic fathers of the church and its doctrines and creeds do not measure up, and Marcion ends up being the only one who understood Paul. The picture of Paul given, for example, by Irenaeus of Lyons (ca. 130–ca. 200) in opposition to Marcion is intent on documenting his continuity both with the Old Testament and with the other apostles, including Peter; the conflict between Peter and Paul described in the second chapter of the Epistle to the Galatians, which for

Marcion as well as for some historians of the New Testament in the nineteenth century was the decisive event in the separation of the early Christian community from Israel and its eventual HELLENIZATION, became at the hands of Irenaeus evidence that "Paul acceded to [the request of] those who summoned him to the apostles . . . and went up to them, with Barnabas, to Jerusalem." As the champion of a harmonious and homogenized apostolic tradition, Irenaeus set the pattern of a Paul comfortably part of the "one holy catholic and apostolic church," which, as he was believed to be saying, was "built upon the foundations laid by the apostles and prophets" (Eph. 2:20), himself included; for, as he continued, "There is one body and one spirit . . . one Lord, one faith, one baptism" (Eph. 4:4–5).

Irenaeus wrote in Greek but in the West, and that Catholic picture of Paul as spokesman for authentic tradition was shared by the Greek East and the Latin West. Each of the Cappadocians drew portraits of him: in the second of his *Orations* Gregory Nazianzus employed the rhetorical techniques of classical panegyric to describe Paul's life and ministry through a catena of the more personal passages in the epistles. On the assumption that the Catholic picture was a correct one, Augustine emerges with profound affinities to Paul. It was, he said in the *Confessions,* a verse from Paul, "Let us behave with decency as befits the day: no revelling or drunkenness, no debauchery or vice, no quarrels or jealousies!" (Rom. 13:13), that in his conversion summoned him from his own debauchery and vice to Christian discipleship and membership in the Catholic Church; "I wanted to read no further," he explained, "nor did I need to." It is surprising that in his activity as a biblical exegete Augustine did not occupy himself very much with the Pauline Epistles, only Galatians having received a complete commentary, and that a relatively brief one; by contrast, he commented at great length on the Gospels, especially in his *Tractates on the Gospel of John* and in his exposition of the Sermon on the Mount, and on 1 John. On the other hand, in his polemical writings, especially in the treatises against the Pelagians, the Pauline Epistles (and above all the

Epistle to the Romans) became central. Here as elsewhere, it was Paul's continuity with the Catholic tradition—and therefore his own continuity with it—that he stressed.

The same Paul, and the same Epistle to the Romans, provided the most effective ammunition of Martin Luther against such notions of continuity and tradition. As he said in 1519, when confronted by his opponent Johann Eck (1486–1543) with a battery of quotations from patristic and medieval sources, "Saint Paul and I will withstand them all!" His *Lectures on Romans* were a primary force in his "discovery of the gospel," whereas the successive versions of *Lectures on Galatians* may well be the most comprehensive statements of his theological position. The doctrine with which he, and the Protestant Reformation generally, were the most closely identified, JUSTIFICATION BY FAITH—which in Romans 3:28 he translated as "by faith alone"—was a Pauline doctrine; references to it elsewhere in the New Testament, notoriously in James 2:21, 24, were explained in the light of Romans. The more "Catholic" parts of the Pauline corpus, namely the Epistles to the Ephesians and Colossians for theology and the pastoral Epistles for churchmanship—significantly, Protestant historical criticism eventually denied the Pauline authorship of every one of these Epistles—were less central. Calvinism, more consistently than Lutheranism, incorporated into its central system of doctrine the entire progression of the argument of Romans, from sin and justification in chapters 1–3 to election in chapters 8–11. On the other hand, John Wesley (1703–1791) also found his inspiration in Paul; and when his heart was "strangely warmed" at Aldersgate on 24 May 1738, it was the reading of Luther's preface to Romans that converted him.

It was, however, not the continuity of Paul with the Catholic tradition, but another dimension of continuity in his teaching that became the focus of attention for the historical criticism of the Enlightenment: the continuity, or lack of it, between Paul and the teachings of Jesus. Paul was cast as the principal architect of the "religion about Jesus" that had replaced the "religion of Jesus" and had gone on to become the orthodoxy of the church. As the study of the Gospels sought to distinguish between authentic sayings of Jesus and later additions by the church, so it disengaged Jesus from Paul. Yet the career of Paul as the *agent provocateur* of theological revolution could not be dismissed so easily as all that. Just when he had been relegated to history, "a bombshell fell into the playground of the theologians": *Der Römerbrief (The Epistle to the Romans)* by Karl Barth (1886–1968) broke upon the theological world of post–World War I Protestantism with an impact that changed it forever. It seems safe to predict that the Pauline Epistles will go on having that kind of impact.

▪ Reformation

For every generation since the sixteenth century, the Reformation has been a source of theological renewal to its "heirs and assigns in perpetuity." The oft-quoted axiom, *Ecclesia Reformata semper reformanda* (The church of the Reformation continually stands in need of reformation), has been seen as no less applicable to the teaching of the church than to its structure.

The applicability of that axiom has extended far beyond theology and the church, to the entire cultural and intellectual history of the lands and peoples who participated in the Reformation. Thus when T. G. Masaryk (1850–1937), the native of Moravia and philosopher who was to become the first president of Czechoslovakia after the First World War, was seeking to make sense of Czech history as a resource for the reawakening of national consciousness, he was led by his reading of the Czech historian of the Reformation, František Palacký (1798–1876), to the heritage of the Hussite Reformation, in which he believed he had found the authentic spirit of Bohemia and Moravia; thereby Masaryk made this understanding of the Czech Reformation normative within Czechoslovakia but also beyond its borders. Palacký's better-known contemporary and colleague in historiography, the German polyhistor Leopold von Ranke (1795–1886), likewise developed his philosophy of history and his historical methodology through the scholarly study of the Reformation. His *Deutsche Geschichte im Zeitalter der Reformation,* published in 1839–1847 and republished many times (also in

English translation), reached a far broader public than Palacký's work did; it acquired, and in many respects still holds, a similar canonical status for Reformation scholars in training.

The primary importance of the Reformation, however, has always been seen in its impact on the life and teaching of the church. Although individual Reformation leaders, above all MARTIN LUTHER, have been celebrated as religious geniuses and heroes of the faith and have thus occupied a prominent place within the history of religious and philosophical ideas, most subsequent church history has been determined by the ecclesiastical and theological structures that emerged from the several Reformation establishments. The Augsburg Confession of 1530, eventually incorporated into the *Book of Concord* of 1580, has been the official definition of Lutheranism ever since. It was characteristic of the Reformed and Calvinist churches that they did not elevate any one Reformation confession to a similar status, but allowed each of the national churches to adopt its own, producing CREEDS in great variety. In this respect as in others, the English Reformation took a distinctive form, because the Thirty-Nine Articles of 1563, as the official confessional document of the Church of England, have occupied a secondary position to that of the *Book of Common Prayer* in its successive revisions. Enforced as they were by civil law, these various Reformation establishments shaped public education and public order throughout Protestant Europe and colonial America.

Noticeably absent from standard catalogues of the outcome of the Reformation, the dissenting groups of Anabaptists and Antitrinitarians on "the left wing of the Reformation" did not achieve recognition at law. Only with the gradual disestablishment, intellectual as well as political, of the churches of what George H. Williams aptly terms "the magisterial Reformation" have these radicals come into their own as legitimate children of the Reformation. During the scholarly lifetime of senior Reformation historians still active, editions of primary sources and monographic studies concerned with the radical Reformation have enriched—and complicated—scholarship, with the result that no respectable history of the Reformation today could avoid giving the radicals proper place alongside the groups that used to be regarded as the only genuine Reformation churches. That scholarly evolution has been accompanied and stimulated by a sense, among the theological heirs of the magisterial Reformation, that the very issues of DOGMA on which the radicals departed from the mainstream of Reformation doctrine—such as the Trinity, the church, and the sacraments—were among the most questionable and vulnerable doctrines in the Reformation confessions themselves. By its advocacy of the freedom of conscience and its call for the separation of church and state, moreover, the radical Reformation had anticipated many of the political and moral-theological emphases that all the heirs of the Reformation in the nineteenth and twentieth centuries were finally making their own.

At the same time, Reformation scholarship has also been reaching in the opposite direction, toward the movements that used to be lumped together under the heading "Counter-Reformation." Underlying the use of that term, which was standard among Roman Catholics as well as Protestants until comparatively recent times, was the assumption that the Roman Catholic Church had been primarily reactive during the events of the Reformation era. Therefore the *Canons and Decrees* of the Council of Trent (1545–1563) were read principally as the church's answer to the attacks of "the Reformation," that is, of Protestantism. In this area, too, critical editions and monographic studies published during the twentieth century have helped to restore the balance. Protestantism had not exhausted the reformatory dynamic in the church; nor was the continuing agitation for change and renewal only a reaction to its message. One of the most exciting aspects of this new research has been the discovery of the inseparable connections, positive and negative, between the Reformers of the sixteenth century and the spiritual and intellectual movements of the fourteenth and fifteenth centuries; the former Institute for Reformation History at the University of Tübingen is now called the Institute for the

Late Middle Ages and Reformation. The ecumenical movement and other theological shifts of the twentieth century have made their contribution to this changing perspective as well. The deepening awareness on both sides that there were losses as well as gains entailed in the Reformation inaugurated a new style of Reformation scholarship among Roman Catholic historians, as well as a new sympathy among Protestants toward those who retained their allegiance to ROME during the sixteenth century; the rising prestige of Sir Thomas More (1478–1535) as "a man for all seasons" could serve as an index of this change in the scholarly and theological climate.

Events of the twentieth century have redefined Reformation study in yet another fundamental way, with the coming-of-age of Marxist scholarship in the field. Beginning already with *Der Bauernkrieg* (1850 and 1870), the study of the Peasant War of 1525 by Friedrich Engels (1820–1895), Marxists had recognized that the study of the Reformation was fundamental to their historical diagnosis of the end of feudalism and the rise of capitalism, and such Marxist scholars as Karl Kautsky (1854–1938), who had been private secretary to Engels, kept that interest alive. The political outcome of the Second World War made Marxism-Leninism the dominant political ideology of Reformation territories such as East Germany and Bohemia, whose scholars have applied the methodology of historical dialectic to the events of the sixteenth century, with results that have compelled the attention of Reformation scholars everywhere. The impact of those results on the debates over historiography has not only put the standing controversy between social history and intellectual history into new perspective, but has also served to reconfirm the crucial position of the study of the Reformation in scholarship and theology.

• Renaissance

The courses in the history department that now bear the title "Early Modern Europe" used to be called "Renaissance and Reformation" (or, in the vernacular, "Ren 'n' Ref"). Like the hyphen in "Judeo-Christian"—or for that matter in "Greco-Roman"—it was the "and" that created the most problems, intellectually as well as pedagogically. And because not only the REFORMATION but also the Renaissance was preoccupied with the themes and issues of the Christian faith, such problems were, and are, perforce theological problems as well.

For generations scholarship in Reformation studies and scholarship in Renaissance studies have been moving in opposite directions, and the way young scholars have been prepared for research and teaching in the two fields has abetted this trend. Typically, a university that had a faculty of theology or a divinity school as well as a history department would assign the Reformation to the first and the Renaissance to the second; budgetary constraints permitting, there could be a Reformation position in each, but it was much more likely that a second Renaissance position would be located in art history or in the literature of one of the Romance languages than in religious studies. That allocation of resources was reflected in the academic paths taken by the incumbents of such positions when they were in graduate school. Hajo Holborn (1902–1969), who was ambidextrous in "Ren 'n' Ref," used to reminisce with considerable amusement about being told by ADOLF VON HARNACK at the University of Berlin that he should probably go into *Profangeschichte*. Most Reformation scholars, at least until this generation, came to the field with considerable background in the "other" fields of theological study, including their languages (Greek as well as Latin), and often with enough interest in normative questions of Christian doctrine to be called closet theologians. By reciprocity, their research was often subject to immediate exchange into the coinage of the systematic theologians; this was particularly true of Luther research in Scandinavia and Germany. Renaissance scholars—with a few notable exceptions, also in this generation—had been prepared only in the humanities, in literature or philosophy, and were as unacquainted firsthand with theology as were Reformation scholars with these humanistic disciplines. Italian was a requirement for a Ph.D. in Renaissance history, but not in Reformation studies.

It is the lesson of church history that schisms tend to perpetuate themselves long after the original occasion for the separation has been forgotten. While it is of course an exaggeration to say, as is sometimes heard, that Jacob Burckhardt (1818–1897) "invented the Italian Renaissance," it is true that his *Civilization of the Renaissance in Italy,* first published in 1860, did for Renaissance studies in the century that followed it much of what the work of his teacher, Leopold von Ranke (1795–1886), had done for Reformation studies. Even now, a critical review of Burckhardt's book in the light of more recent research not only orients neophytes to the present state of the field but reveals the degree to which his interpretation of "the state as a work of art" and of "the discovery of the world and of man" still sets the questions for Renaissance scholars. Significantly, there was relatively little room for religion, and considerably less for theology, in Burckhardt's version of the Renaissance. Even his constant use of DANTE as a point of reference, which enabled him to recognize some profound continuities between medieval and Renaissance culture, paid less attention to Dante as theologian than the themes of the *Divine Comedy* and *De Monarchia* would have warranted. When *The Civilization of the Renaissance in Italy* is seen, as Burckhardt evidently wanted, in the light of his total oeuvre—and specifically of *The Age of Constantine the Great,* his work on the Christianization of the Roman Empire and the origins of the Middle Ages—it becomes the closing act of the theocratic drama and the opening act of the new era. Yet almost every one of the writers and thinkers in Burckhardt's narrative of the Italian Renaissance dealt with theology as well as with the political or artistic topics with which they are identified.

Although there was more of a Reformation in Italy than may be generally recognized, at least until it was quashed by the

Counter-Reformation, the very definition of the Renaissance as an Italian rather than a pan-European movement almost guarantees that its theological dimensions will be overshadowed. John Calvin (1509–1564) and most of the other leaders of the magisterial Reformation repeatedly interpreted their theologies as the application of the Renaissance slogan *Ad fontes!* (Back to the sources!) to the sources of the Christian message, above all to the Bible. For example, Luther's translation of the Bible into German, which may well be his most important accomplishment, would have been impossible without the work of Renaissance scholars like ERASMUS. The same professors of Greek taught the classics and the New Testament, apparently with no awareness that, in the eyes of scholars in the nineteenth and twentieth centuries, they would be seen as engaging in distinct or even contradictory enterprises. (That circumstance would also seem to render doubtful the repeated effort to claim the authority of the Reformation for the attack on orthodox Christian doctrine as the Hellenization of the gospel.)

This reappraisal of the place of the Renaissance in the history of Christian thought has been brought about also by the even more fundamental reappraisal of the connection between the Reformation and the later Middle Ages. As a few Renaissance scholars of the nineteenth century recognized, "the discovery of the world and of man," celebrated by Burckhardt as the central theme of the Renaissance, derived its inspiration in considerable measure from the rediscovery of nature and the revaluation of humanity associated during the late medieval period with the Franciscan revival. The Franciscan spirituality in the work of various Renaissance artists, for example Giovanni Bellini (ca. 1430–1516), bears out that interpretation. Although Luther's own attitude to the Franciscan movement was often highly critical, it is undeniable that a broader definition of the Reformation to include the Radical and the Catholic Reformations also lends new importance to the thought of Franciscan theologians during the fourteenth and fifteenth centuries, when in many fields they were the dominant force. A redefined Reformation and a redefined Renaissance emerge as twin children of the redefined Middle Ages.

None of this should, however, be permitted to obscure the legitimate claim that the Enlightenment descended from certain important aspects of Renaissance thought. As the writings of Erasmus illustrate, there was in the program of the Christian humanists a drive toward the reduction of the content of the gospel through the elimination of elements that seemed to be either contradictory to reason or irrelevant to morality. It stopped well short of denying such teachings of orthodoxy as the deity of Christ, but it did tend to elevate the message of the Sermon on the Mount over them. Those leaders of Enlightenment thought who believed themselves to be engaged in a "new Reformation" as they purified theology of its later excrescences adopted Erasmus, often in preference to Luther, as their patron saint: with Erasmus and against Luther, they defended the freedom of the human will as indispensable both to a sound morality and to a sensible faith.

▪ Revelation

Like the question of AUTHORITY, with which it is closely related though by no means identical, the doctrine of revelation is not simply one doctrine among others, but a doctrine by which every other doctrine may be said to stand or fall. If the claim to divine revelation is groundless, the entire fabric of Christian belief and life will have to be called fundamentally into question.

The Greek word for "revelation" in the New Testament is *apokalypsis,* and the final book of the New Testament is alternately called the Book of Revelation and the Apocalypse. That suggests one of the earliest and most persistent of the several meanings of revelation: the disclosure of the hidden future. Both the CANON OF THE HEBREW BIBLE (OLD TESTAMENT) and the CANON OF THE NEW TESTAMENT in their present forms contain apocalyptic literature, although its status, especially in the New Testament, remained doubtful for a considerable time; it is important to remember as well that the inclusion of Ezekiel, Daniel, and the Apocalypse simultaneously involved the exclusion of a vast body of other apocalyptic literature, Jewish and Christian. As a supposed divine revelation, an apocalypse imparts details of information concerning questions of ESCHATOLOGY, and it usually lays claim also to privileged information about the eschatological timetable. Some answer to the question of how to handle the apocalyptic elements in the revelation that is conveyed in the teaching of Jesus himself would seem to be demanded by the literary form of our Gospels, as a key to the interpretation of such central and cherished portions of the New Testament as the Sermon on the Mount and as an especially troubling test case of the genuineness and completeness of the human nature of Jesus Christ. The critical study of the Gospels in the twentieth century seems to have made it impossible ever again to dissociate "revelation" from "apocalypse," not only in etymology but in theology.

Even as apocalypse, however, revelation is not simply a message about future events; it is itself an event. Biblical religion set itself apart from other claims to revelation by its emphasis on history. It took the nature festivals of various nations, in which the changing of the seasons and other phenomena were thought to disclose MYSTERY, and made them into festivals commemorating the events of a historical revelation: Passover did not celebrate the coming of spring, but the Exodus from Egypt; Christmas was the observance not of the *Sol invictus* (Unconquered Sun) at the winter solstice, but of the birth of Christ. The God revealed in such events was present and active in nature and in other events, indeed in all the events of history, but had become knowable in those special acts to which a revelatory word was attached. Israel was seen as the chosen people of God, not by virtue of some moral superiority or cultural progress, but because the history of ZION had been selected to bear a particular revelation that was, in principle, universal. That historical particularity made biblical claims of revelation subject to the investigations of a critical historiography, whose skepticism about the historicity of the events that were believed to be revelatory was bound to affect the concept and the content of revelation.

Christianity inherited and appropriated the Jewish definition of revelation as event, but through the doctrine of the incarnation it added to this definition a special conception of revelation as person: "When in former times God spoke to our forefathers," the opening words of the Epistle to the Hebrews affirm, "he spoke in fragmentary and varied fashion through the prophets. But in the final age he has spoken to us in the Son." The revelation conveyed through the Son took several forms. As the author of Hebrews implies, Jesus was presented in the apostolic message as one who stood in the succession of the prophets of Israel, through whose sayings God was believed to have spoken. To this primitive Christian belief we owe the larger part of our Gospels—the parables, the sayings and discourses, and the Sermon on the Mount—in all of which Jesus as prophet and as rabbi communicated the word and will of God. Speaking on behalf of the life and proclamation of the early church, however, the writers of the Gospels went on from the teachings of Jesus to his deeds: the miracles in which the power and the compassion of God were made manifest, but above all the suffering, death, and resurrection of Christ. In its later doctrines of the atonement the church insisted that the gift of Good Friday and Easter had to be seen as redemption and grace, therefore as more than revelation; but it was never less than revelation. The most explicit language in the Gospels about the death of Christ as "ransom" and redemption (Matt. 20:28) came in the context of revealed moral instruction.

The prophetic message about revelation as event and the apostolic emphasis on revelation as person both interpreted revelation as the coming of the Word of God in person: "These are the words of the Lord to the men of Judah and Jerusalem," the prophet announced (Jer. 4:3); "the Word became flesh," continued the evangelist (John 1:14). As the word of God, revelation served as the explanation of the deeds of God in history, but it was also the medium for communicating the truth about the will and the nature of God. That biblical accent became the basis for a developing concentration on an understanding of revelation as the transmittal of doctrine. *O Timothee, depositum custodi!* (O Timothy, guard the deposit of the faith; I Tim. 6:20): this New Testament exhortation of the Vulgate was taken to mean that the revelation had taken the form of a heavenly doctrine, entrusted to the apostles and by them "handed on" (Latin *traditum*) as a holy tradition to their successors through the history of the church. At each stage in the development of doctrine, what the church now confessed as dogma was equated with that apostolic revelation of doctrine, and heresy was defined as the rejection of revealed truth. Although there have been some theologians who spoke about two sources of revelation, in Scripture and in non-Scriptural traditions, it has been the preponderant view that revelation ended with the last apostle and that the traditions of the church have been the means by which the church has made explicit the doctrine that had been present in Scripture all along.

Although each of these definitions of revelation has brought it into conflict with other systems, revelation as doctrine has been the concept that has most often occasioned such conflict throughout its history; for this is the definition that has figured in the conflicts over the relation of revelation and reason. In the patristic era, such conflicts were central to the thought of Origen, Augustine, and the Cappadocians, each of whom strove to give reason its due (enough of its due to bring upon them the charge of Hellenization from later theologians and historians), while affirming the finality of revealed truth. Their affirmation was the foundation on which Thomas Aquinas constructed his version of theology as SACRED SCIENCE, according to which revelation did not abolish reason, but perfected it. How much of a theological consensus those several views of revelation in the history of Christian thought represented, despite their pronounced differences, became evident during the critiques of the Enlightenment, when, for the first time, the very notion of revelation, howsoever defined, came into doubt. It was at least partly in response to those critiques that theologians reopened the question. Such typical twentieth-century book titles as *The Idea of Revelation in Recent Thought* and *The Meaning of Revelation* are an index of its continuing importance.

▪ Rome

It is customary to speak of "the primacy of Rome." But if it is at all legitimate to attribute something called "primacy" to any one place in the church of the first century, that place would have to be Jerusalem, where Jesus Christ had died and been raised from the dead and where all twelve of his apostles had exercised their ministries after receiving the Holy Spirit at Pentecost. Even Paul had to admit in the defense of his apostolicity to the Galatians, where he was intent on documenting the independence of his authority as an apostle from that of Peter and the others, that some years after his miraculous conversion he "did go up to Jerusalem to get to know Cephas [Peter]" (Gal. 1:18). But with the sack of Jerusalem by the Roman armies in 70 C.E., the early church not only made a decisive break with Israel, but also gravitated away from that Holy City toward another Holy City and a new center of primacy: "And so to Rome!" (Acts 28:14).

That dramatic phrase in the final chapter of the Acts of the Apostles reinforces the intuitive sense that the eventual primacy of Rome in Christendom was obvious, indeed almost inevitable. The medieval proverb, "All roads lead to Rome," merely stated what everyone in the West has believed for two millennia, that Rome is the capital of the civilized world. The primacy of the church of Rome is certainly a function of the unique status of the capital city itself, as the early usage of Christians both in Rome and elsewhere suggested. This basis for its primacy suddenly became problematical with the decision of Emperor Constantine I (d. 337) to move the capital of the Roman Empire from Rome to BYZANTIUM in 330 C.E. For if his new capital city of Constantinople was to be called "New Rome," as he decreed, this could be taken to mean that not only the political seat of empire but also the ecclesiastical primacy had been transferred. No one was to have the temerity to make that suggestion out loud for many centuries, but the attempts at early church councils in 381 and 451 to place the patriarchate of Constantinople alongside that of Rome "because it is the New Rome" did appear to base the authority of New Rome as well as that of Old Rome itself on political rather than religious criteria.

The spokesmen for Rome, only some of whom were also bishops of Rome, found those political criteria unacceptable, and from the beginning had been putting forth other grounds for Roman primacy. Principal among these was the unchallenged primacy of the apostle Peter. In the various lists of the apostles in the New Testament, his name always appears first; in the Gospels, he repeatedly assumes a leadership position; and although some of his other prerogatives are shared by all the apostles, it is to him alone that Jesus addresses the words, "You are Peter, the Rock; and on this rock I will build my church, and the powers of death shall never conquer it" (Matt. 16:18). Peter had been in Jerusalem and then in Antioch, but (despite the absence of his name from the catalogue of greetings sent by Paul to the church there, in the final chapter of the Epistle to the Romans) he was all but universally believed to have then come to Rome and to have died there. Rome became "the see of Peter," whose primacy in the church was acknowledged by every other see, including that of Constantinople. As history proved, transferring the capital of the Roman Empire to Constantinople actually strengthened Rome's claim to primacy in the church, because the bishop of Rome now became the natural heir to its aura: the title of Supreme Pontiff (*Pontifex Maximus*) had belonged to the emperors, but now it gradually devolved on the popes.

The special status of the church of Rome within the whole of Christendom likewise benefited from the jurisdictional and theological clashes between various parts of the church. In such a controversy, both sides would appeal their case to Rome, implicitly and often explicitly affirming its right as an appellate court to arbitrate between the parties—at least pending a final adjudication by an ecumenical council, in which Rome would of course take a (or the) leading part. Rome also managed to choose the "right" side, namely, the one that was eventually to be declared orthodox by the first four ecumenical councils (Nicea in 325, Constantinople in 381, Ephesus in 431, Chalcedon in 451), in the doctrinal controversies of the fourth, fifth, and sixth centuries. At the fourth ecumenical council, that of Chalcedon, the sometime bishop of Constantinople, Nestorius, was condemned, and Leo I, bishop of Rome (440–461), had supplied much of the decisive dogmatic language for the orthodox outcome; and the participants at the council were heard to declare: "Peter has spoken through the mouth of Leo!" The one major exception to this unchallenged track record of orthodoxy came in 681, when the sixth of the ecumenical councils of the church, held at Constantinople, condemned Pope Honorius I (625–638) for having taught that there were not two wills in the person of Christ, one divine and one human, but only a single will. Ever after, the case of Honorius would come up whenever, as at the First Vatican Council of 1869–1870, there was an attempt to claim not only primacy but infallibility for the see of Rome, and proponents of that claim would have to (and did) scramble to find explanations for the condemnation of Honorius.

The physical separation of the papacy from the city of Rome and its location at the French city of Avignon during the "Babylonian captivity of the church" from 1309 to 1377 was a prelude to widespread denunciation of its corruption. The title from the Apocalypse, "Babylon the great, the mother of whores and of every obscenity on earth" (Rev. 17:5), originally applied to the pagan city of Rome, was now transferred by late medieval advocates of reform to the Rome of the popes; and a loyal son of the church like Erasmus was a scathing critic of abuses within it. After their break with the authority of Rome, whether through its excommunication of them or their separation from it, most Protestant Reformers were convinced that the Pope was the fulfillment of the prophecies of the New Testament about the Antichrist (1 John 2:22–23) and the "wickedness revealed in human form, the man doomed to perdition"(2 Thess. 2:3). In addition, among many of those who sided with Rome against the Protestant Reformation, vigorous protest developed against the medieval centralization of authority. As formulated by the eminent historian and anti-Protestant apologist, Jacques Bénigne Bossuet (1627–1704), "Gallicanism" in the church of France was only the most clearly articulated statement of the widespread Catholic position that each national church should be allowed a large measure of local discretion, though always with the proviso that it keep itself doctrinally subject to the authority of the Apostolic See in Rome. With the codification of the principle of collegiality by the Second Vatican Council of 1962–1965—encapsulated in the slogan that the other bishops were to be joined "with Peter"—local discretion in liturgical and administrative areas did return in considerable measure to the national churches, again with the proviso that they were at the same time to remain "under Peter" in their doctrine and ecclesiastical obedience.

After these two millennia of almost unbroken continuity, the special status of Rome in the history of the church and of its teaching remains, to use the word of Christ to Peter, a "rock." But the debate is as heated as ever over whether this rock is, as the words inside the dome of Saint Peter's in Rome declare, the rock on which Christ has built his church, or a "stone to stumble against," over which honest seekers after truth will continue to trip whenever they try to enter the temple of God.

· Sacrament

The Greek word usually translated as "sacrament" is *mystērion;* yet nowhere in the New Testament does *mystērion* mean primarily what we now call "sacrament," and even *sacramentum* in patristic Latin is often better translated as "mystery." Individually and above all collectively, the sacraments not only bulk large in the history of Christian doctrine, but they also are an especially striking instance of the DEVELOPMENT OF DOCTRINE.

The concept of sacrament has been part of liturgical and theological thought for so long that we naturally assume it to be the starting point: identify the nature of a sacrament, specify the necessary components of its definition, and then you can decide how many sacraments (whether two or three or seven) there are. It is important for the understanding of the sacraments to recognize that in the New Testament and the early church the thought process moved in the opposite direction. Each of the sacred actions now identified as sacraments (whether two or three or seven) was considered in its own terms, and only very gradually did the relation between them produce a mature doctrine *de sacramentis in genere.* The statements of the New Testament about water and blood flowing from the side of the crucified Christ (John 19:34; 1 John 5:6) and about the typology of the water from the rock and of the manna during the Exodus of Israel from Egypt as "symbols to warn us" (1 Cor. 10:1–6) may originally have implied what they eventually came to mean in patristic and medieval exegesis, a coordination of BAPTISM and the EUCHARIST; if they did, they stood virtually alone in suggesting such a coordination, and the meaning of "sacrament" had to be worked out *a posteriori*.

According to the New Testament, Jesus instituted and commanded various practices, among them baptism, a common meal, the washing of feet, anointing, and the casting out of demons. Some of these were continued by Christians; some were dropped; some additional practices were adopted and attributed to the institution of Christ. Consideration of all these rites and ordinances led to the development of the concept of sacrament, but both the definition and the exact number remained fluid well beyond the end of the first millennium of church history. As finally set forth by Peter Lombard (ca. 1100–1160), codified by Thomas Aquinas, and promulgated by the seventh session of the Council of Trent on 3 March 1547, the sacraments were said to be seven in number (baptism, confirmation, Eucharist, penance, anointing or extreme unction, holy orders or ordination, and matrimony) and to be efficacious signs of the grace of God instituted by Christ for permanent observance by the church. The Reformation questioned both the definition and the number of the sacraments taught by the scholastics, as well as the use of the sacraments in medieval piety, liturgy, and churchmanship.

Two issues in sacramental theology have been unavoidable for all theologians regardless of their tradition. Everyone agreed that a sacrament involved the use of external means or signs, which scholastic theology called the "matter" of the sacrament: a physical element and the action of using that element. Theologians in the Platonic tradition—by whom the entire external world has been seen as a "sign" or "symbol" of the spiritual world, and for some of whom it seems to have been little more than that—have had very little difficulty regarding any of the seven sacraments as signs of the efficacious presence of God. Their problem has been to extricate these signs from the welter of symbols around them. For quite different reasons, the heirs of the Radical Reformation have also faced the issue of finding a qualitative distinction between the sacraments and other "signs," such as the cross. The Council of Trent proclaimed that "the sacraments of the New Testament contain the grace that they signify," instead of being "merely outward signs . . . and some sort of marks of the Christian profession"; this seemed to many critics, also within Roman Catholic theology, to underemphasize the role of the sacraments as signs of the personal reality of the presence of grace in the recipient.

The vigorous efforts of the proponents of each of these traditions to meet such objections are themselves worthy of note. Augustine transcended his Neoplatonic propensities to develop a theory of signs and sacraments, albeit one that was better equipped to deal with infant baptism than with the Eucharist, as the ninth-century controversies over his eucharistic doctrine were to show. Even very radical Protestants have treated baptism and the Eucharist with utmost seriousness (as Emerson was to discover when he announced that he did not regard Communion, even in its minimalist Unitarian observance, as a rite instituted by Jesus for permanent observance); much of the history of Roman Catholic sacramental theology from the Council of Trent to the Second Vatican Council has been marked by a combination of the traditional stress upon the sacraments as means of grace with a further clarification of the difference between this and any magical interpretation of the effect of the sacraments. The differences among Christians on this issue have remained profound and in many ways basic; no less significant, however, is the rapprochement between those Protestants who seek to avoid the rationalism of a theory of "mere symbols" and those Roman Catholics who seek to avoid the superstition of a theory of "efficacity apart from the disposition of the recipient."

Part of almost every definition of a sacrament has been the requirement that it have been, in some sense, instituted by Christ. Of the seven sacraments accepted by Eastern Orthodoxy and Roman Catholicism, such institution can be incontrovertibly documented from the New Testament only for baptism and the Eucharist; the very concept of institution as a criterion appears to have entered sacramental theology from the consideration of the Eucharist. The references to baptism in the sayings of Jesus (John 3:5; Matt. 28:19) seem to presuppose its prior existence, and there are no words of institution for it that correspond to the four versions of such words for the Eucharist (Matt. 26:26–29; Mark 14:22–25; Luke 22:17–19; 1 Cor. 11:23–26).

During the debates of the sixteenth and seventeenth centuries, the language of the New Testament was strained by both sides in an effort to prove that the historical Jesus really did, or really could not have, instituted matrimony, ordination, and so on as sacraments. Protestant biblical scholarship eventually came to recognize that even the accounts of the institution of the Eucharist by Christ are, in their present form at least, part of the tradition of the primitive Christian community rather than verbatim transcripts of the sayings of the historical Jesus. Roman Catholic theology likewise surrendered the effort to find explicit historical support for each of the seven sacraments in such sayings, and concentrated instead on the implicit significance of the very establishment of the church: those sacraments that do not appear as such in the Gospels were instituted by Christ in a "theological sense" when he founded the church and empowered it to become what it is, even though there is no way of proving that the historical Jesus instituted each of the eventual seven sacraments in a "historical sense." Baptism and the Eucharist are unquestionably primary for all theology. Was confirmation a necessary adjustment to the development of infant baptism, as a sacrament to incorporate the confession of faith and the beginning of adult responsibility that were originally a part of adult baptism? Was penance the answer of the church to sin after baptism, which the New Testament sometimes appeared to treat as beyond forgiveness (Heb. 6:4)? Such questions as these have made conventional debates obsolete, while at the same time putting the concerns of an earlier generation into a new light.

▪ Sacred Science

Theology is a disciplined reflection upon the truth of Christian REVELATION. The earliest uses of the word "theology" (*theologia*) in Greek referred to the critical interpretation of the classical myths—a sense that the word has sometimes had in Christian usage as well. Therefore the history of the term "theology," which has engaged the attention of scholars during the nineteenth and twentieth centuries, is, despite its interest, no reliable guide to that meaning of theology which Richard Hooker (ca. 1554–1600) had in mind when he called it "the science of things divine." In Thomas Aquinas, one of the common terms for theology was "sacred science." An age like our own, which has become accustomed, so rapidly and so completely, to the use of the term "science" exclusively for the empirical investigation of the data of the natural world—known until very recently as "natural philosophy"—finds the application of the term "science" to the area of religion anomalous or even quaint. Yet theology is fully entitled to be called scientific if by this one means that it has a prescribed function, a disciplined methodology, and a rational structure.

The two other disciplines with which Christian theology has most often been compared and contrasted are philosophy and HISTORIOGRAPHY. An obvious and common distinction between theology and philosophy is derived from the more basic distinction between reason (or experience) and revelation, or between nature and grace. Philosophy is a product of the natural reason and concerns the realms of reality that are accessible to reason; theology as "sacred science," on the other hand, is charged with the interpretation of a truth that is said to have been revealed supernaturally. Thomas Aquinas put the distinction succinctly: "There is no reason why those things which are treated by the philosophical sciences, in so far as they can be known by the light of natural reason, may not also be treated by another science in so far as they are known by the light of the divine revelation. Hence the theology included in sacred doctrine differs in genus from that theology which is part of philosophy."

But the very theology of Thomas Aquinas shows that this formal distinction between the tasks of philosophy and of theology does not prevent a theologian from interpreting the data of revelation in a particular way because of a prior commitment to a particular philosophy. Dealing as it does with the nature of being and the rules of human thought, philosophy affects the work of the theologian throughout any system of Christian doctrine (and there were philosophical systems before there were theological systems of Christian doctrine). Therefore Christian theology has not been able to avoid philosophy even when it wanted to; although Tertullian (ca. 160–ca. 225) and Luther denounced the incursion of philosophy into Christian thought as a perversion, both found themselves obliged to draw upon philosophical sources for their own expositions of Christian thought. Conversely, even the most philosophically inclined theologians have been unable to bend the facts of Christian revelation into total conformity with their metaphysics; for Christianity as a history, as a proclamation, and as a sacramental life has refused to become completely malleable even in the hands of ancient Neoplatonists or modern Hegelians. An awareness that the HELLENIZATION of Christianity had resulted when theologians were overly attentive to the claims of philosophy (whether they recognized and admitted it or not) has caused Christian thought in the nineteenth and twentieth centuries to tie the work of theology more closely to that of history. When Schleiermacher defined dogmatic theology as "the science which systematizes the doctrine prevalent in a Christian church at a given time," he made the task of the dogmatic theologian primarily a historical one, namely, to determine the doctrines that are prevalent and then to reflect upon them in a systematic fashion.

The very concentration of Christian theology upon revelation—the account of God's dealing with the world through the history of Israel, through the incarnation of Jesus Christ, and through the establishment and development of the church—makes it a historical discipline. Yet the outcome of the historical preoccupation of theology has raised some fundamental questions about the propriety of identifying it so closely with historical SCHOLARSHIP. For historical scholarship has the result of making its data relative—relative to the processes of research themselves and relative to the age and culture in which the data occurred. Historical study of the Bible, for example, has related central elements of the creed, such as the virgin birth and the ascension of Christ, to the religious and mythological conceptions of the ancient world. The outcome has been to discredit the biblical narratives in the eyes of many, and even those who continue to regard the narratives as basically trustworthy have learned to recognize the historically conditioned character of biblical language and imagery. A simplistic equation of theology as "sacred science" with the science of historiography is an absurdity.

Equally absurd is the assertion that because theology does not conform to either philosophy or history it is fundamentally irrational and intuitive, more akin to poetry or song than to the orderly work of the intellect. As a protest against the excessive intellectualism of some theologians or of some periods in history, such a "theology of the heart" makes a valid point, but it is incapable of going on to do the work of theology, which is then assigned by default to other disciplines—especially, and not surprisingly, to philosophy and history. Ironically, the Pietist attack upon theology in the name of true religion may bring on the loss not only of theology as "sacred science" but also of "true religion." Conversely, a scientific theology that knows its limits and that is open to the discipline that philosophy, history, philology, and other sciences can provide for it, even as it pays primary attention and yields fundamental loyalty to the data of revelation, may serve the cause of the "religion of the heart" more faithfully than does the anti-intellectualism of the enthusiast.

• Schleiermacher, Friedrich Daniel Ernst (1768–1834)

Translator of Plato into German, Romantic apologist for religion to "the cultured among its despisers," and the most influential Protestant theologian since the Reformation.

Romanticism has been defined by a perceptive contemporary interpreter, René Wellek, as "that attempt, apparently doomed to failure and abandoned by our time, to identify subject and object, to reconcile man and nature, consciousness and unconsciousness by poetry which is 'the first and last of all knowledge.'" Earlier Wellek had observed that "Romanticism was more completely victorious in Germany than elsewhere." Although Wellek does not refer to him by name, Schleiermacher could well be taken as a textbook case of the definition, with the added stipulation that by the term "poetry" in the quotation from William Wordsworth (1770–1850) with which the definition closes, Schleiermacher (and perhaps Wordsworth himself) would have meant something like Christian poetic theology or a Christian theological poetics, as the force that integrates the antithetical pairs of subject and object, man and nature, consciousness and unconsciousness. Schleiermacher's Christian theology redefined his Romantic poetry as profoundly as his Romanticism shaped—and, in the judgment of his critics ever since, corrupted—his interpretation of the meaning of the Christian faith.

Schleiermacher burst upon the literary and intellectual scene just as the eighteenth century was ending, with *On Religion: Addresses to the Cultured among Its Despisers* (*Über die Religion: Reden an die Gebildeten unter ihren Verächtern*), published in Berlin in 1799. Like Emerson's first book, *Nature,* which was to be published in 1836, Schleiermacher's was anonymous. Nor is that the only point of resemblance. Both books were appeals by clergymen beyond the borders of the institutional church. One difference between them was that Schleiermacher remained a churchman all his life, putting his academic theology to the ultimate test of the pulpit and the pew, whereas Emerson resigned from the active ministry of the Unitarian Church and did his preaching through lectures and books. Although he did not try to hide his profession in the *Addresses,* Schleiermacher explicitly dissociated himself from conventional religiosity and even morality, reaching out to the poetic sensibilities of his readers as to a MELODY that was more genuinely religious than run-of-the-mill religion. "What you worship but do not know—this is what I now proclaim": this appeal of Paul to the Athenians (Acts 17:23), echoed by Christian apologists since Origen and even earlier, now became an affirmation of the sensitivity to nature and yearning for the Transcendent, which was being expressed by the aesthetes of the Romantic era, despite (or even because of) their hostility to the church. Then, by a series of transitions, he brought his statement of the case for religion back to the church, which needed "the cultured among its despisers" at least as much as they needed it.

So scintillating has been the effect of *On Religion* that the estimate of Schleiermacher's place in the history of theology has tended to be unduly dominated by this work of his youth. Not only did he heavily revise it in subsequent editions; but his appointment to the theological faculty of the newly founded university at Berlin made it possible and necessary for him to lecture on all the major fields of theology, which is said to have evoked from one of his colleagues the comment that he was carrying on his private education in public. Even in a discipline as seemingly remote from his tastes as church history he made substantial contributions. Those who dismiss him as a Romantic (and who regard that as a way of dismissing someone) have often forgotten that he possessed sufficient mastery of languages to carry out the translation of Plato from Greek into German. In the process of studying the problem of the historical Socrates, he became, as Werner Jaeger (1888–1961) says, "the first to express the full complexity of this historical problem in a single condensed question." Philological training enabled him also to be among the first to raise questions about the authorship of the pastoral Epistles. One of his principal contributions to scholarship was the refinement of the methodology of HERMENEUTICS, setting the lines of discussion for much of the nineteenth century.

But Schleiermacher's most important theological work was his systematic theology, *The Christian Faith* (*Der christliche Glaube*), which first appeared in 1821–1822. The *Glaubenslehre*, as it came to be called, set itself off from most books of dogmatics through the author's overt desire to make an ecumenical statement, albeit from an unabashedly Protestant perspective; Schleiermacher was speaking here in the name of the union of Lutheran and Reformed churches that had been consummated in Prussia. Discontinuities as well as continuities with his earlier apologetics were evident in this work. The principal continuity lay in the definition of religion as "a feeling of utter dependence" (*schlechthinnige Abhängigkeit*), from which all other affirmations, whether dogmatic or moral, were to be derived. That definition enabled Schleiermacher to propose that every doctrine could be described in relation not only to the sources of revelation or to divine attributes, as had traditionally been done in systematic theology, but to the experience and self-consciousness of the believer. Far more than he had earlier, he related that experience to the corporate expressions of the faith of the church, as set down in the creeds and confessions both of the universal church and of the Protestant Reformation, whether Lutheran or Calvinist. His critics questioned the sincerity, and denied the reliability, of these appeals to authority, seeing them as a cover for pantheist or even ATHEIST/AGNOSTIC beliefs that the author was afraid to espouse. Yet even they could not deny the power of thought and language in this highly idiosyncratic statement of Christian dogma.

Perhaps the best way to decide whether the thought and work of any theologian should be called "epoch-making" is to measure its use not only by his disciples but by his detractors in succeeding generations. Measured by that criterion, Schleiermacher and *The Christian Faith* must certainly qualify. It seems safe to say that most of the major Protestant theologians of the nineteenth and twentieth centuries, on the right or on the left, have taken the thought of Schleiermacher as a point of departure: the left moved toward a philosophical or psychological subjectivism that put the particularity of Christian teaching behind and transformed theology into the philosophy of religion, while the right substituted an "organic" concept of the church's self-consciousness for the self-consciousness of the individual. Such a characterization of Schleiermacher's importance would apply in the first instance only to German-speaking (or German-reading) Protestant theologians. *On Religion* was known in English in the nineteenth century, but the full text of *The Christian Faith* did not appear in English translation until a full century after its original publication. Other and far lesser German theologians were translated into English during their lifetimes, sometimes in multivolume works, but Schleiermacher was not. The lag is all the more surprising in light of the profound affinities between the outlook of the *Glaubenslehre* and the emphasis on experience in the theology and worship of Anglo-Saxon Protestantism. One can only speculate—it is almost irresistible to do so—about what would have ensued from a confrontation between Schleiermacher and his far younger contemporary, JOHN HENRY NEWMAN, who shared so much and yet so little. No such confrontation took place in person, but it has repeatedly taken place in the work of those who are more deeply in debt to these two than to any other theologians of the nineteenth century.

• Scholarship

The Jewish scholar and philosopher Gershon Scholem (1897–1982) was one of the most rational of men; yet his research dealt not only with *Major Trends in Jewish Mysticism* (the title of his best-known book, which considered the specific forms of the mystical in Jewish spirituality) but with the apocalyptic speculations of Jewish eschatology, some of which, like their Christian counterparts, could be fairly wild. When Professor Scholem was once asked about this anomaly, he replied (in an epigram whose original authorship is disputed among his colleagues): "Nonsense is always nonsense, but the history of nonsense is scholarship."

A lifetime of research into the history of Christian thought has also uncovered a substantial amount of nonsense. At one council, a Byzantine monk was so confident of the correctness of his doctrine of the incarnation that he prayed God to vindicate his orthodoxy by raising the body of a colleague who had died during the council; we are solemnly informed in the *Acta* of the council that the prayer remained unanswered. Over and over during the Second World War, Protestant Evangelicals recited incidents in which a soldier's life was saved when a pocket New Testament stopped a bullet (which could, presumably, have been stopped also by a copy of *Das Kapital*). Without multiplying such anecdotes unnecessarily, it should perhaps be added that the history of nonsense, too, is an ecumenical phenomenon. Yet it would be difficult to imagine a lifetime of research on the history of theology and of religion whose scholarship was only "the history of nonsense." For that matter, *Major Trends in Jewish Mysticism* provides brilliant and irrefutable evidence that Professor Scholem did not confine his own scholarship to nonsense either.

If anything, the opposite danger—of using scholarship as an escape from responsibility—seems to have been more of a temptation. Considering the careers of such figures as ADOLF VON HARNACK, Karl Barth (1886–1968) once observed astutely that the nineteenth century presented "the not altogether edifying spectacle of a flight of the very best brains into history" away from theology, because the manipulation of historical sources permitted them to theologize furiously and yet to hide behind all those footnotes. As Søren Kierkegaard (1813–1855) once put it, it was for One to be crucified, but for others to become professors of the fact that that One had been crucified. In the twentieth century, too, the lure of becoming a theological scholar can appear to be a substitute for taking a stand, even when (as in the Nazi period, but not only in the Nazi period) the existence of everything sacred is at stake. Measured against the ministry and martyrdom of Dietrich Bonhoeffer (1906–1945), author of *The Cost of Discipleship,* for example, scholarship can appear to be an evasion of moral and political responsibility, the ultimate ivory tower. As a brilliant graduate student Bonhoeffer had been chosen to speak the farewell on behalf of the students to Adolf von Harnack, upon his retirement and again at his funeral, and his future was bright. Yet he gave up a promising career in research and teaching to serve Christ and the church in the battle against Antichrist, and he paid for this commitment with his life when he was executed for his part in a conspiracy to assassinate Adolf Hitler.

It does not appear extreme to urge that no one has a moral right to the scholarly life in any discipline, above all in theology, who has not faced with utmost seriousness the decision between the scholarly *vita contemplativa* and the existential *vita activa.* During the Pietist period, Gilbert Tennent (1703–1764) spoke about "the danger of an unconverted ministry." When applied to theological scholarship, this question took the form of an inquiry into the possibility of a "theology of the unregenerate" (*theologia irregenitorum*): Was it necessary for a theologian to have had a personal experience of regenerating grace in order to understand the message of the Bible or the teachings of the church from within? Pietism was an attack on the established churches and their professional scholarly élites for having ignored the seriousness of that question. Yet to answer the question in the negative, as most theological scholars then and since have done—and properly so—is to define scholarship in theology as a vocation that has its own technical autonomy and to insist on the analogies between theological scholarship and empirical scholarship in history, philology, or other supposedly objective disciplines. When theological scholarship in the UNIVERSITY is evaluated by criteria that can also be applied to history or philology, the distinctiveness of the theological task and the centrality of the church to it may easily be forfeited.

The question of the apostle Paul, "Where is your wise man

now, your man of learning, or your subtle debater—limited, all of them, to this passing age?" (1 Cor. 1:20) may be read, and often has been, as an attack on the pretensions of the learned and on the tyranny of scholarship in the theology of the church. Yet only the most reactionary would deny that theology and the church as we know them are unthinkable without the activity of scholars: even to decide that the Greek word *grammateus* in that question may be translated "man of learning" requires a measure of lexicographical learning. And when, as for many earlier centuries in the Latin West (and again now), there have been "theologians" who were not in a position to make their own responsible scholarly judgments about the languages of Scripture and theology, it has been necessary for them and their churchly theology to be rescued by scholarship—the dry-as-dust (and sometimes not very pious) philological scholarship of those who, in the words of "A Grammarian's Funeral" by Robert Browning (1812–1889),

> settled *Hoti*'s business—let it be!—
> Properly based *Oun*—
> Gave us the doctrine of the enclitic *De*,
> Dead from the waist down.

Although such scholarship may not be what the church and its theologians want, it can be what they need. And when the institutional church fails to recognize that, the scholarship will be cultivated elsewhere—as it often has been throughout modern history. The price has been a concentration of scholars on problems of research that appear individually important to them rather than on the problems of immediate (or even long-range) concern to the life and message of the church, as well as the development of a scholarly methodology that may be more appropriate to secular concerns than to the doctrines of the church.

Conversely, it is also useful to be reminded that the institutional church often has, and at considerable sacrifice, given priority in the use of its own resources and manpower to scholarly projects and has supported them generously, without seeking to dictate how they were supposed to turn out. Because of such support for scholarly clerics, Edward Gibbon, for all his hatred of monks, had to acknowledge his debt to their tireless scholarship, on which he relied for the very data with which he attacked the church for its pride and oppression. And speaking of pride, scholars for their part have not always been known for modesty in relation to the church and its prelates either. When N. F. S. Grundtvig (1783–1872) denounced "the papacy of the biblical scholar," he was referring to the prestige and authority of professors who, exercising their own version of infallibility, felt qualified to pass highly individualistic judgments on questions over which the tradition of the church had been brooding for centuries—and who then proceeded to hurl an anathema against anyone who taught otherwise. In a special category are those who began by devoting their lives to theological scholarship and who suddenly had ecclesiastical responsibility thrust upon them; LUTHER, NEWMAN, and SÖDERBLOM have at least this in common. The suspicion of their new colleagues in the church has often been matched by the disappointment of their former colleagues in the world of scholarship, and the case study of their intellectual and theological consistency before and after their relocation has fascinated their biographers.

• Sermon on the Mount

The collection of the words of Jesus in the fifth, sixth, and seventh chapters of the Gospel of Matthew is usually called the "Sermon on the Mount"; the "Sermon on the Plain" in Luke 6:20–49 provides many parallels with it, as well as significant contrasts.

Most scholars today would probably agree that in its present form (or forms) the sermon is not the transcript of any one sermon delivered by Jesus, but a compilation of many sayings. It is not, however, a random compilation. Opening with the

Beatitudes, which in the history of interpretation have had a life of their own—among the Cappadocians, for example, they are the subject of a special discourse by Gregory of Nyssa—the Sermon on the Mount proceeds to a series of discourses of instruction and warning to the disciples. It also contains the Lord's Prayer, which in Luke's Gospel (Luke 11:1–4) appears in response to the disciples' request, "Lord, teach us to pray, as John [the Baptist] taught his disciples," but which here is incorporated into a longer discourse about the distinction between vain and authentic prayer. With the rise of interest in the concrete situation or *Sitz im Leben* of GOSPEL sayings within the history of the early Christian community, scholars have connected individual passages of the Sermon on the Mount to specific situations in the ancient church; thus the addition of the words "for the cause of right" and "for my sake" to the Beatitudes (Matt. 5:10–11) about suffering persecution have been taken as a warning that not all persecution was *eo ipso* blessed, and the admonition "not to make a show of your religion" (Matt. 6:1) as a critique of the formalistic Christianity that developed in the next generations as well as of the Pharisaic Judaism which it appears to address.

Whatever its origin and purpose, the Sermon on the Mount has been the object of repeated expositions, many of them in the form of "sermons on the Sermon"; two of the most influential among these were delivered by AUGUSTINE in the early years of his priesthood and by LUTHER in 1530–1532. Naturally, it has also received close attention as part of full-length commentaries on the Gospel of Matthew as a whole, the earliest preserved of these being the *Homilies on the Gospel of Saint Matthew* delivered at Antioch around 390 by John Chrysostom (ca. 347–407). Into modern times, the Sermon on the Mount has continued to evoke special interest not alone among professional theologians and biblical scholars but among serious believers of every persuasion. Thus L. N. Tolstoy (1828–1910), as part of his campaign to replace Russian Orthodoxy with the authentic religion of Jesus, devoted polemical and theological writings to an exposition of its literal applicability in everyday life, but also discussed it at length in his novel of 1899, *Resurrection,* which can be read as a series of radical glosses on the Sermon on the Mount, written in defense of Russian sectarians against persecution by the Orthodox Church. A history of the interpretation of the Sermon on the Mount throughout the past two millennia would virtually amount to an introduction to the entire development of Christian theology and ethics.

Consideration of the Sermon on the Mount has repeatedly provided theologians with the occasion for a discussion of the relation between the Old and the New Testament and, more generally, of the relation of the Christian Church to the Jewish people. Over and over in his treatise against Marcion, the second-century heretic who denied the authority of the Old Testament, Tertullian (160–ca. 225) quoted the words from the Sermon on the Mount: "Do not suppose that I have come to abolish the law and the prophets; I did not come to abolish, but to complete" (Matt. 5:17). Yet in the text those words stand as the introduction to an entire series of contrapuntal statements (Matt. 5:21–48), in which what "our forefathers were told" in the law of Moses is followed by a magisterial "But what I tell you is this." The sermon as a whole is followed immediately by the invidious comparison that "unlike their own teachers he taught with a note of authority" (Matt. 7:29). Patristic interpreters such as Chrysostom and Augustine concluded from all of this that Jesus was restoring the correct and original meaning of the Old Testament, which had been corrupted by the later developments of Judaism; despite occasional echoes of a Marcionite antithesis between the two Testaments, Luther usually agreed with that interpretation. But more heterodox interpreters like Tolstoy, as well as those in the evangelical tradition of the Radical Reformation, explained the Sermon on the Mount as the epitome of the "new law" or "evangelical law" that Christ had come to teach.

Because of his emphasis on the contrast between the law and the gospel, Luther was uncomfortable with such terms as "new law" and "evangelical law," despite their patristic and even biblical precedent. Because the distinction between the law and the gospel was, for Luther, not tantamount to the distinction between the Old Testament and the New Testament (there being both law and gospel, by his definition, in each), he read the Sermon on the Mount, at least at one level, as the supreme instance within the teachings of Jesus of the absolute demands of the law, raised to a high standard of perfection that was obviously beyond reach. When Christ demanded avoidance not merely of adultery but of sexual desire, not merely of murder but of anger, this was not intended to describe the life of Christian discipleship under the conditions of historical existence. Rather, in keeping with his doctrine of justification by faith, Luther insisted that by such demands Christ was seeking to make the hearer recognize the impossibility of such perfection and the need for grace. Luther's commentary was also a vigorous polemic against the fundamental assumptions of monasticism. During much of Christian history, as obiter dicta in the commentaries of Chrysostom and Augustine suggest, the demands for perfection had been dealt with by stratifying the divine commandments into those that were binding on all believers, summarized in the Decalogue (Ex. 20:3–17), and those "evangelical counsels" or "counsels of perfection," above all absolute poverty and total chastity, that could be obeyed only by those who had received a special gift.

The radical rediscovery of the ESCHATOLOGY of the Gospels in the New Testament criticism of the nineteenth and twentieth centuries proposed a drastically different method of coping with this troublesome perfectionism. Luther had been right in urging that it was not meant to be a commonsensical guide to everyday living, but he had not seen that it was instead a set of instructions for the Messianic community on how to live during the brief interval between the first and the second comings of the Son of Man, an "interim ethic." Only after the expectation of the second coming had been disappointed was it necessary to remove the message of the Sermon from its eschatological context and try to find its relevance to a world that was not about to end. When the radical eschatological reading of the Sermon on the Mount was in its heyday and students of theology in the generation of Martin Luther King (1929–1968) coming out of a variety of seminaries were struggling to find its possible bearing upon their own life and ministry, he said, "my mind, consciously or unconsciously, was driven back to the Sermon on the Mount, with its sublime teachings on love, and to the Gandhian method of nonviolent resistance." The Sermon on the Mount, illumined by the life and teachings of Mahatma Gandhi (1869–1948), who had in turn been a disciple of Tolstoy, became King's program and the basis for a new summons to the social and individual imperatives of authentic discipleship.

By that time, the Sermon on the Mount had been used for an astonishing variety of purposes. Constantine I (d. 337), after the Christian takeover of the Roman Empire, saw it as Christ's "invitation to the practice of virtue." Gregory of Nyssa read it as a way to set forth a Neoplatonic theory of forms. Beginning with Chrysostom for Eastern monasticism and Augustine for Western monasticism, it was a description of the true "evangelical life" of the monks. On the basis of it, Luther preached the proper distinction between law and gospel, Tolstoy called the Russian Orthodox Church to judgment, and Gandhi challenged the authority of the British Empire. In the light of this history, it is difficult to imagine circumstances to which this resilient document could not speak.

▪ Sin

"The real trouble with our times," Étienne Gilson once observed, "is not the multiplication of sinners, it is the disappearance of sin." He was, unfortunately, speaking not only— not even primarily—about the opponents of the Christian message, but about its professed adherents and even its professional expositors. The gospel of self-acceptance and of "feeling good about yourself," which once could be thought of as characteristic of Enlightenment thought and of theologians infected by it, can now be proclaimed by popular evangelists and pastoral counselors (many of whom would characterize themselves as "conservative" or "Evangelical" in their theology) as the authentic meaning of the Christian faith.

For this moralistic confusion the churches have, in many ways, only themselves to blame. In their diagnosis of the human condition and their denunciation of evil, they have so often concentrated on the "sins of the flesh" that in popular parlance—exemplified by such a phrase as "living in sin"—sexual transgressions dominate, or even define, the understanding of human sinfulness. From the evidence of the Gospels the definition of sin in the teaching of Jesus is quite different. One of the most remarkable bits of such evidence is made all the more forceful by its questionable textual status. As scholarly study of the text of the New Testament has shown, the narrative of "the woman seized in adultery" (*pericope adulteriae*), which usually appears as John 8:3–11, has wandered around the manuscripts of the Gospels; it is printed in *The New English Bible* as an appendix to the Fourth Gospel. In this familiar incident, a woman apprehended in adultery flagrante delicto is dragged before Jesus by his adversaries, who demand to know whether the capital punishment set down in the Mosaic law (Lev. 20:10) should be carried out. Jesus replies, "That one of you who is faultless shall throw the first stone," and one by one her accusers disappear, until there is no one left to condemn her. "Nor do I condemn you," Jesus says to her. "You may go; do not sin again." From what we know of the church in the second century it is difficult to imagine that such a story could simply have been made up: then as now, there were "faultless" people aplenty in the church who were ready to do their Christian duty by throwing the first stone. The pericope did not find a definite place as the Gospels were being assembled and fixed, but it could not quite be discarded either. The very absence of textual attestation would seem to be, in a curious way, evidence of its authenticity as a *logion tou Kyriou*, a "saying of the Lord."

The theologians who have contributed most to the development of the Christian doctrine of sin have been those whose own experience has compelled them to come to terms with its power:

above all, perhaps, PAUL, AUGUSTINE, and LUTHER. Each of these had come to recognize through intense personal struggle the tyrannical hold that pride and self-will could exercise over him, and each had learned that it was a snare and a delusion to suppose that instruction or exhortation was sufficient to break that tyranny. Beyond any moralistic catalogue of evil deeds was rebellion against God; for according to the psalm, when David repented of his sins of adultery and murder, he was moved to confess to God: "Against thee, thee only, I have sinned and done what displeases thee" (Ps. 51:4). As the use of that psalm in various formulas of confession suggests, the acknowledgement of sin became a prerequisite to forgiveness. In the medieval sacrament of penance three steps came to be distinguished: contrition over the sin as a sin against God; confession of the sin to a priest qualified to pronounce the absolution; and restitution or "satisfaction" rendered to those who had been aggrieved by the sin, that is, to God and to the person against whom the sin had been committed. The last of these steps was the origin of the practice of indulgences, by which the penitent was able to obtain remission of the temporal penalty for sin. Although the abuse of indulgences provoked Luther's public attack and caused him to reject the penitential system, he did retain the sequence of contrition, confession, and absolution as the steps through which God granted salvation and forgiveness to the sinner; he even called absolution a "sacrament." That sequence was likewise retained in catechisms and systematic theologies, both Roman Catholic and Protestant.

The inherent logic of the sequence makes it all the more surprising that historically the doctrine of sin and the doctrine of salvation should have developed in the reverse order. Throughout the second, third, and fourth centuries (and well beyond), theology was engaged in probing the content and the implications of what had happened in Christ. The doctrines of the Trinity and of the incarnation dominated the controversies, and almost every early heresy was in some way connected to those doctrines. It was only after the councils of Nicea in 325 and of Constantinople in 381 had settled the Trinity as dogma, and the process of defining the doctrine of the person of Christ, which was to achieve definitive formulations at the councils of Ephesus in 431 and of Chalcedon in 451, was well along, that doctrinal attention turned to clarification of the doctrine of sin. Seemingly the church had first to identify the cure before it could diagnose the nature of the illness. When it did so, a clinching argument was the practice of infant baptism, which by then was universally accepted. If infants were to be baptized, so the reasoning ran, and if baptism was "for the forgiveness of sins" (Mark 1:4), which sins could it forgive in someone who had not yet had the opportunity to commit sin?

In part, this inversion of the logical sequence was a function of the personal religious development of Augustine as documented in his *Confessions*. As has often happened in the development of doctrine, his opponents, eventually condemned as heretics, were holding to formulations of the doctrine of sin that had been appropriate and orthodox earlier, when the defense of free will had been the primary need, but that were now being superseded. Against them he argued that if every person were morally neutral and confronted the same choice that Adam and Eve had, it was difficult to account for the regularity with which every person made the same choice that Adam and Eve had made—unless there were an innate proclivity in that direction. More profoundly and more generally, however, the development of the doctrine of sin indicates that alienation from God could not be confronted in all its magnitude and horror until it could be viewed in the light of the cross.

That suggests, in turn, that the doctrine of sin has proved to be too hot to handle when the doctrines of incarnation and salvation have, for whatever reason, lost their specificity and power. One of the most forceful modern reformulations of the Christian doctrine of sin, in the first volume of the Gifford Lectures of Reinhold Niebuhr entitled *The Nature and Destiny of Man,* states the paradoxes and conflicts of human nature so eloquently that the corresponding discussion of human destiny in the second volume seems pale by comparison. In much of contemporary literature and drama, more perhaps than in theology, the Augustinia.ı awareness of sin and of demonic EVIL has found clear expression. Less clear, whether in literature or in theology, is the Augustinian awareness of salvation. By a curious reversal of polarity, a gospel that had been criticized by the Enlightenment as excessively gloomy in its estimate of human capacity is now often criticized as excessively rosy in its estimate of human destiny. In both circumstances the temptation has been to adjust the message to suit the zeitgeist. Conversely, Gilson's complaint about "the disappearance of sin" points to the continuing need for the development of doctrine to rehearse the tradition faithfully and yet to find within it the resources for change.

• Slavs

As a consequence of the awakening of national consciousness toward the end of the Middle Ages and its reawakening in the nineteenth century, many nations have reflected on what makes them distinctive, often in self-deprecating ways (as when Luther spoke about his bibulous countrymen as *die vollen, tollen Deutschen*) but also with serious attention to the special quirks of national development, perhaps even of "national character," that have contributed to their special place in the history of culture. The peculiarities of languages frequently occupy a special place in such reflection, especially when it has been necessary to defend the national language against those deemed to be its enemies foreign and domestic, which included at various times colonialism, linguistic snobbery, and the Latin Mass. The role played by Christianity both in the establishment of national identity and in the codification of language has given an additional theme to the debate over national character, as in quite different ways the phenomena of the German Christians in the Nazi period and of the Americanist heresy in nineteenth-century Roman Catholicism demonstrated.

The special Slavic forms of this reflection go back to the way

Christianity came to the Slavs. Although it was through Christianization that various of European nations such as the Germans were united, the Slavs were divided by becoming Christian. When the "apostles to the Slavs," Cyril (826–869) and Methodius (ca. 815–885), brought the gospel to the Greater Moravian Empire from BYZANTIUM, they brought with it the characteristic belief of Eastern Christianity that each nation was to carry on the worship of God in its own language; therefore they translated the Bible and the Divine Liturgy into Slavonic, devising for it the first Slavic alphabet (which was apparently not the Cyrillic alphabet, despite its attribution to Cyril, but the Glagolitic). Meanwhile there had already been some mission work among the Western Slavs by monks coming from the Franks in the Carolingian period, but this had consisted in the introduction of the Latin Mass together with the authority of the Apostolic See.

The two ways of worship came into conflict already during the lifetime of Cyril and Methodius, and the case was quite naturally appealed to the supreme court in Rome. It was eventually resolved, and the Slavs were compelled to choose between two ways of following Cyril and Methodius: those who followed them in adhering to Rome (for example, Poles, Croats, Slovenians, Czechs, Slovaks) received the Latin Mass and became Roman Catholic; but those who followed Cyril and Methodius in the use of the Slavonic liturgy (including Russians, Ukrainians, Serbs) retained their ties with Constantinople and became Eastern Orthodox. This occurred just at the time when, in the conflict between Pope Nicholas I (d. 867) and Patriarch Photius (ca. 810–ca. 895), Rome and Constantinople were drifting apart.

Ever since the ninth century, Slavs have been seeking to come to terms with the reality of this division. The sheer statistical preponderance of the Orthodox Slavs has repeatedly meant that the awareness of being a Slav has necessitated a clarification of one's relation to Slavic Orthodoxy and therefore to Russia. Johann Gottfried Herder (1744–1803) in his *Ideen zur Geschichte der Menschheit* stimulated the growth of "Pan-Slavism" in the nineteenth century, and with it the awareness of Orthodoxy as a possible way of reuniting what history had put asunder. Some Slavs have striven to have it both ways: Ukrainian Catholics have, often with opposition from both East and West, sought to be Eastern in worship and if possible in polity, while maintaining or recovering union with the Holy See.

• Sobornost'

There are comparatively few Slavic words in the current vocabulary of English. One of them is "robot," which, by way of Karel Čapek's *R.U.R.*, is derived from the word *robota* (work). Apparently related to the Slavic word *grom* (thunder), the universally recognizable term "pogrom" is a reminder that the roots of antisemitism within Christendom know no ethnic or national boundaries. The slightly precious word "kudos" (a singular, by the way) seems to be connected with the Slavic root for "wonder" or "miracle," *čud.* Because of Russian scientific leadership in the study of soils, many of the technical terms from that research have been Anglicized. And everyone knows the meaning of *trojka* or *sputnik.*

There is, however, one Slavic word that has found its way into the theological vocabulary of the twentieth century: the attribute of the church that Russian theology refers to as *sobornost'.* *Sobornaja* appears in the Church Slavonic version of the Nicene Creed as a rendering of the Greek *katholikē,* which is of course the same as the English word "catholic." Just how early that term came to be used in the Slavonic text of the creed is a matter of some debate. The Russian theologian and literary critic A. S. Chomjakov (1804–1860) maintained that it had appeared very early, but his view is contested by others. Because the word for "church council" is *sobor,* the term served to express the insistence of Eastern Christendom, in opposition to theories of papal monarchy, that it was not one apostolic see, not even the see of Rome, but all of the sees together, in ecumenical council assembled, that had the right to legislate on behalf of the entire church. The church, then, was "catholic" if it adhered to the universal tradition set down by an ecumenical *sobor*.

The domestication of *sobornost'* in the theological vocabulary of the Western churches during the period between the two world wars was an outgrowth of the ECUMENICAL movement, and specifically of the deepening participation of Eastern theologians and churchmen in its deliberations. The Bolshevik Revolution had caused a considerable emigration of Russian intellectuals, including theologians, to such Western centers as Prague and Paris, eventually also to the United States. Eastern Christian philosophers such as N. S. Berdyaev (1874–1948), who wrote chiefly in French, became a significant force in the West. But in 1925, thanks in great measure to the pioneering vision of NATHAN SÖDERBLOM, the Ecumenical Patriarch of Constantinople was persuaded to attend the Universal Conference on Life and Work held at Stockholm. That conference was an ecumenical milestone, and ever since, despite occasional setbacks of Eastern or Western provocation, the Eastern Orthodox presence has represented a tertium quid in ecumenical discussions. Specifically, in the doctrine of the church it has come to be seen as a way out of the false dilemma posed by the conflict between Roman Catholic institutionalism, which was in danger of equating the church with a particular historical structure, and Protestant individualism or idealism, which was in danger of making the church into an abstraction or an afterthought. For by its emphasis on tradition as a living reality, Eastern Orthodox ecclesiology made the church visible, but visible as an article of faith.

For all of those emphases and the contribution they seemed to bring to the ecclesiological impasse that has gripped Western theology since the Reformation, *sobornost'* has become a welcome addition to the theological vocabulary of several Western languages—even if that soft "t" at the end is almost never sounded by any non-Slavic tongue.

• Söderblom, Nathan (1866–1931)

Historian of religions, Swedish archbishop, Nobel laureate, and ECUMENICAL pioneer.

It was said of Nathan Söderblom that he could be "a Catholic at the altar, an Evangelical in the pulpit, and a Modernist in the study"—and all of these with a sense of complementarity rather than of contradiction. For a historical-theological scholar who has preferred a method of both/and to one of either/or, this complementarity (which Söderblom termed "Evangelical Catholicity") has demonstrated that it is not necessary to choose between particularity and universality, nor in the name of the Cross as the once-and-for-all gift of God to humanity to say no to the reality of divine truth wherever it has appeared within the history of that humanity. Those qualities made themselves evident in each of the several vocations of Söderblom's lifework.

As a scholar, he took a leading part in the acceptance of the history of non-Christian religions as a standard component of the curriculum both in the faculty of arts and sciences (where it could seem relatively harmless to Christian absolutism) and in the faculty of theology (where even his revered friend HARNACK did not want it to be a full-fledged participant). He taught the history of religions at his own University of Uppsala beginning in 1901, and in 1912 assumed an additional appointment as professor of the history of religions at Leipzig. His particular scholarly contribution lay in the history of Persian religion, with his Sorbonne thesis of 1901, *La vie future d'après le Mandéisme*. When, near the end of his life, he was invited to undertake the Gifford Lectures, which were published posthumously under the title *The Living God,* he turned again to his studies of the Persian tradition, finding deep affinities between its form of "personal religion" and that expressed in the work of the Hebrew prophets and of Jesus. Like his contemporary, the philosopher of religion Rudolf Otto (1869–1937), Söderblom recognized that although the idea of God was not universal throughout human history, the idea of the Holy was; for every religion, primitive or "advanced," carried the notion of that which was set apart from the ordinary—a holy place or time or person or object—even if there were no identifiable *Gudstro* (faith in God). The history of religion was, in that sense, a proof of the existence of God for him, but Söderblom could heighten even that paradox to assert that the uniqueness of the revelation in the incarnation of Christ enabled one to listen sympathetically to every disclosure of the word and will of God anywhere.

The election of Nathan Söderblom as archbishop of Uppsala and primate of the (Lutheran) Church of Sweden in 1914, shocking though it was to conservative and Pietist elements in that church, meant for him not a reversal of roles, but a change of venue for the practical execution of his theological and philosophical position. An interpretation of the history of religion in which the practice of the religious life rather than doctrine as such had been the key to understanding now expressed itself in his leadership, first within the Swedish Church itself and then on a broader stage, of the effort to reform the liturgy and to bring it more into line with the "Evangelical Catholicity" which the church professed. Recognizing the special position of Sweden during and after World War I, Söderblom worked for international understanding, and in the aftermath of the suffering he took the lead in relief and reconstruction; for this work he was awarded the Nobel Prize for Peace in 1930. He took a special interest in the intellectual and spiritual strivings of the university communities, and some of his most moving addresses are the talks he gave, as professor and then as archbishop, to students in Sweden and in other countries.

The depth of his scholarship and the breadth of his experience, including his facility with languages, made Söderblom a natural leader of the ecumenical movement. The preservation of the apostolic succession of ordaining bishops since the Reformation in the Church of Sweden provided a common ground with Anglicanism, while his own Evangelical piety permitted him to understand the special concerns of Dissenters and

Methodists. Believing that (as he quoted a German Lutheran friend) "doctrine divides but service unites," he took the lead in convoking a Universal Conference on Life and Work, which met at Uppsala in 1925, attended also by the Ecumenical Patriarch. Paul the apostle of faith was there, Söderblom observed, looking at his fellow Lutherans and other Protestants; now John the apostle of love had come, in the person of the Eastern Orthodox; "only Peter still stands by the fire and warms himself." From his own studies of the Reformation, assembled in his book of 1919, *Humor and Melancholy in Luther and Other Studies,* he recognized both the depth of Luther's faith and the far-reaching implications of the Reformation for Roman Catholicism no less than for Protestantism; and he strove, almost half a century before the Second Vatican Council, to find a way for Roman Catholicism to give and to receive in its relation to the other churches of Christendom.

Those who knew Nathan Söderblom personally have unanimously invoked words like "magical" and "unforgettable" to describe the effect that even one hour with him could have on an entire lifetime.

• Solitude

The time seems to have come for someone to say a good word again on behalf of solitude, and to do so specifically in the interests of theology and of scholarship. As a corrective to the individualism that seemed endemic to modern Protestantism, the Social Gospel rediscovered the collective dimension of the Christian message: sin was not merely an evil act by an evil person, but a social condition, and salvation had to be the transformation of a society rather than the rescue of an individual from society. Similarly, the ecumenical movement has been responsible for a new birth of Christian "togetherness," as a counterforce to the sectarianism and isolation that has dogged so much of Christian history. Every generation, it seems, is doomed to be alienated by the very processes of change that had brought it into being; and as that was true of the Social Gospel and the ecumenical movement in relation to their past, so it would seem to be true again in relation to their emphasis on social context. The Christian doctrine of the church has long been involved in this very tension: to be a Christian believer is to be a member of the church as the communion of saints; and yet, in Luther's phrase, "you must do your own believing as you must do your own dying." Whenever either pole has received exclusive emphasis, the other pole has demanded attention.

There is an entire chapter of *Walden* that bears the title "Solitude," in which Henry David Thoreau (1817–1862) expounds what can only be called his "theology of solitude." In it he confides to his readers his impression that people are "still a little afraid of the dark, though the witches are all hung, and Christianity and candles have been introduced"; yet he has found it "wholesome to be alone the greater part of the time," whereas "to be in company, even with the best, is soon wearisome and dissipating." In justification of this attitude he argues that "God is alone,—but the devil, he is far from being alone; he sees a great deal of company; he is legion." Nor was Thoreau the first to have such preferences. The history of Christian asceticism, as documented in such collections as *The Sayings of the Desert Fathers* as well as *The Life of Antony* by Athanasius of Alexandria (ca. 296–373), is replete with cases of solitary monks who withdrew from the world—but also from the church, and even from other monks—and who served God alone in their vocation as hermits. Their great model was John the Baptist in the deserts of Judea. Similarly, "anyone who wants to be a scholar," Harnack said in 1920, "has to be a bit of a monk, and give up something of life, and I know that to amount to anything in scholarship it is necessary to start very young." Yet the hermit Antony, like John the Baptist before him, became a public figure, almost against his will, and so have many scholars, including Harnack. But to carry out their public service, they had to have first learned the lesson of solitude.

So it is that the solitude of the library has frequently been a seedbed of revolution, because it provided revolutionaries with a diagnosis of society and its ills. For any such transforming vision of the world, be it constructive or destructive, solitude and study can be a better preparation than cultivating the habit of making ethical, political, or theological choices on the basis of what other people think. Change will continue in theology as in society, but which programs for change will prove to be sound and which will be a delusion will be significantly affected by the study and reflection that their leaders have been carrying on in solitude. This does not mean that the study of history, including the history of theology, is an infallible reference point for change. It does mean that the change will simultaneously manifest continuity and development if there has been an opportunity for tradition to speak before it is either rejected or affirmed. And it is very difficult for tradition to speak when its voice is being drowned out by the trendy voices of the moment.

The function of solitude for contemporary theology is something that used to be the function of society: to introduce us to our ancestors. What the Greek church fathers denounced as "novelty-mongering" (*kainotomia*) is often purchased at the price of heritage; and it is no longer possible, as it once was, to rely on worship or creed to redress the balance through socialization or group pressure. Therefore the recovery of historical continuity often becomes dependent on what one does when one is by oneself. So likewise does the cultivation of moral realism, and the sense of what Reinhold Niebuhr (1892–1971) once called "the irony of history." In 1870, a man whose awareness of that irony during the battle over slavery had been far more acute than his critics recognized, RALPH WALDO EMERSON, published a book called *Society and Solitude*. In it he spoke about "the necessity of solitude," and yet he also recognized that "a man must be clothed with society, or we shall feel a certain bareness and poverty." Hence, he said, "a scholar is a candle which the love and desire of all men will light." "But," he continued, "the people are to be taken in very small doses. If solitude is proud, so is society vulgar." The fundamental tension expressed in that oscillation between society and solitude was a theme through all of Emerson's own life and thought, but it has also been a leitmotiv throughout the history of thought and the history of theology.

▪ Text of the New Testament

The text of the New Testament has probably received more attention and careful study than any other document in history, ancient or modern. In fact, many of the techniques of textual criticism now applied to literary sources of all kinds were developed originally for the establishment of the text of the New Testament. Textual criticism is important for theology as part of the process by which the church and SCHOLARSHIP seek to determine what belongs in the Bible and what does not. Questions about the CANON OF THE NEW TESTAMENT and questions about its text are technically distinct, but they often intersect. For example, the question of the "long ending" of Mark's Gospel (Mark 16:9–20) involves both textual and canonical judgments. Did the last chapter of the Gospel of Mark originally end where it now does in the best manuscripts, or did it end with one of the endings attached to it in other manuscripts and in several translations, or with a conclusion now lost? And on the other hand, when the Gospel of Mark became part of the canon, was the "long ending" already a part of the accepted text? Usually, however, canonical study determines which books belong in the Bible, whereas textual study determines which text of each of those books is closest to being authentic.

Textual criticism of the New Testament is necessary because of the thousands of variants in the existing manuscripts and versions. Some of these variations are inconsequential, involving three different forms of the name "Jerusalem" in Greek or three different renderings of the name "Gerasenes/Gadarenes" (Matt. 8:28; Mark 5:1; Luke 8:26). Other variations, however, affect the meaning of an entire passage or verse. If the apostle Paul, writing to the Romans, said (Rom. 5:1) "We have (Greek *echomen*) peace with God," he meant one thing; but if the correct reading is "Let us have (Greek *echōmen*) peace with God," it would seem to mean another thing. When scholars set about to decide which of two or more variant readings should be adopted, they must consult the available textual evidence.

The main sources are the manuscripts of the New Testament, dating from the second to the tenth century or even later. In the process of copying, these manuscripts underwent the revisions that necessitate textual criticism. Some of these revisions were unintentional, as the scribe skipped a word or a line or mistook one character for another. Other revisions came from the desire of the scribe to harmonize the text of one GOSPEL with another or of one Testament with the other, or from a pious wish to "correct" or clarify the text at another point. Such variants in the text make collation of the manuscripts a difficult task.

Nor are the manuscripts of the Greek New Testament the only source of textual evidence. Versions in other languages sometimes reflect variants in the original text that correct the readings of the Greek manuscripts. Although these versions do not figure so prominently in the study of the text of the New Testament as does the Septuagint in the study of the text as well as of the CANON OF HEBREW SCRIPTURE (THE OLD TESTAMENT), they must not be ignored in any attempt to establish its text. Especially important among the LANGUAGES of Christian source material for this purpose are Latin and Syriac.

Examining the manuscripts and the ancient versions does not exhaust the evidence for the New Testament text. New Testament textual criticism must call on patristics for help, because the writings of the early Christian fathers often reflect yet another form of text. In some cases these writings represent the only access to textual traditions that have long since disappeared; and therefore their witness to the text, especially as it corroborates readings from other sources, belongs to the testimony that textual critics must consult before forming their conclusions. The work of assembling and collating the evidence from all these sources is one of the greatest existing monuments to Christian SCHOLARSHIP, and the task is not finished yet. Origen and Erasmus may be counted among the founders of textual criticism, but it was with the work of the Lutheran Pietist Johann Albrecht Bengel (1687–1752) that the science moved into its modern phase.

From all the evidence collected by these and other editors, how does a scholar settle upon one reading in preference to all the others? Merely counting the manuscripts pro and con will not decide the question; for they are not all of equal value, and the same manuscript is not of equal value for various books of the New Testament. The date of a manuscript does not necessarily indicate its relative worth, because a later manuscript may reflect a more trustworthy or an earlier text. Even grouping the manuscripts by families or by the quality of their text is not a satisfactory method, because this quality is not constant throughout a manuscript or a group of manuscripts. Selection of the reading that conforms to custom or to some regional tradition or to some arbitrary definition of orthodoxy is no solution either. Each of these methods has some contribution to make, but the only defensible procedure would have to include all of them—and other considerations besides.

The method that most textual critics follow begins with the accumulation and evaluation of the external evidence. This evidence must be assigned relative weight according to the usefulness of a particular manuscript or version or quotation by a church father for the passage being studied. Once this has been done—and opinions as to the relative usefulness of these witnesses vary widely—the textual critic must also consider internal evidence, examining the context of the passage, the style of the writer, and the structure of the sentence and paragraph; these may provide a clue to the proper reading. Weighing the witness of the manuscripts, versions, and church fathers leads to the question: Which of the variants most satisfactorily explains the rise of the other variants? The variant that does this deserves consideration as the possible source of the entire textual tradition. When all the possibilities supplied by both the external and the internal evidence have been exhausted, there remains the possibility that no existing text provides the original reading and that this reading can be arrived at only by conjectural emendation. Such conjectural emendation is as hazardous as it is necessary. Some conjectures have been dramatically substantiated by later discoveries; others have received no support at all.

Textual criticism and Christian doctrine stand in a complex and reciprocal relation, as a striking epitome of the delicate balance between scholarship and theology. In principle it would seem that those whose view of biblical AUTHORITY is the highest, and whose theory of biblical inspiration is the most comprehensive, should also be the most zealous about determining precisely which textual variant has been verbally inspired by the Holy Spirit, because they unanimously insist that verbal inspiration applied only to the original manuscripts (now lost). In the history of biblical study, however, these theologians have frequently resisted scientific textual criticism, especially because it is so often obliged, after all of its research, to leave the question of the exact *Urtext* undecided—or because, as in the notorious case of 1 John 5:7, it took away a favorite proof text. Conversely, the assertion of Enlightenment critics that the very existence of these thousands of textual variants makes a reliance on the message of the New Testament impossible is contradicted by the witness of history: it seems safe to claim, albeit impossible to prove, that no one has ever missed the point of the message of the Christian gospel because of a mistaken variant in a text.

• Thomas Aquinas (ca. 1225–1274)

Dominican theologian, author of *Summa Theologiae* and *Summa contra Gentiles,* and Angelic Doctor.

There are some theologians, such as Augustine or Luther, whose thought it is impossible to understand without knowing more than a little about their personality and biography. Their "systems"—if that is the right word—were forged in the crucible of doubt and personal experience. To such theologians, Schleiermacher's definition of doctrine as an expression of the "pious self-consciousness" of the believer certainly applies, as he himself recognized when he cited them as historical evidence for the correctness of his definition. But there are other theologians who seem, at least to the superficial observer, to be working on an assembly line of systematic theology and who can go on for hundreds and even thousands of pages without more than the very slightest of hints about themselves. As Emerson said in an intentional hyperbole about a preacher he once heard, "The capital secret of his profession, namely, to convert life into truth, he had not learned. Not one fact in all his experience had he yet imported into his doctrine."

Such a caricature has frequently been imposed on Thomas Aquinas, sometimes even by his disciples or epigones. "The Art of Misunderstanding Saint Thomas" was the title of one of the last public lectures of Étienne Gilson (1884–1978). As he was the first to acknowledge, it was an art that Gilson himself had practiced from time to time; but because he was, *sit venia verbis,* an even greater historian of philosophy than he was a philosopher, he was able to exorcise that art. And because he understood Saint Augustine as well as Saint Thomas, he was in an almost unique position to recognize their important differences but also their even more important affinities. And that enabled him to give, in the conclusion of a highly personal essay on "The Terrors of the Year Two Thousand," this highly personal characterization of Thomas Aquinas: "There was in the thirteenth century a philosopher to whom the sight of the world did not give nausea, but a joy ever new, because he saw in it only order and beauty. Man did not seem to him a Sisyphus hopelessly condemned to the liberty of the absurd, for he read in his own heart the clear law of practical reason."

That could stand as a description either of Thomas or of Augustine, and Thomas would not have been surprised at all to be found in agreement with Augustine. From his first public utterances to his last, Thomas was, wanted to be, and wanted to be known as, an Augustinian. As a teacher at the University of Paris, he was commissioned in 1252 to lecture on the *Sentences* of Peter Lombard (ca. 1100–1160), the standard textbook of doctrine on which literally thousands of MEDIEVAL theologians, including Martin Luther, were to comment. As there were more quotations from Augustine in the *Sentences* than from any other ecclesiastical writer, an *explication de texte* of Peter Lombard was perforce an exposition of Augustine. Over the next two decades, Thomas deepened his study of the writings of Augustine, particularly of those against the Pelagians. As a result, when he came to deal with the doctrine of GRACE in his mature works, above all in the appropriate questions and articles of his *Summa Theologiae,* he demonstrated that a development of doctrine had been taking place in his own thought. This was not, as some modern textbooks suggest, a growing away from Augustine but on the contrary a far surer grasp of PATRISTIC doctrine— sometimes surer than the patristic doctrine itself had been. The fundamental change that came about in Thomas, and through Thomas, was not the substitution of Aristotle for Augustine, but an effort, in loyalty to Augustine and through him to the entire tradition of patristic theology, to clarify Augustine.

In that clarification, Aristotelian philosophy provided the best available documentation of just how much (and also how little) human reason was able to discover about reality without the revelation of the gospel. It was necessary to draw on philosophy for this service, just as, in Thomas's judgment, a certain version of Platonic (we would say today, Neoplatonic) philosophy had played an important part in confusing Augustine's theological judgment. Carrying out the task begun in earlier

medieval development, of straightening out Augustine's doctrine of the sacraments, especially of the Eucharist, Thomas was
able, with the help of Aristotle, to identify how the Eucharist
had to be differentiated from other symbols, in which the visible
reality pointed beyond itself to an invisible one. The Eucharist
did that also, of course, but it also contained that which it symbolized, the body and blood of Christ. To describe how these
were present, Thomas made use of the Aristotelian distinction
between "substance" (as "that which exists in itself and not in
another thing") and "accident" (as "that which is other than the
essence," such as color or taste). Most changes in everyday experience were changes of accident, as when a tree became a
board or a board became a chair. But in the miracle of the
Eucharist, the accidents of the elements remained and the
substance was changed from bread and wine to the true body
and blood of Jesus Christ. Whether that technical Aristotelian
sense of "substance" was intended by the Fourth Lateran Council in 1215 when it decreed transubstantiation as a dogma may
be questioned, but that was how Thomas read the decree in the
light of what he had meanwhile learned from the Aristotelian
distinctions.

Such assistance to Catholic theology from Aristotelian philosophy could have been very costly. Although atheist was
probably not the right name for the philosophy of Aristotle, it
was not quite theistic either, and certainly not monotheistic in
the sense in which Christianity had learned monotheism from
Judaism and had affirmed it in its doctrine of the Trinity. Aristotle seemed to have taught quite unambiguously that the world
of matter was eternal, and thus coeternal with whatever gods
may be, and he seemed to have taught this as a truth that could
be demonstrated by reason. Some Christian Aristotelians—
whom Thomas labels "Averroists," as the followers (whether
they really were or not) of the Muslim philosopher Averroes
(Ibn Rushd, 1126–1198)—tried to teach simultaneously that the
world was eternal, as a truth of philosophical reason, and that it
had been created by God, as a truth of revelation. Thomas
resolved the antinomy by identifying certain truths, such as the

existence of God, that could be known by reason and not only by revelation, and by distinguishing from these those other truths, such as creation *ex nihilo,* that could be known by revelation alone; these latter did not contradict reason, but they did transcend it. All of that was an application to epistemology of the axiom, which epitomizes much of Thomistic theology, that grace was the perfecting of nature. Although the axiom in that form came from the *Summa Theologiae* as a work of theology and dogma, it was no less the fundamental presupposition for the *Summa contra Gentiles* as a work of apologetics and philosophical theology.

"The art of misunderstanding Saint Thomas" may therefore be seen, at least in the present context, as the unwillingness to take him at his word when he propounded his philosophical ideas and his commentaries on the Aristotelian corpus as a part of—and a prolegomenon to—the theological enterprise in which he was engaged when he wrote *De veritate* and the *Summa Theologiae.* Neo-Thomism may be said to have grown into Thomism during the twentieth century by reversing that trend and identifying more accurately the authentically theological MELODY that Thomas Aquinas claimed to be singing, for it was this that made him the "Angelic Doctor."

• Tradition

According to an epigram whose pedigree seems impossible to track down, "Tradition is the living faith of the dead, traditionalism is the dead faith of the living." Like DEVELOPMENT OF DOCTRINE, tradition is a fundamental concept in Christian theology, but one whose importance extends far beyond Christian theology to the very definition of culture. As modern anthropology has documented in great detail, culture is transmitted chiefly by means of tradition, which during most of the history of the human race has taken the form of oral transmission and ritual action. The encounters of Milman Parry (1902–1935) in

Yugoslavia with peasants who could recite thousands of lines of folk epic led to the recognition that whoever "Homer" (he or they or even she) may have been, it would have been possible for the *Iliad* and the *Odyssey* to have been passed on through oral tradition long before there was written Greek. At about the same time as Parry, Protestant students of the New Testament began interpreting the Gospels as the written deposit, produced relatively late, of the early Christian *kērygma,* which was oral in its original form and which continued to be oral also after the composition, collection, and canonization of the Gospels; for example, one of the best-known of the sayings of Jesus, "Happiness lies more in giving than in receiving," does not appear in the Gospels at all, but is quoted by the apostle Paul, who is in turn quoted by Luke in Acts 20:35. The narratives in the Pentateuch likewise came, whether through Moses or through later writers, from the traditions of the people of Israel.

If there was, then, a tradition before there was a Bible—a Hebrew tradition before there was a Hebrew Bible, a Christian tradition before there was a Christian Bible—what did that do to the status of postbiblical tradition? The apostle Paul was ashamed of his earlier "boundless devotion to the traditions of my ancestors" (Gal. 1:14), and early Christians rejected the postbiblical traditions of contemporary Judaism and other received doctrines as "traditions of man-made teaching" (Col. 2:8), which had usurped the divine AUTHORITY of the word of God. Following that precedent, and citing these very passages of the New Testament, the Protestant Reformers had rejected the postbiblical traditions of Catholicism as superfluous at best and subversive at worst. During the twentieth century, however, a deepening uneasiness with both of these rejections has led, in the first instance, to an increasing recognition of the postbiblical tradition of Judaism as a legitimate expression and extension of biblical faith, and, in the second instance, to an affirmation of the inevitability, but also of the legitimacy, of postbiblical tradition in Christianity. This affirmation has coincided with a deepening awareness of development of doctrine as the necessary corollary to tradition. For if, as mainline Protestantism teaches in concord with Roman Catholicism and Eastern Orthodoxy, it was good and proper for the church in 325 to go on from the scattered statements of the New Testament about Father, Son, and Holy Spirit to the full-blown doctrine of the Trinity, which is not explicitly taught in the Bible, then both the concept of development of doctrine and the concept of tradition have to be accorded a place in Christian doctrine. They are, in any event, indispensable to an understanding of its history.

As they stand, however, tradition and development of doctrine are mutually antithetical principles, and tradition at any rate has frequently (or one should perhaps say "traditionally") been interpreted as precluding the very notion of any development. Until comparatively modern times, HERESY has likewise represented itself as the guardian of the tradition against innovation. The history of various heresies suggests that they frequently were the effort to retain or to revive a position that had been outgrown. But orthodoxy, too, has often defined CONTINUITY in static terms. Such definitions have helped to render both tradition and orthodoxy vulnerable to critical historiography, which, by comparing the orthodoxy of one era with that of another, succeeded in relativizing the concept of tradition as well as its authority. That discovery was the permanent accomplishment of the Enlightenment, whose historiography of doctrine reached the pinnacle of its influence at the end of the nineteenth and the beginning of the twentieth century in the *History of Dogma* of Adolf von Harnack.

But many of the disciples of Harnack and the Enlightenment drew from that discovery the unwarranted conclusion that tradition was no more than the "detritus" of the past. As both a product and a critic of the Enlightenment, Edmund Burke (1729–1797), by his definition of the social contract as "a partnership not only between those who are living, but between those who are living, those who are dead, and those who are to be born," had put the concept of tradition (in this case political and social tradition) in a new light. His definition was paraphrased and applied to theology by G. K. Chesterton (1874–1936), who in his book *Orthodoxy* of 1908 defended the thesis "that tradition is only democracy extended through time." "Tradition," Chesterton continued, "may be defined as an extension of the franchise. Tradition means giving votes to the most obscure of all classes, our ancestors. It is the democracy of the dead." But in order to keep from becoming the dead faith of the living, tradition needed to be connected with what had been valid in the Enlightenment's discovery of change. It was the historic importance of Newman to have made that connection. And so, in the summary statement of Yves Congar, "with Newman—not that he was the only one, but he was and remains to this day the *locus classicus* for the question—the idea of development became an inner dimension of that of tradition."

Once it is seen to have had a history of its own, the idea of tradition-as-development may become the object of the historian's research as well as of the theologian's exposition. Some of the processes by which a supposedly changeless truth has changed can be charted, and some of the differences in the rate and in the nature of that change can be observed. The doctrine of the incarnation went on developing for many centuries, but the doctrine of the Holy Spirit did not; the Catholic doctrine of baptism sprang almost full-grown from the brow of patristic theology in the second-century church, whereas the Eucharist did not achieve a similar formulation (if indeed it ever did) until the controversies of the medieval and Reformation periods. Yet each of these doctrines had, in some sense, been an integral part of "the tradition" from the first, as remembered in the church's deposit of faith and teaching about Jesus Christ and as "re-presented" in its creed and worship—but in what sense? The answer to that question, if there is one, must be sought in the relation between what tradition is and what tradition becomes. Newman saw correctly that this was a task for both the historian and the theologian, but in his thought the theologian consistently won out over the historian. It need not do so.

The work of both theologians and historians since Newman, however, does suggest—*pace* Emerson's question, "Why should not we have a poetry and philosophy of insight and not of tradition?"—that the concept of tradition has proved to be a fruitful source of insight. The insight, moreover, leads not only to a more complex and profound grasp of tradition than Emerson's question expresses, but to a subtler and more sophisticated method of understanding other ideas and doctrines.

• Trinity

During almost the entire history of the church, the doctrine of the Trinity has been the normative expression of the Christian doctrine of God. Yet there is perhaps no doctrine of Christianity, not even the doctrine of the atonement, on which the development of the last three centuries has diverged as much from that of the first fifteen centuries of church history as the doctrine of the Trinity. From having stood as the unquestioned, and unquestionable, confession shared by all who were acknowledged as Christian, the Trinity has often been denied—or, worse yet, ignored, and with impunity—by those who are now acknowledged as Christian.

This change may be seen as the doctrinal counterpart of a political development. The universal consensus on the doctrine was not simply a theological position, but a legal requirement. Under the date of 27 February 380 the *Theodosian Code* specified: "We desire that all peoples who fall beneath the sway of our imperial clemency should profess the faith . . . that, according to apostolic discipline and evangelical teaching, we should believe in one deity, the sacred Trinity of Father, Son, and Holy Spirit." Anyone who refused to accept this trinitarian faith was guilty of heresy and therefore of sedition. So long as this legal requirement was enforceable, the police power of the state could see to it that trinitarian orthodoxy remained intact. This was one of the reasons, though not the only one, that the doctrine of the Trinity was the first article of the confession of faith that Luther's followers presented to the Diet of the Holy Roman Empire at Augsburg in 1530. Defending their right, under the law of the empire, to reform the churches in their own principalities, the Lutheran princes and free cities began by pledging their allegiance to a doctrine that had always, or almost always, been the distinguishing mark of orthodox Christian teaching. Conversely, once the political authorities were no longer in a position to back up the demand with the sanctions of the state, the doctrine of the Trinity began to wither away and its hold on the Christian mind was relaxed.

Yet it would be political reductionism (not an unknown phenomenon, especially in the twentieth century) to dismiss the trinitarian orthodoxy of the Cappadocians and Augustine, or of Thomas Aquinas and Luther, as no more than obedience to the civil law. In the name of *sola Scriptura,* the sole authority of the Bible over against tradition, the Protestant Reformers of the sixteenth century gave up some of the most cherished beliefs and practices of the Catholic centuries, including many of those associated with the Virgin Mary and with the sacraments. But on the doctrine of the Trinity the major Reformers stood firm, and they provided it with a biblical support that it had not had since the early church. Although Protestant liberals like HARNACK regarded the trinitarianism of the Reformation as a vestigial remnant that could (and should) be shed, such central Reformation documents as Luther's Small Catechism would be inconceivable without it.

This was true despite the lack of any one passage of Scripture in which the entire doctrine of the Trinity was affirmed. Strictly speaking, the Trinity is not a biblical doctrine, but a church doctrine that tries to make consistent sense of biblical language and teaching. From its roots in the faith of ZION, the church received an unwavering commitment to monotheism, which nothing could be allowed to compromise or contradict. But regardless of how early we look, we also find the church using language about Jesus Christ that did appear to compromise or even contradict that monotheistic faith. Jesus at his death had said, "Father, into thy hands I commit my spirit" (Luke 23:46); but the first Christian martyr, Stephen, cried out, "Lord Jesus, receive my spirit" (Acts 7:59). "Lord" (Greek *kyrios*) was an early title for Jesus, but it was also the Greek rendering of the unpronounceable divine name in the Hebrew Bible ("YHWH"). The earliest Christian sermon we have after the New Testament, the so-called Second Epistle of Clement, opens with the admonition: "Brethren, we ought so to think of Jesus Christ as of God." Meanwhile the church, following what it believed to be the parting command of its Lord (Matt. 28:19), was baptizing "in the name of the Father and of the Son and of the Holy Spirit."

The doctrine of the Trinity may be interpreted as the effort of the early church to say and do all of this and yet to affirm the *Shema* of Israel's faith: "Hear, O Israel, the Lord is our God, one Lord" (Deut. 6:4). During the second and third centuries there were various attempts at a construction of the doctrine of God that would simultaneously preserve the monotheism of the *Shema* and do justice to the new reality of Christ. In the formula of Harnack, "Is the Divine that has appeared on earth and reunited man with God identical with the supreme Divine, which rules heaven and earth, or is it a demigod?" The eventual formulation on which the Christian church (led by the newly Christianized emperor) agreed at Nicea began with the *Shema*: "We believe in one God." But then it went on to speak about the Father, the Son, and the Holy Spirit as the sacred three, for whom the term "person" (Greek *hypostasis*) was to become the standard way of speaking. Enacted by the councils of Nicea in 325 and of Constantinople in 381 and enforced by the "all-Christian" emperors, this doctrine of the Trinity came to represent the non-negotiable creed of the entire church.

Yet the imposition of this creed did not mean theological uniformity. For it has usually been characteristic of ORTHODOXY that it has drawn a circle within which theological thought was to be carried on, but has within that circle continued to tolerate an astonishing variety and creativity. Far from stifling such creativity, therefore, the doctrine of the Trinity has provided an opportunity for speculation and reflection. In the Latin West, the most celebrated instance of such trinitarian reflection is almost certainly Augustine's construction of "psychological analogies" to the divine Trinity, as part of his doctrine of the IMAGE OF GOD. No less courageous and creative was the attempt by the Cappadocians to use the doctrine of the Trinity as a means for coping with the ancient philosophical problem of "the one and the many." As his analogies between the one human psyche and the one divine being suggest, it was characteristic of Augustine's thought about the Trinity, and of that of other Western theologians, that it took its start from the One rather than from the Three, and that it found the distinction between the three "persons" problematical. In the Greek East, on the other hand, the reality of the Christian experience of Father, Son, and Holy Spirit tended to make the Three the starting point; Gregory of Nyssa wrote a treatise under the title *That We Should Not Think of Saying There Are Three Gods*. Opposed though he was to speculation, as a subversion of the authentic task of theology, Karl Barth (1886–1968) nevertheless succeeded in rescuing the doctrine of the Trinity from the obscurity into which, thanks in considerable measure to Schleiermacher, modern theology had relegated it, and in making it once more the fundamental doctrine of church dogmatics.

▪ University

Most of the theologians in the early church were bishops, most of the theologians in the medieval church were monks, and most of the theologians in the modern church have been university professors. Pope Gregory I (590–604) was a bishop and a monk; Martin Luther was a monk and a professor. Particularly for those aspects of the theological enterprise that define themselves as scholarship more than as creed, the university context has been decisive, but it has also generated special problems of its own for theology, especially in its normative functions but also in its descriptive tasks.

Despite their beginnings in the cathedral schools and monastic centers of the Middle Ages, the universities did not arise simply to meet the needs of theology. Both the university at Byzantium for the East and those in Oxford, Cambridge, and other places for the medieval West served as centers for the study of rhetoric, medicine, or law as well; but in those Christian societies such study could not be unrelated to the theological enterprise. It was the teaching not only of the civil law (the law codes of the Germanic tribes in relation to Roman law) but of canon law (the legislation of synods and church councils) that gave the University of Bologna its preeminence. The study of canon law, moreover, stimulated much of the investigation into the nature and function of tradition that was to become, in the thought of the scholastics, a decisive force in theological study as well. Theology as SACRED SCIENCE took its place alongside the other sciences as "queen of the sciences" (in the sense that by dealing with revelation it had a transcendent point of reference), but also as a partner in the university dialogue. The career of THOMAS AQUINAS at the University of Paris illustrates the partnership, for he lectured in the philosophical faculty on the newly translated writings of Aristotle as well as on Scripture in the theological faculty. The University of Paris was to become in the later Middle Ages a major arbiter of doctrinal disputes in the church, and with the decline in the authority of Rome its theological faculty functioned in the fifteenth century as a kind of corporate pope.

Universities performed a similar function for the theology of the Reformation, as was evident in the reformatory careers of John Wycliffe (ca. 1330–1384) at the University of Oxford, Jan Hus (ca. 1372–1415) at the University of Prague, and Martin Luther at the University of Wittenberg. Luther came to his insights into the meaning of Christian doctrine through the exercise of his responsibility as a university professor and a *Doctor in Biblia*. That responsibility in the university, and not his position in the church as monk and priest, likewise supplied him with his principal justification for speaking out in public, and it was to become his protection against his theological and political adversaries. So although Luther could never be accused of softness toward false teachers or of excessive tolerance, it was in the name of a sixteenth-century version of academic freedom that he carried out his program of theological reform. For these favors from the university, Luther and his theological colleagues, above all Philip Melanchthon (1497–1560), reciprocated by reforming university education. Because such reform owed much also to the scholarly ideals of the Renaissance, theology was defined within the university as a field of learning, and the ministry as a learned profession, alongside medicine and law, for whose practice one prepared by undertaking a disciplined program of study.

To these origins the theologies of all the major Christian traditions owe much of their definition and inspiration. But as has happened also with law and medicine, the constituency often found much to criticize in the preparation that the university faculties of theology were offering, and frequently it was the university context that was identified as the very source of the problem. Not only were the morals of the theological students corrupted by the loose living of their classmates from the other faculties, but the emphasis of the universities on scholarship and dialectics often seemed inimical to the primary task of theology within the community of the church. As part of its program of Catholic reform, the Council of Trent (1545–1563) charged the bishops of the church with the task of establishing theological seminaries in their dioceses, as a means of assuring the church a professionally qualified but ecclesiastically accountable priesthood. Criticism of university theology was one of the items in the programs of both Pietism on the Continent and Methodism in England. Eventually this complaint helped to produce in Protestant Germany several church schools or *theologische Hochschulen,* to supplement with training that was both practical and churchly the offerings of the university faculties of theology. And when, in America, the churches faced the necessity and the opportunity of redesigning theological education *de novo,* they created colleges and seminaries that were intended to avoid the evils of the Old World universities.

Many of these colleges and seminaries evolved into universities in the United States, and with that evolution the problems of the place of theology in the university continued to demand attention. The disestablishment of the churches and the constitutional doctrine of the separation of church and state meant that state universities could not train clergy or teach Christian theology as a normative discipline. Because that limitation was often seen as a prohibition not only of the normative but also of the descriptive teaching of theology, it foreshortened the teaching and research of the humanities in disastrous ways. In the private universities, most of which had originated in the churches and many of which continued to maintain at least some connection with their roots, the primary obstacles to the study and teaching of theology were not constitutional but intellectual. Faculties of divinity were often retained in universities of this kind; but historically some of these could be dismissed as professional schools without any role within the university as defined by the arts and sciences, whereas others achieved such a role at the cost of their Christian particularity and of their professional mission as schools for the ministers of the church.

The rise of "religious studies" as a field or department within the arts and sciences has been designed to meet many of these obstacles. Amalgamating existing departments of religion with the scholarship and teaching on subjects of religious importance in such other departments as philosophy, classics, history, and the social sciences, religious studies became a way of introducing students to the phenomena, traditions, and literatures of the world religions, including Christianity. Some traditional areas of theological study—for example, the history of the church, especially the history of the Reformation—have found this university setting congenial, but it has raised serious questions for other areas. For so direct a scholarly need of the church as the investigation of the text of the New Testament or of patristics, for example, the scholarly priorities of the arts and sciences will only rarely have room. Even more problematical is the status of theology in this setting. Comparative studies of Christian ethics and other ethical systems have made a major contribution to theology as well as to the social sciences and philosophy, and a description of the Christian theology of a particular denomination or historical tradition (whether or not the expositor happens to be a participant in that denomination or tradition) does, in simple justice, seem to have a right to the same platform as the exposition of a secular or anti-Christian position. But the tensions are acute, as are the questions that these developments raise about the future of scholarship in the church and about the continuity of scholarly interest and training not only in the traditional languages of theological study and research but in its very subject matter.

▪ Worship

"Worship" as a word is a treasure of English theological LAN-GUAGE. As a concept, it is a major force in the history of theology. "The rule of prayer is the rule of faith" (*Lex orandi lex credendi*) was a principle articulated after the death of Augustine by his defenders, in response to the charge, heard already during his lifetime, that his view of grace was a violation of tradition. Initially the actual wording was slightly different—*ut legem credendi lex statuat supplicandi* (that the rule of praying should lay down the rule of believing); but the principle, as formulated by Prosper of Aquitaine (ca. 390–ca. 463), affirmed that the authentic tradition was to be found not only in the formal theological treatises of the early fathers, where for apologetic and polemical reasons free will and moral accountability had been defended more vigorously than the reality of inherited sin or the sovereignty of unearned grace, but also in the prayers and liturgies employed by those same fathers in their worship, in which they confessed their total sinfulness and begged for divine mercy. It is a bit of historical whimsy to note that the same controversy over Augustine's doctrine of grace evoked from his critics, specifically from Prosper's contemporary and opponent, Vincent of Lérins (d. ca. 450), the most widely disseminated principle by which to measure continuity of doctrine, the so-called Vincentian canon: *quod ubique, quod semper, quod ab omnibus creditum est* (what has been believed everywhere, always, and by all). Measured by that criterion, Vincent of Lérins contended, Augustine's anthropological doctrines could not stand as authentically orthodox and ecumenical.

Apart from its theological validity or invalidity, the principle of worship as *lex orandi lex credendi* has proved to be far more useful historically, as a guide to the patterns of the DEVELOPMENT OF DOCTRINE, than has the Vincentian canon. The history of many doctrines is difficult to document solely on the basis of the surviving theological literature. For the doctrine of the Eucharist, for example, the first full-length theological treatises do not appear until the Carolingian period; before that, a defender of continuity must argue, in the words of Newman, that "the real presence appears, by the liturgies of the fourth or fifth century, to have been the doctrine of the earlier, since those very forms probably existed from the first in divine worship." The doctrine of the Trinity itself can be interpreted as the effort to find satisfactory formulas by which to defend the established practice, followed also by the opponents of the Nicene doctrine, of speaking to and about the person of Jesus Christ in the language of worship and adoration. Conversely, the absence of such language in the early history of the doctrine of the Holy Spirit helps to account for the difficulties experienced in its development and eventual codification.

• Zion

From the beginning, Christians have spoken in the language of Zion, but the twentieth century will almost certainly be remembered in the history of Christian thought as the period when Christians rediscovered its theological significance. It took the Nazis to accomplish this, but it would be a disastrous oversimplification as well as a crass injustice to give them all the credit.

Although it is often true of novel ideas that it is difficult for their adherents to imagine a time when they were not held, the Jewishness of early Christianity does seem now to be so obvious that it could never have been overlooked. And in a sense it never was overlooked: a book that appears to be one of the least Jewish in the New Testament, the Gospel of John, represents Jesus as saying that "it is from the Jews that salvation comes" (John 4:22); and in the ninth, tenth, and eleventh chapters of the Epistle to the Romans the apostle PAUL set forth his anguish and his hope about his people, climaxing with the expectation that when "the Gentiles have been admitted in full strength," the promise would be fulfilled and "the whole of Israel will be saved" (Rom. 11:25–26).

Yet the ingenuity of theologians is almost boundless, as is their capacity to evade the obvious implication of a biblical text if it does not square with their philosophical or moral assumptions. During the very years of the Nazi *Endlösung,* or "final solution," seminary courses on the exegesis of the Epistle to the Romans and the Gospel of John were interpreting those chapters to say that Paul's words, "the whole of Israel will be saved," could not of course refer to the Jews as the people of Israel, but must be applied solely to the Christian Church as "the spiritual Israel"; similarly, "it is from the Jews that salvation comes" meant that salvation had come away from the Jews and to the Christians exclusively. Some bolder spirits had been heard to suggest that before the end of time there would be a wholesale conversion of Jews to Christianity and that by this means "the whole of Israel will be saved"—not, certainly, as Israel but as Christians. At that very time, however—and sometimes through the work of theologians and scholars who retained the conventional Christian anti-Jewish prejudices, even in a virulent form—Christian theology was discovering lines of affinity with the Jewish tradition that would, in counterpoint and response to the events of world history, reopen the question of the relation between Zion and the church in a new and yet a very old way.

One powerful theological force in that direction was the *Theologisches Wörterbuch zum Neuen Testament* edited by Gerhard Kittel, which began appearing in the fateful year of 1933. Its method of word study is not beyond scholarly reproach, for it is a DICTIONARY and therefore runs the danger of isolating individual vocables from the narrative line or the rhetorical argument of a larger passage or of the writing as a whole, and even of giving the impression of a greater lexicographical consistency than the texts warrant. Nevertheless, word study did have the great advantage of focusing attention on the backgrounds of New Testament terms drawn from the Hebrew Bible, the Septuagint, and Hellenistic Judaism (as well as from non-Jewish Greek usage), even where the New Testament is not overtly quoting the Old Testament or alluding to it. As a result, words and concepts that had generally been assumed to reflect only the influence of Gentile literary or philosophical sources were seen to bear unmistakable marks of the Jewish heritage: there may not have been a Hebrew word for "conscience" (Greek *syneidēsis*) as such, but both in the Jewish sacred writings and in postbiblical Jewish reflection on them much thought had been given to the notion of an inner law through which the voice of God spoke.

Conversely, the Jewish theological renaissance during the twentieth century could not fail to have a powerful impact on Christian thought. To begin with the obvious issue of LANGUAGE, the revival of spoken Hebrew and its establishment as the official language of a national state and an entire society meant that for the first time since before the days of Jesus the language of the Pentateuch, the Psalms, and the prophets had once more become a vernacular, in which ordinary people could converse, debate, make love, buy and sell, and go on writing poetry or scholarly books. Christian interpretation of the "Old" Testament could not long ignore this new antenna for the language of the Scriptures; and as a command of biblical Hebrew had become, in the period of the Renaissance and the Reformation, the indispensable preparation for serious scholarly work on the Bible (at any rate within Protestantism), so it seems likely that a reading knowledge, if not also a speaking knowledge, of modern Hebrew will be seen as an asset to being able to hear the Bible as one reads it.

The substantive implications of Jewish exegesis are even more profound. To the extent that the HELLENIZATION of Christianity has caused a distortion in the reading of the Bible by placing in the framework of metaphysics and ontology biblical statements that were originally spoken in (for want of a better term) a "personalistic" or "existential" context, a non-Hellenic reading of those statements may compel Christian exegetes to examine their own presuppositions more carefully. Throughout Christian history, and especially in the Reformed tradition and in its Puritan expression, the centrality of the biblical concept of "covenant" has served as a hermeneutical tool for both ethics and theology. But even before the rise of Zionism, Jewish interpretation of the covenant linked it—as did the language of the Pentateuch and the prophets—to the biblical promises about "the land." The status of those promises in the Christian reading of the Hebrew Bible has raised many problems throughout all the churches, as they have wrestled with the need to reexamine age-old prejudices in the light of both new scholarship and recent history. A special place in the history of the Christian rediscovery of Judaism during the twentieth century is occupied by the Second Vatican Council, at which, in a manner that had not been heard before in the official declarations of the churches, the permanence of the divine covenant with Zion was affirmed and at least the outlines for a doctrine of two covenants appeared.